Motivational Interviewing Skills for Probation and Parole Officers

A Practical Guide for Criminal Justice and Community Corrections Professionals

Shepherd Travis Humphrey

Motivational Interviewing Skills for Probation and Parole Officers: A Practical Guide for Criminal Justice and Community Corrections Professionals

First Edition

ISBN: 978-1-923646-59-9

Table of Contents

Preface 1

PART I: FOUNDATIONS & FRAMEWORK 4

Chapter 1.0: Why Traditional Approaches Don't Work 5

1.1 The Confrontation Problem 5

1.2 Evidence for MI Effectiveness 6

1.3 Understanding Mandated Populations 7

1.4 Case Study: The Cost of Confrontation 8

1.5 Financial and Human Costs 10

1.6 Case Study: Breaking the Cycle 11

1.7 What This Book Offers 12

1.8 Chapter Summary 12

Chapter 2.0: Understanding Motivational Interviewing 14

2.1 Defining Motivational Interviewing 14

2.2 The Spirit of MI 15

2.3 The Four Processes 16

2.4 Case Study: Engaging the Disengaged 18

2.5 MI and Evidence Based Practice 19

2.6 Case Study: Addressing Criminogenic Needs 20

2.7 Common Misconceptions 21

2.8 Chapter Summary 22

Chapter 3.0: Authority and Ally Together 24

3.1 Understanding the Dual Role 24

3.2 Transparency About the Role 25

3.3 Case Study: Establishing the Frame 26

3.4 Sanctions Within MI Framework 27

3.5 Case Study: Handling a Violation 28

3.6 When Authority Must Lead 30

3.7 Case Study: Safety First, Then MI 31
3.8 Maintaining MI Long Term 32
3.9 Chapter Summary 33
PART II: CORE SKILLS FOR THE FIELD 34
Chapter 4.0: The Fundamental OARS Skills 35
4.1 Open Questions Explained 35
4.2 Affirmations That Work 36
4.3 Reflections as Core Skill 37
4.4 Case Study: Questions and Reflections 38
4.5 Summaries in Practice 40
4.6 Case Study: Affirmation and Summary 41
4.7 Putting Skills Together 42
4.8 Chapter Summary 42
Chapter 5.0: Recognizing Change Talk 44
5.1 The DARN CAT Framework 44
5.2 Hearing Change Talk 45
5.3 Case Study: Recognizing Subtle Forms 46
5.4 Evoking Change Talk 48
5.5 Responding to Strengthen 49
5.6 Case Study: Evoking and Responding 50
5.7 Context in Criminal Justice 51
5.8 Core Concepts Recap 52
Chapter 6.0: Sustain Talk and Discord 53
6.1 Sustain Talk Versus Discord 53
6.2 Responding to Sustain Talk 54
6.3 Case Study: Sustain Talk Response 55
6.4 Reducing Discord 56
6.5 Case Study: Discord Repair 57
6.6 The Righting Reflex 58
6.7 Case Study: Resisting the Reflex 59

6.8 Essential Points Recap 61
Chapter 7.0: MI Throughout Supervision 62
7.1 The Initial Interview 62
7.2 Collaborative Case Planning 63
7.3 Case Study: Intake and Planning 64
7.4 Routine Supervision Visits 65
7.5 Post Violation Conversations 66
7.6 Case Study: After Violation 67
7.7 Successful Termination 69
7.8 Case Study: Termination Conversation 69
7.9 Bringing It Together 71
PART III: SPECIAL POPULATIONS & CRIME-SPECIFIC APPLICATIONS 73
Chapter 8.0: Substance Use and MI 74
8.1 MI Origins in Addiction 74
8.2 Substance Use Conversations 75
8.3 Case Study: Treatment Resistance 76
8.4 Responding to Relapse 78
8.5 Case Study: After Relapse 78
8.6 Treatment Provider Coordination 80
8.7 Core Principles Recap 81
Chapter 9.0: Intimate Partner Violence Cases 82
9.1 Evidence for MI in IPV 82
9.2 Accountability in MI Framework 83
9.3 Case Study: Minimization and Accountability 84
9.4 Common IPV Conversations 85
9.5 Victim Safety Priority 86
9.6 Chapter Synthesis 87
Chapter 10.0: DUI and Impaired Driving 88
10.1 Evidence Base for DUI 88
10.2 Exploring Drinking and Driving 89

10.3 Case Study: First Offense Minimization.......90
10.4 MI Across DUI Supervision.......91
10.5 Assessing Treatment Needs.......92
10.6 Essential Points.......93
Chapter 11.0: Drug and Specialty Courts.......94
11.1 MI and Treatment Court Philosophy.......94
11.2 Team Member Applications.......95
11.3 Case Study: Team Consistency.......96
11.4 Phase Advancement Conversations.......97
11.5 Mental Health Court Considerations.......98
11.6 Chapter Overview.......99
Chapter 12.0: Sex Offender Supervision.......100
12.1 Evidence and Possibilities.......100
12.2 Engaging Resistant Clients.......101
12.3 Case Study: Engaging Through Values.......101
12.4 Specific MI Applications.......103
12.5 Risk Management Balance.......103
12.6 Summary and Implications.......104
Chapter 13.0: Working with High Risk.......105
13.1 Why MI Matters More.......105
13.2 Intensive Supervision Techniques.......106
13.3 Case Study: Intensive Supervision.......106
13.4 Gang Involved Individuals.......108
13.5 Criminal Thinking Patterns.......108
13.6 Bringing It Together.......109
Chapter 14.0: Reentry and Parole.......110
14.1 The Reentry Challenge.......110
14.2 Pre Release Conversations.......111
14.3 Case Study: Pre Release Planning.......111
14.4 Reentry Challenges.......113

14.5 Service Coordination....113
14.6 Concluding Thoughts....114
PART IV: IMPLEMENTATION & SUSTAINABILITY....115
Chapter 15.0: Integrating MI Into Practice....116
15.1 Stages of Learning MI....116
15.2 Starting With Practice....117
15.3 Self Assessment Methods....118
15.4 Case Study: Skill Development....119
15.5 Common Pitfalls....120
15.6 Avoiding the Pitfalls....121
15.7 Putting Knowledge Into Practice....121
Chapter 16.0: Agency MI Implementation....123
16.1 Making the Evidence Case....123
16.2 Effective Training Models....124
16.3 Case Study: Failed Implementation....125
16.4 Supporting Officer Practice....126
16.5 Measuring Success....127
16.6 Case Study: Successful Implementation....127
16.7 Chapter Synthesis....128
Chapter 17.0: Self Care and Sustainability....130
17.1 Compassion Fatigue in Corrections....130
17.2 MI Under Pressure....131
17.3 Case Study: Preventing Burnout....132
17.4 Finding Meaning....133
17.5 Continued Professional Growth....134
17.6 Case Study: Sustained Growth....134
17.7 Core Principles Recap....135
PART V: CASE STUDIES....137
Chapter 18: Foundation Cases....138
Case Study 1: Initial Intake Interview with Resistant Client....138

Case Background 138
Session Script 138
MI Skills Demonstrated 143
Reflection 143
Outcome Analysis 144
Case Study 2: Using Open Questions to Build Engagement 146
Case Background 146
Session Script 146
MI Skills Demonstrated 151
Reflection 152
Outcome Analysis 153
Case Study 3: Strategic Affirmations with a Defensive Supervisee 155
Case Background 155
Session Script 155
MI Skills Demonstrated 161
Reflection 161
Outcome Analysis 162
Case Study 4: Reflective Listening with an Ambivalent Client 164
Case Background 164
Session Script 164
MI Skills Demonstrated 170
Reflection 171
Outcome Analysis 172
Case Study 5: Summarizing to Consolidate Change Talk 174
Case Background 174
Session Script 174
MI Skills Demonstrated 180
Reflection 180
Outcome Analysis 181
Chapter 19: Change Talk and Sustain Talk Cases 183

Case Study 6: Recognizing and Evoking DARN-CAT Change Talk 183
Case Background 183
Session Script 183
MI Skills Demonstrated 189
Reflection 189
Outcome Analysis 190
Case Study 7: Responding to Sustain Talk Without Amplification 192
Case Background 192
Session Script 192
MI Skills Demonstrated 198
Reflection 198
Outcome Analysis 199
Case Study 8: Rolling with Resistance in a High-Conflict Session 201
Case Background 201
Session Script 201
MI Skills Demonstrated 207
Reflection 208
Outcome Analysis 209
Case Study 9: The Decisional Balance Conversation 211
Case Background 211
Session Script 211
MI Skills Demonstrated 219
Reflection 219
Outcome Analysis 220
Case Study 10: Using Importance and Confidence Rulers 222
Case Background 222
Session Script 222
MI Skills Demonstrated 228
Reflection 229
Outcome Analysis 230

Chapter 20: Special Population Cases 231
Case Study 11: Substance Abuse and Recovery Motivation 231
Case Background 231
Session Script 231
Reflection 237
Outcome Analysis 238
Case Study 12: Mental Health and Co-occurring Disorders 239
Case Background 239
Session Script 239
Reflection 246
Outcome Analysis 246
Case Study 13: Domestic Violence Perpetrator Accountability 248
Case Background 248
Session Script 248
Reflection 254
Outcome Analysis 255
Case Study 14: Sex Offense Supervision and Denial 256
Case Background 256
Session Script 256
Reflection 261
Outcome Analysis 262
Case Study 15: Juvenile Justice and Adolescent Engagement 263
Case Background 263
Session Script 263
Reflection 269
Outcome Analysis 269
Chapter 19: Supervision Cycle Cases 271
Case Study 16: Post-Violation Conversation 271
Case Background 271
Session Script 271

Reflection 276
Outcome Analysis 276
Case Study 17: Case Planning Session 277
Case Background 277
Session Script..277
Reflection 282
Outcome Analysis 282
Case Study 18: Routine Office Visit with Stalled Progress 283
Case Background 283
Session Script..283
Reflection 287
Outcome Analysis 288
Case Study 19: Crisis Intervention and Safety Planning 289
Case Background 289
Session Script..289
Reflection 294
Outcome Analysis 294
Case Study 20: Successful Termination and Transition 296
Case Background 296
Session Script..296
Reflection 301
Outcome Analysis 301
Conclusion 304
Appendix A: Quick Reference MI Skills 305
A.1 OARS Summary..305
A.2 Change Talk Types..305
A.3 Responding to Sustain Talk...306
A.4 Common Phrases...307
Appendix B: Sample Dialogues..309
B.1 Initial Interview Excerpt...309

B.2 Routine Visit Brief MI 309
B.3 Violation Conversation 310
B.4 Post Relapse Conversation 311
Appendix C: Assessment and Planning Tools 313
C.1 MI Informed Case Plan Template 313
C.2 Change Talk Tracking Form 314
C.3 Self Assessment Checklist 314
C.4 Supervision Meeting Agenda 315
Appendix D: Resources for Learning 317
D.1 Books and Training Manuals 317
D.2 Training and Professional Development 317
D.3 Fidelity Instruments 317
Appendix E: Research Summary Tables 319
E.1 MI in Criminal Justice 319
E.2 MI Effectiveness by Population 319
E.3 Training Effectiveness 319
Glossary of Terms 321
References 323

Preface

Community corrections stands at a crossroads. After decades of policies emphasizing surveillance, compliance monitoring, and swift punishment for violations, the evidence has become impossible to ignore: traditional approaches to probation and parole supervision consistently underperform. Recidivism rates remain stubbornly high despite massive investments in supervision intensity. Officers experience burnout and frustration while supervisees cycle through the system repeatedly. Something fundamental needs to change in how officers communicate with the people they supervise.

The communication approach presented in this book represents that change. Motivational interviewing emerged from addiction treatment research in the 1980s, where clinicians discovered that confrontational methods produced worse outcomes than supportive, client-centered conversations. Over four decades, the evidence base expanded dramatically. Researchers documented MI effectiveness across diverse populations and settings, including the criminal justice contexts where practitioners face the unique challenge of supporting change while enforcing accountability. The research consistently demonstrates that how officers talk with supervisees matters as much as what they talk about.

Writing a practical guide on this topic required wrestling with a fundamental tension. Professional utility demands accessible language, concrete examples, and skills that officers can apply in their next supervisee contact. Academic credibility demands thorough documentation and precise explanations. The goal throughout has been to honor both demands: to provide practical guidance that enables immediate implementation while maintaining the theoretical foundation that explains why these approaches work. Every technique described here rests on research evidence, and every significant claim includes verifiable citations.

Each chapter follows a consistent structure designed to build competence progressively. Opening discussions establish relevance by describing situations that practitioners encounter regularly. Core content explains the underlying principles and specific skills with sufficient depth to support genuine understanding. Case studies illustrate concepts in action through composite examples drawn from authentic probation and parole scenarios. These fictional vignettes were crafted to feel authentic precisely because they reflect common patterns that experienced practitioners will recognize immediately.

The case studies deserve particular mention regarding their fictional nature. All names, circumstances, identifying details, and dialogue are entirely created for educational purposes. No case study represents any actual individual, case, or agency. The scenarios were developed by combining common elements from typical supervision situations into illustrative composites. Any resemblance to actual persons or cases is coincidental. Readers should not attempt to identify any real individuals in these examples because none exist.

Part One establishes the foundation by examining why traditional confrontational approaches fail and how motivational interviewing offers a research-supported alternative. Readers will understand the spirit that underlies MI and the processes that structure MI conversations. The dual role challenge receives extended attention because probation and parole officers occupy a position unlike any other helping profession: simultaneously supporting change and enforcing consequences when change does not occur.

Part Two develops the core skills that every MI practitioner needs. The OARS skills of open questions, affirmations, reflections, and summaries provide the building blocks for all MI conversations. These skills may appear simple on the surface, but skilled application requires practice, feedback, and refinement over time. The text provides detailed guidance on each skill along with examples demonstrating common errors and effective alternatives.

Part Three addresses the strategic elements that distinguish MI from other empathic approaches. Recognition and evocation of change talk predicts whether supervisees will actually modify their behavior following supervision contacts. Responding to sustain talk and discord without escalation enables officers to maintain engagement even when supervisees push back against the supervision process. These chapters address the most challenging moments in supervision relationships.

Part Four applies MI skills across the supervision cycle and to special populations. Initial interviews, case planning sessions, routine contacts, post-violation conversations, and successful terminations each present distinct opportunities for MI application. Specialized chapters address substance abuse, mental health conditions, domestic violence, sex offenses, and juvenile justice contexts that require adapted approaches.

No single book can transform practice. Skill development requires ongoing effort, practice with actual supervisees, feedback from supervisors or peers, and refinement over time. Reading about MI differs fundamentally from practicing MI in real supervision contacts. What a practical guide can do is provide the conceptual framework, the evidence base, and the detailed guidance that support deliberate practice. The goal is to equip readers with sufficient understanding to begin that practice and to continue developing competence throughout their careers in community corrections.

The officers who will benefit most from these pages are those willing to examine their own communication patterns honestly. Recognizing the righting reflex in oneself, acknowledging when conversations have become arguments, and genuinely seeking to understand supervisees' perspectives all require professional humility. MI is not a technique to be applied on people but rather a way of being with people that expresses respect for their autonomy while supporting their capacity for positive change. Officers who approach these skills with openness to examining their own practice will find substantial rewards in more productive supervision relationships and better outcomes for the individuals and communities they serve.

PART I: FOUNDATIONS & FRAMEWORK

Chapter 1.0: Why Traditional Approaches Don't Work

Every day, thousands of probation and parole officers across the country sit down with individuals whose lives hang in the balance. The officer reviews the file, notes the conditions of supervision, and begins what should be a conversation about change. Instead, it becomes a lecture. The officer explains what the person needs to do, lists the consequences of failure, and watches as their words bounce off an invisible wall of resistance. By the end of the meeting, both parties feel frustrated, and nothing meaningful has shifted. This scenario repeats itself millions of times each year, and we keep wondering why recidivism rates remain stubbornly high.

This chapter examines why traditional approaches to offender supervision consistently underperform and presents the evidence for a fundamentally different way of engaging with justice-involved individuals. You will learn:

- Why confrontational communication strategies increase resistance rather than reduce it
- What research tells us about the effectiveness of motivational interviewing in criminal justice settings
- The hidden costs of maintaining adversarial relationships with supervisees
- How this book will help you develop practical skills for better outcomes

1.1 The Confrontation Problem

The criminal justice system has long operated on a simple assumption: if people understand the consequences of their actions, they will change their behavior. This assumption drives the confrontational approach that dominates most probation and parole interactions. Officers tell supervisees what they must do, warn them about what will happen if they fail, and expect compliance to follow naturally. When it does not, the response typically involves more confrontation, more warnings, and eventually, more sanctions (Clark, 2005).

The problem is that this approach contradicts decades of research on how human beings actually change. **Psychological reactance** refers to the motivational state that occurs when people perceive their freedom is being threatened or restricted. When someone tells us what to do, especially in a forceful or authoritative manner, our natural response is to resist (Brehm & Brehm, 1981). This reaction is not defiance for its own sake. It represents a fundamental human drive to maintain autonomy and self-determination.

Consider what happens in a typical probation office visit. The officer says, "You need to get a job within 30 days, or I'll have to report you to the court." The supervisee hears a threat to their autonomy. Their internal response, even if unspoken, often sounds like: "Who are you to tell me what I have to do?" This reaction occurs regardless of the fact that employment is genuinely in their best interest. The confrontational framing triggers resistance that would not exist if the conversation had unfolded differently.

Miller, Benefield, and Tonigan (1993) conducted a landmark study that quantified this phenomenon. They examined how therapist communication style affected client outcomes in alcohol treatment. Clients who received a confrontational approach showed twice as much resistance during sessions compared to those who received a supportive, client-centered approach. More striking was the finding about actual drinking outcomes: the more the therapist confronted, the more the clients drank at twelve-month follow-up. The confrontational style did not merely fail to help. It actively made things worse.

This research has profound implications for criminal justice settings. When officers adopt a confrontational stance, they inadvertently create the very resistance they are trying to overcome. Each warning, each threat, each "you need to" statement builds a wall between the officer and the supervisee. Behind that wall, the person's motivation to change remains untouched or even diminishes further (Walters, Clark, Gingerich, & Meltzer, 2007).

The "righting reflex" compounds this problem. This term describes the natural tendency of helping professionals to want to fix problems, give advice, and direct people toward better choices (Miller & Rollnick, 2013). Officers see clearly what their supervisees should do. Employment, sobriety, stable housing, and prosocial relationships all represent obvious paths toward successful completion of supervision. The temptation to simply tell people these things feels overwhelming. Yet the research consistently shows that this telling approach produces poor results precisely because it triggers reactance and fails to engage the person's own motivation.

1.2 Evidence for MI Effectiveness

If confrontation makes things worse, what actually works? Over the past four decades, motivational interviewing has accumulated an impressive evidence base across diverse populations and settings. Originally developed for addiction treatment, MI has demonstrated effectiveness in promoting behavior change across healthcare, mental health, and increasingly, criminal justice contexts (Hettema, Steele, & Miller, 2005).

A systematic review and meta-analysis examining MI effectiveness with justice-involved populations analyzed 22 studies involving individuals convicted of various offenses including intimate partner violence, violent crimes, sexual offenses, property crimes, and driving while intoxicated. The findings were clear: interventions incorporating MI proved more effective than other approaches in preventing and reducing offending behavior (Pinto e Silva et al., 2022). This conclusion held across different types of crimes and different correctional settings.

The Motivational Assessment Program to Initiate Treatment (MAPIT) study provides particularly relevant evidence for community corrections. This multisite randomized controlled trial compared motivational interviewing delivered by counselors against supervision as usual for probationers with substance use disorders. Researchers found that MI improved treatment participation, with greater gains observed for high-risk offenders in both study sites (Taxman et al., 2015). The MI approach proved especially effective with the very populations that traditional supervision struggles to engage.

Research with driving while intoxicated offenders demonstrates the durability of MI effects. Brown and colleagues (2015) followed DWI recidivists for nearly five years after they received either a single 30-minute brief motivational interviewing session or a control intervention involving information and advice. The brief MI session was more effective in delaying subsequent DWI arrests and other dangerous traffic violations, particularly among younger drivers. These findings suggest that even brief MI interventions can produce meaningful long-term changes in behavior.

Studies examining MI with intimate partner violence perpetrators reveal its value in increasing treatment engagement. A review of the literature found that MI interventions improved session attendance, homework compliance, and overall engagement in batterer intervention programs (Soleymani et al., 2018). Given the high dropout rates that plague domestic violence treatment programs, these findings have significant practical implications. When perpetrators remain engaged in treatment longer, outcomes improve and victims are safer.

Perhaps most compelling is research showing that brief MI interventions with prisoners reduce reconviction rates. Anstiss, Polaschek, and Wilson (2011) studied male prisoners who received a brief offending-focused MI intervention. Men who completed MI were significantly less likely to be reconvicted than those who did not receive the intervention. The study also validated the stages of change model, showing that prisoners who received MI increased their readiness to change by an average of one stage.

1.3 Understanding Mandated Populations

A common objection to using MI in criminal justice settings centers on the mandatory nature of supervision. Officers frequently argue that MI cannot work with people who did not choose to seek help. This objection reflects a misunderstanding of both MI and human motivation (McMurran, 2009).

First, mandated populations are not uniformly resistant. Research consistently shows substantial variation in motivation levels among justice-involved individuals. Some supervisees desperately want to change and simply lack the skills or resources. Others feel ambivalent, seeing both reasons to change and reasons to maintain current patterns. Only a minority actively want to continue offending behavior. Treating all supervisees as resistant creates resistance where it may not have existed (Ginsburg, Mann, Rotgers, & Weekes, 2002).

Second, external pressure does not eliminate internal motivation. Many people entering the criminal justice system have thought about making changes long before their arrest. The legal consequences may actually represent a catalyst that pushes ambivalent individuals toward action. When officers meet these individuals with confrontation, they squander an opportunity to harness existing motivation. When they meet them with MI, they can amplify and support change that the person was already considering (Clark, 2006).

Third, MI explicitly acknowledges and works with the reality of coerced treatment. MI practitioners do not pretend that supervisees have complete freedom. Instead, they honestly discuss the constraints while focusing on choices that remain available. A probation officer using MI might say: "The court has ordered you to complete substance abuse treatment. You didn't choose that requirement. What you do get to choose is how you approach it. What would make this something useful for you rather than just something you have to get through?" This framing respects the reality of the mandate while engaging the person's autonomy within it (Walters et al., 2007).

Research specifically comparing MI to other approaches with mandated clients shows that coercion does not prevent MI from working. A meta-analysis by Lundahl and Burke (2009) found that MI produced positive effects regardless of the fact that participants were mandated. In some studies, MI showed stronger effects with mandated populations than with voluntary treatment seekers. The authors speculated that mandated clients may have more room to improve and therefore more potential to benefit from effective intervention.

1.4 Case Study: The Cost of Confrontation

Background

Marcus, a 26-year-old man on probation for drug possession, had been labeled "non-compliant" after three months of supervision. His officer, frustrated by missed appointments and positive drug tests, had escalated to increasingly stern warnings. Case notes described Marcus as "resistant," "unmotivated," and "making excuses."

Presentation

During a review of the case, a supervisor asked to observe the next interaction. The officer began the meeting by reading a list of violations and stating, "You're on thin ice here. If you don't get your act together, you're going back to jail." Marcus slouched in his chair, arms crossed, offering only monosyllabic responses. When asked about his positive drug test, he said, "I don't know what you want me to say." The meeting ended with another warning and scheduled follow-up.

Analysis

This case illustrates the confrontation trap in action. The officer's directive approach triggered psychological reactance, visible in Marcus's closed body language and minimal engagement. Each warning further entrenched the adversarial dynamic. The label "resistant" became a self-fulfilling prophecy: the officer expected resistance, communicated in ways that produced it, and interpreted the resulting behavior as confirmation of the initial assessment. Meanwhile, Marcus's actual situation, including housing instability, untreated anxiety, and ambivalence about his drug use, remained unexplored.

Intervention

Following consultation, the officer agreed to try a different approach. At the next meeting, instead of listing violations, the officer began with an open question: "What's been going on for you lately?" Marcus, surprised, started talking about losing his housing and feeling overwhelmed. The officer listened, reflected what Marcus said, and eventually asked, "Where does the drug use fit into all this?" Marcus acknowledged that he was using to cope with stress but admitted it was creating more problems than it solved.

Outcome

Over subsequent meetings using MI techniques, Marcus's engagement increased substantially. He began arriving on time and talking openly about his struggles. His drug use decreased as he connected with treatment services. The case that had seemed headed toward revocation instead progressed toward successful completion.

Teaching Points

- Confrontational approaches often create the resistance they aim to overcome
- Labels like "resistant" can become self-fulfilling prophecies that prevent accurate assessment
- The same individual can appear completely different when approached with MI techniques

1.5 Financial and Human Costs

The failure of traditional approaches carries enormous costs, both financial and human. In the United States, approximately 4.5 million adults are under community supervision at any given time (Kaeble, 2021). Of these, roughly 40% will experience a supervision failure within three years, either through new arrests or technical violations (Pew Center on the States, 2011). Each failure generates cascading expenses: court costs, incarceration costs, lost productivity, and the ripple effects on families and communities.

Incarceration alone costs an average of $35,000 to $45,000 per person per year, with substantial variation across jurisdictions (Vera Institute of Justice, 2019). When probation officers cannot effectively engage supervisees, violations mount, and revocations follow. A single revocation to prison can cost taxpayers more than three years of intensive community supervision services. Multiply this by hundreds of thousands of revocations annually, and the economic impact becomes staggering.

Beyond financial costs, the adversarial approach extracts a toll on officers themselves. Burnout rates among probation and parole officers consistently exceed those in comparable professions (Lewis, Lewis, & Garby, 2013). Officers who spend their days in conflict with supervisees experience chronic stress that affects their health, their job performance, and their personal lives. High turnover in community corrections departments disrupts relationships with supervisees and undermines continuity of supervision.

The individuals under supervision bear the heaviest burden. Failed supervision often means return to incarceration, disruption of employment and housing, separation from family, and the accumulation of additional criminal justice involvement. Children of incarcerated parents experience elevated rates of behavioral problems, academic difficulties, and their own later involvement with the justice system (Murray, Farrington, & Sekol, 2012). What begins as a supervision approach becomes a mechanism for intergenerational transmission of criminal justice involvement.

1.6 Case Study: Breaking the Cycle

Background

Theodora, a 34-year-old woman, had cycled through the criminal justice system six times over fifteen years, always for offenses related to substance use. Each time, she received probation, failed to comply with treatment requirements, and eventually returned to custody. Her file contained hundreds of pages documenting the same pattern repeated again and again.

Presentation

At intake for her seventh probation term, Theodora presented as withdrawn and pessimistic. She told her new officer, "Just tell me what hoops to jump through. We both know how this ends." Her posture and tone suggested someone who had given up on the possibility of a different outcome.

Analysis

Theodora's presentation reflected learned helplessness developed through repeated cycles of failure within a system that consistently approached her the same way. Previous officers had given her the same lectures, the same warnings, and the same referrals to treatment programs she never engaged with meaningfully. Nothing in her experience suggested that this time would be different. Her cynicism represented a rational response to her history.

Intervention

The assigned officer, recently trained in MI, chose not to follow the familiar script. Instead of launching into conditions and consequences, she said, "You've been through this process before. Several times, from what I can see. What's that been like for you?" Theodora, expecting the usual lecture, paused before responding. For the next thirty minutes, she talked about her experiences in the system, her struggles with addiction, and her sense that no one had ever really listened.

Outcome

This initial conversation began a fundamentally different supervisory relationship. The officer continued using MI throughout Theodora's supervision, exploring her ambivalence about drug use rather than demanding abstinence. Over time, Theodora developed her own reasons for seeking recovery, connected with peer support services, and began rebuilding her life. After two years, she successfully completed probation for the first time in her adult life.

Teaching Points

- Repeated system failure may reflect the approach rather than the individual
- Individuals labeled as "chronic offenders" can change when met with effective engagement
- MI techniques can disrupt patterns that have persisted through multiple system contacts

1.7 What This Book Offers

This book provides practical guidance for integrating motivational interviewing into community corrections practice. It is not a theoretical treatise or an academic exercise. Every chapter focuses on skills you can use in your next supervisee interaction. The approach recognizes the realities of community corrections work: high caseloads, limited time, complex populations, and the genuine need to maintain public safety.

In the chapters that follow, you will learn the fundamental MI skills of asking open questions, offering affirmations, making reflections, and providing summaries. You will discover how to recognize and respond to change talk, the language that signals movement toward behavior change. You will develop strategies for handling resistance without escalating conflict. And you will learn how to integrate MI into every phase of supervision, from the initial intake interview through successful discharge.

The case studies throughout this book draw from real scenarios in probation, parole, and related settings. Names and identifying details have been changed, but the situations reflect the genuine challenges that community corrections officers face daily. Each case illustrates specific skills in action and provides models you can adapt to your own practice.

Perhaps most importantly, this book addresses the dual role challenge that makes criminal justice work unique. Unlike therapists or counselors, probation and parole officers must simultaneously support change and enforce accountability. Chapter 3 tackles this challenge directly, showing how MI techniques can be maintained even when sanctions must be imposed. You will learn that being an agent of change and an agent of the court are not incompatible roles.

1.8 Chapter Summary

Traditional confrontational approaches to offender supervision fail because they trigger psychological reactance, creating resistance rather than reducing it. Research spanning decades demonstrates that the more we confront, the more people push back, and outcomes suffer accordingly. Motivational interviewing offers an evidence-based alternative that has proven effective across diverse criminal justice populations including probationers, parolees, DWI offenders, domestic violence perpetrators, and incarcerated individuals preparing for reentry.

The costs of maintaining ineffective approaches are substantial. Financial costs include the billions spent on reincarceration for supervision failures. Human costs include officer burnout, family disruption, and the perpetuation of intergenerational criminal justice involvement. These costs are not inevitable consequences of working with difficult populations. They are, in large part, consequences of how we have chosen to work with these populations.

Change is possible. The evidence reviewed in this chapter demonstrates that different approaches produce different results. When officers learn and apply MI skills, supervisees engage more meaningfully, treatment participation improves, and outcomes change. The following chapters will equip you with the specific skills to produce these results in your own practice.

Chapter 2.0: Understanding Motivational Interviewing

Picture yourself in a conversation where someone genuinely wants to understand your perspective. They ask thoughtful questions rather than jumping to conclusions. They reflect back what you say in ways that help you understand yourself better. They express confidence in your ability to make good decisions, even when you doubt yourself. By the end of the conversation, you find yourself saying things you had not realized you believed, discovering motivations you had not acknowledged, and feeling ready to take steps you had resisted before. That experience captures what motivational interviewing looks like when done well.

This chapter provides a comprehensive introduction to motivational interviewing adapted specifically for criminal justice professionals. You will learn:

- What MI is and what distinguishes it from other communication approaches
- The underlying spirit that makes MI effective
- The four processes that structure MI conversations
- How MI aligns with evidence-based correctional practice frameworks

2.1 Defining Motivational Interviewing

Motivational interviewing is a collaborative, goal-oriented style of communication with particular attention to the language of change (Miller & Rollnick, 2013). This definition contains several important elements worth examining closely.

First, MI is collaborative. It represents a partnership between the practitioner and the client rather than an expert-to-recipient relationship. The officer using MI does not position themselves as the authority who knows what the supervisee should do. Instead, they work alongside the person to explore options, examine ambivalence, and develop plans that the person genuinely owns.

Second, MI is goal-oriented. It is not aimless conversation or passive listening. MI practitioners have clear direction in their work. In criminal justice settings, that direction typically involves reducing criminal behavior, increasing compliance with supervision conditions, and supporting positive life changes. The difference between MI and traditional approaches lies not in having goals but in how the practitioner pursues them.

Third, MI pays particular attention to the language of change. This feature distinguishes MI from other client-centered approaches. MI practitioners listen strategically for statements that signal movement toward change and respond in ways that strengthen and amplify that movement. This active, directional quality makes MI especially suitable for settings where behavior change is the explicit purpose of the encounter.

Many practitioners initially confuse MI with general "good listening" or "being nice." While MI certainly involves skillful listening and respectful treatment, it requires much more. An officer who listens patiently to a supervisee describe their struggles but then proceeds to lecture about what they should do is not practicing MI. Genuine MI maintains its collaborative, evocative quality throughout the entire conversation, even when addressing difficult topics or uncomfortable truths (Moyers, 2014).

Similarly, MI is not a technique for getting people to do what you want them to do. This misunderstanding leads some practitioners to view MI as a more sophisticated form of manipulation. In reality, MI works precisely because it is not manipulative. It draws out the person's own values, goals, and motivations. The practitioner may shape the conversation, but the motivation comes from the person themselves. When MI is used as a manipulation tool, people typically sense the inauthenticity, and the approach fails (Miller & Rollnick, 2013).

2.2 The Spirit of MI

Technical skills alone do not produce effective MI. Behind every successful MI conversation lies a particular spirit or way of being that the practitioner embodies. This spirit has four interrelated components: partnership, acceptance, compassion, and evocation. Together, they create the foundation upon which all MI techniques rest (Miller & Rollnick, 2013).

Partnership represents a fundamental shift in how the practitioner relates to the client. In traditional criminal justice interactions, the relationship is hierarchical. The officer holds power; the supervisee complies or faces consequences. Partnership does not eliminate the power differential entirely, but it changes how that power is exercised. The officer working from partnership seeks to create a collaborative atmosphere even within the constraints of mandatory supervision. They communicate, implicitly and explicitly, that the supervisee has valuable knowledge about their own life and that positive change requires working together rather than one person directing another.

Acceptance involves four elements: absolute worth, accurate empathy, autonomy support, and affirmation. Absolute worth means communicating that the person has inherent value regardless of their behavior. This does not mean approving of criminal behavior or pretending that harmful actions are acceptable. It means recognizing the fundamental humanity of every person, even those who have caused serious harm. Accurate empathy involves understanding the person's perspective and internal frame of reference, seeing the world through their eyes without losing one's own perspective. Autonomy support acknowledges the person's right and ability to make their own choices, recognizing that ultimately they will decide what they do regardless of external pressure. Affirmation involves recognizing and reflecting the person's strengths and efforts (Miller & Rollnick, 2013).

Compassion means that the practitioner's actions are fundamentally oriented toward the client's welfare. The officer using MI genuinely cares about what happens to the supervisee. This caring provides motivation for the hard work of MI practice and communicates to supervisees that someone is on their side. Compassion does not mean being a pushover or ignoring accountability. It means that even when enforcing consequences, the officer maintains genuine concern for the person's wellbeing and wants them to succeed (Stinson & Clark, 2017).

Evocation reflects the assumption that people already have within themselves what they need to change. The practitioner's task is not to install motivation but to draw out motivation that already exists. This represents a profound shift from the traditional "education" model where the expert provides information and advice. In MI, the conversation is structured to help the person discover and articulate their own reasons for change. These self-generated reasons prove far more powerful than externally imposed ones (Miller & Rollnick, 2013).

2.3 The Four Processes

MI unfolds through four overlapping processes: engaging, focusing, evoking, and planning. These processes do not follow a rigid sequence. Practitioners may move among them fluidly within a single conversation and return to earlier processes when needed. Understanding each process helps practitioners know where they are in the conversation and what their primary task is at any given moment (Miller & Rollnick, 2013).

Engaging establishes a working relationship and therapeutic alliance. Without engagement, the other processes cannot proceed effectively. In criminal justice settings, engaging faces particular challenges because the person did not choose to be there and may view the officer as an adversary. Engagement requires demonstrating trustworthiness, showing genuine interest in the person beyond their criminal behavior, and creating a space where honest conversation becomes possible.

Engaging is not a one-time event that happens at the beginning of supervision and then remains settled. Officers must continually monitor and maintain engagement throughout their work together. When engagement weakens, perhaps after a difficult conversation or a violation, the officer returns to this foundational process before attempting to move forward (Walters et al., 2007).

Focusing involves developing and maintaining a specific direction in the conversation. MI is not aimless. The practitioner and client need to establish what they are talking about and why. In community corrections, multiple possible foci exist: substance use, employment, relationships, housing, mental health, and compliance with specific conditions. Focusing helps ensure that conversations have clear purpose and that both parties understand what they are working toward.

Sometimes the focus emerges naturally from the person's concerns. Other times, the officer may need to introduce topics that the person has not raised. MI provides strategies for introducing topics in ways that maintain engagement rather than creating resistance. The key is negotiating an agenda collaboratively rather than imposing one unilaterally (Miller & Rollnick, 2013).

Evoking is the heart of MI. Once engaged and focused, the practitioner works to draw out the person's own motivations for change. This involves listening for **change talk**, statements that favor movement in the direction of change, and responding in ways that strengthen and amplify such statements. Evoking also involves recognizing **sustain talk**, statements that favor maintaining the status quo, and responding in ways that do not strengthen it.

The evoking process distinguishes MI from other empathic approaches. A non-directive counselor might reflect all client statements equally, giving no particular attention to change-related language. The MI practitioner, while remaining client-centered, actively guides the conversation toward change. This strategic direction makes MI particularly effective in settings where change is the explicit goal (Moyers et al., 2009).

Planning emerges when the person demonstrates sufficient readiness for change. The practitioner shifts from evoking motivation to consolidating commitment and developing specific plans for action. Planning should not be rushed. Premature planning, before sufficient motivation has developed, often produces plans that the person does not follow through on. The experienced MI practitioner reads signs of readiness and times the transition to planning appropriately.

Planning in MI remains collaborative. Rather than the officer creating a plan and presenting it to the supervisee, planning involves joint exploration of options, consideration of barriers, and development of steps that the person genuinely commits to. This collaborative quality increases the likelihood that plans will be implemented (Miller & Rollnick, 2013).

2.4 Case Study: Engaging the Disengaged

Background

Remigius, a 41-year-old man, began parole after serving eight years for armed robbery. During his first month of supervision, he presented as withdrawn and minimally communicative. He answered questions with the shortest possible responses, avoided eye contact, and seemed to be waiting for each meeting to end. His parole officer noted him as "disengaged" but also recognized that this presentation might reflect something other than lack of motivation.

Presentation

When asked about his transition back to the community, Remigius typically responded with shrugs and brief statements like "It's fine" or "Whatever." Previous officers had interpreted similar behavior as evidence that the person did not care about supervision or their future. This officer chose to explore further.

Analysis

Remigius's presentation illustrated the engaging challenge common in criminal justice settings. After eight years of incarceration, he had learned to protect himself by revealing nothing. Engagement required demonstrating that this supervisory relationship might be different from others he had experienced. The officer recognized that pushing for information would likely increase Remigius's guardedness rather than reduce it.

Intervention

Instead of pressing for details about his adjustment, the officer spent several meetings focusing on topics where Remigius showed any interest. When Remigius mentioned offhandedly that he had been watching basketball, the officer asked about his team preferences. When Remigius mentioned his sister, the officer explored that relationship with gentle curiosity. Over time, as these non-threatening conversations accumulated, Remigius began to relax.

After several weeks, the officer said, "You know, we've been meeting for a while now, and I realize I've done most of the talking about the official stuff. I'm curious what you think about how parole is going. Not what you're supposed to say, but what you actually think." Remigius paused, then began talking about his fears, his frustrations with finding work, and his determination not to return to prison.

Outcome

Once engaged, Remigius proved highly motivated to succeed on parole. The apparent disengagement had masked significant anxiety about the transition and distrust of the system. As trust developed, he became increasingly open about challenges and receptive to support. He completed parole successfully, maintaining employment and reconnecting with his family.

Teaching Points

- Apparent disengagement may reflect self-protection rather than lack of motivation
- Engaging requires patience and willingness to build relationship before addressing business
- Non-threatening conversations can create openings for more substantive dialogue

2.5 MI and Evidence Based Practice

Motivational interviewing fits seamlessly within the evidence-based practice frameworks that increasingly guide criminal justice work. The **Risk-Need-Responsivity (RNR) model**, developed by Andrews and Bonta, provides the dominant framework for effective correctional intervention. Understanding how MI aligns with RNR helps practitioners see why this communication style produces better results than traditional approaches (Andrews & Bonta, 2010).

The **risk principle** states that intervention intensity should match the person's risk level. Higher-risk individuals benefit from more intensive services, while lower-risk individuals may actually be harmed by excessive intervention. MI contributes to risk-informed practice by improving the quality of officer-supervisee relationships, which research shows mediates the relationship between supervision and outcomes. When officers use MI effectively, their supervisees engage more meaningfully with whatever level of intervention their risk level warrants (Kennealy, Skeem, Manchak, & Eno Louden, 2012).

The **need principle** holds that interventions should target criminogenic needs, those dynamic factors empirically linked to criminal behavior. These include antisocial cognition, antisocial associates, substance abuse, and deficits in employment, education, family relationships, and prosocial recreation. MI provides a vehicle for addressing criminogenic needs because it increases receptivity to treatment and improves engagement with services targeting these areas. A supervisee who feels heard and respected is more likely to follow through with treatment referrals than one who feels coerced and controlled (Taxman, 2008).

The **responsivity principle** contains both general and specific components. General responsivity indicates that cognitive-behavioral and social learning interventions produce the best outcomes across populations. Specific responsivity calls for tailoring interventions to individual characteristics including motivation, personality, and learning style. MI addresses responsivity directly. It provides a way of communicating that increases receptivity regardless of specific intervention content. Research shows that officers who use MI techniques improve outcomes for their supervisees even when no specific treatment program is involved (Walters et al., 2010).

The relationship between MI and RNR operates bidirectionally. MI enhances the implementation of RNR-based supervision by improving engagement with all aspects of the model. At the same time, the RNR framework provides context for MI application, helping practitioners understand why motivation matters and how it connects to recidivism reduction (Viglione, 2019).

2.6 Case Study: Addressing Criminogenic Needs

Background

Faustina, a 29-year-old woman on probation for theft, had multiple identified criminogenic needs. Her assessment indicated antisocial cognition (rationalizations about stealing), substance abuse (methamphetamine), unemployment, and antisocial associates (friends who also used drugs and engaged in property crimes). Previous officers had addressed these needs by lecturing Faustina about each one and directing her to address them.

Presentation

At her first meeting with a newly assigned officer, Faustina presented defensively, ready for another list of problems and demands. She began by explaining that she knew what she needed to do and just needed to be left alone to do it. Her tone suggested she did not believe this would happen.

Analysis

Faustina's needs were real and significant. Her risk level warranted substantial intervention. The question was how to engage her with those interventions effectively. Previous officers' direct approach, while accurate in identifying problems, had failed to create any movement toward change. The new officer recognized that addressing criminogenic needs required Faustina's active participation, not merely her compliance with directives.

Intervention

Instead of reviewing the problem list, the officer said, "It sounds like you've heard a lot about what other people think you should do. I'm more interested in what you think. If things could be different in your life, what would matter most to you?" Faustina, surprised, thought for a moment before mentioning her daughter. She wanted to be a better mother but felt trapped in patterns she could not break.

From this starting point, the officer helped Faustina explore how her substance use and lifestyle affected her parenting. Rather than telling her these things were problems, the officer asked questions that helped Faustina articulate the connections herself. When Faustina identified discrepancies between her current behavior and her parenting goals, the officer reflected these discrepancies back, strengthening Faustina's own motivation for change.

Outcome

Over subsequent months, Faustina engaged actively with substance abuse treatment, something she had refused in previous probation terms. She began distancing from antisocial associates as she developed new connections through treatment and parenting programs. Her thinking patterns shifted as she examined how her rationalizations had affected her daughter. The same criminogenic needs existed, but addressing them through MI produced engagement that directives had not achieved.

Teaching Points

- Criminogenic needs are addressed more effectively through evocation than direction
- Connecting behavior change to the person's own values increases motivation
- MI enhances rather than replaces RNR-based supervision

2.7 Common Misconceptions

Several misconceptions about MI persist among criminal justice practitioners, and clarifying these helps with effective implementation.

Misconception: MI means being permissive. Some officers fear that MI requires them to accept whatever supervisees say or do. In reality, MI is fully compatible with clear expectations and consequences. The difference lies in how these are communicated. An officer using MI might say, "The court requires you to complete community service, and that hasn't happened yet. I want to understand what's getting in the way so we can figure out how to make it work." This statement maintains the requirement while opening space for problem-solving.

Misconception: MI takes too much time. While learning MI requires initial investment, practiced MI often takes less time than traditional approaches. Confrontational conversations frequently bog down in arguments and resistance, extending sessions without productive movement. MI conversations, by reducing resistance, often reach productive ground more quickly. Research shows that brief MI interventions, sometimes as short as 15 minutes, produce significant effects (Vasilaki, Hosier, & Cox, 2006).

Misconception: MI only works with motivated people. This misconception fundamentally misunderstands what MI does. MI is specifically designed for people who are ambivalent or unmotivated. It would be unnecessary if people were already clearly motivated. The entire purpose of MI is to help people who are stuck in ambivalence move toward change. Research consistently shows MI effects in populations with low initial motivation (Lundahl, Kunz, Brownell, Tollefson, & Burke, 2010).

Misconception: MI is just common sense. While MI principles may seem intuitive after learning them, they do not come naturally to most people, especially in professional helping roles. The righting reflex, the urge to fix and advise, is deeply ingrained. Research on naturally occurring officer-supervisee conversations shows that without training, officers typically dominate conversations with closed questions, advice, and warnings. MI represents a systematic alternative that requires deliberate learning and practice (Walters et al., 2007).

2.8 Chapter Summary

Motivational interviewing offers a distinct approach to communication that fits the unique demands of criminal justice settings. It is collaborative, goal-oriented, and pays strategic attention to the language of change. MI rests on a foundation of partnership, acceptance, compassion, and evocation. These elements of spirit provide the context within which MI techniques become effective.

The four processes of engaging, focusing, evoking, and planning provide a roadmap for MI conversations. Practitioners move among these processes fluidly, returning to earlier processes when needed and timing transitions appropriately.

This fluid movement requires ongoing attention to where the conversation is and where it needs to go.

MI aligns closely with the Risk-Need-Responsivity model that guides evidence-based correctional practice. By improving engagement and increasing receptivity to intervention, MI enhances every aspect of RNR implementation. Officers who use MI effectively create conditions where their supervisees can benefit from assessment and intervention at all risk levels.

The chapters that follow build on this foundation with specific skills, techniques, and applications for criminal justice settings. The concepts introduced here provide the framework for understanding why those skills work and how they fit together into a coherent approach.

Chapter 3.0: Authority and Ally Together

A probation officer sits across from someone who has just tested positive for cocaine, violating a core condition of supervision. The officer knows that reporting this violation could result in the person's return to custody, separation from their family, and loss of their job. The officer also knows that ignoring violations undermines the integrity of supervision and potentially endangers the community. How do you maintain a helpful relationship while enforcing accountability? How do you express genuine care while also expressing that actions have consequences? These questions strike at the heart of what makes criminal justice work distinct from other helping professions.

This chapter addresses the unique position of community corrections officers who must simultaneously support and supervise. You will learn:

- How to understand and navigate the inherent tension between the support and enforcement functions
- Strategies for establishing transparent relationships within appropriate boundaries
- Techniques for delivering sanctions while preserving therapeutic alliance
- When enforcement must take priority and how to return to MI afterward

3.1 Understanding the Dual Role

Community corrections officers occupy a position unlike that of other professionals who work with similar populations. Counselors and therapists focus primarily on client welfare, with confidentiality protecting the therapeutic relationship. Police officers focus primarily on law enforcement, with clear authority and limited ongoing relationships. Probation and parole officers must do both simultaneously, maintaining ongoing relationships with people they may also need to sanction, revoke, or arrest (Skeem & Manchak, 2008).

This dual role creates genuine tension that cannot be eliminated through clever technique. Officers who pretend the tension does not exist, adopting either a purely supportive or purely punitive stance, create problems. Those who act only as helpers may fail to hold supervisees accountable and may endanger communities. Those who act only as enforcers may fail to support change and may increase recidivism by damaging relationships that could have facilitated progress. Effective practice requires holding both roles simultaneously (Trotter, 2015).

Research on officer-supervisee relationships illuminates how this balance affects outcomes. Skeem, Eno Louden, Polaschek, and Camp (2007) developed a measure of relationship quality in probation supervision and found that relationship quality predicted outcomes above and beyond other factors. Supervisees who perceived their officers as fair, caring, and trustworthy showed better compliance and lower recidivism, even after controlling for risk level. This relationship effect persisted regardless of whether officers emphasized a law enforcement or social work orientation.

The concept of **therapeutic jurisprudence** provides a framework for understanding how authority figures can promote wellbeing while exercising their legitimate functions. Developed in the legal context, therapeutic jurisprudence recognizes that legal processes inevitably affect participants' psychological states and that attention to these effects can improve outcomes without compromising legal objectives (Wexler & Winick, 1996). Applied to community corrections, therapeutic jurisprudence suggests that how officers exercise authority matters as much as what authority they exercise.

Officers sometimes assume they must choose between being respected and being liked. This false dichotomy leads some to adopt unnecessarily harsh stances, reasoning that supervisees will comply out of fear if not out of affection. Research contradicts this assumption. Respect and rapport are not opposites; they can coexist and reinforce each other. Supervisees can simultaneously view their officers as authorities who will hold them accountable and as caring individuals who want them to succeed (Kennealy, Skeem, Manchak, & Eno Louden, 2012).

3.2 Transparency About the Role

The foundation for navigating the dual role is transparency. From the first contact, officers should clearly communicate both aspects of their function. This transparency serves multiple purposes: it establishes honest ground rules, prevents later surprises, and models the kind of straightforward communication that effective supervision requires (Walters et al., 2007).

Many officers fear that explicit discussion of the enforcement role will damage rapport. The opposite typically proves true. Supervisees already know that their officers can report violations, recommend revocation, and potentially send them back to custody. Pretending otherwise insults their intelligence and creates mistrust. Honest acknowledgment of the officer's full role actually increases credibility and demonstrates respect (Clark, 2005).

Effective transparency sounds like this: "I want to be straight with you about my job. Part of my job is to help you succeed. I want you to complete supervision, stay out of trouble, and build a good life. I'll do everything I can to support that. Another part of my job is to report accurately to the court about how things are going. If you violate conditions, I have to report that. I don't decide what happens, but I have to give an honest picture. Knowing both parts, how can we work together?"

This statement accomplishes several things simultaneously. It affirms the officer's genuine support for the supervisee's success. It honestly acknowledges the reporting obligation without threatening or moralizing. It positions the officer as someone with a job to do rather than someone choosing to punish. And it invites collaboration within the reality of the situation.

Some supervisees test this transparency, particularly early in supervision. They may make statements designed to see how the officer responds. "So if I told you I smoked pot last week, you'd send me back to jail?" The temptation is to either reassure them that consequences will not follow or warn them about what will happen. The MI-consistent response stays with the question itself: "It sounds like you're trying to figure out how this is going to work. What concerns do you have about being honest with me?"

3.3 Case Study: Establishing the Frame

Background

Galatea, a 23-year-old woman, began probation following conviction for prescription fraud. She had obtained medications illegally to manage chronic pain and anxiety. Her assigned officer met her for an initial intake session, aware that Galatea had a history of distrust toward authority figures stemming from childhood experiences with social services.

Presentation

Galatea arrived guarded, answering questions minimally and avoiding eye contact. When the officer began explaining probation conditions, Galatea interrupted: "I know how this works. You pretend to care, then as soon as I mess up, you send me back. So just tell me what I have to do and let's not play games."

Analysis

Galatea's statement reflected past experiences where helping professionals made supportive statements but ultimately took punitive action. Her defensive stance protected against anticipated betrayal. The officer recognized this as an opportunity to establish a different kind of relationship through transparent acknowledgment of the dual role.

Intervention

The officer paused, then responded: "You've been through this before, and it sounds like it hasn't felt fair. You're right that I can report violations and that violations can have consequences. I'm not going to pretend otherwise. I'm also not pretending when I say I want things to work out for you. Both of those things are true at the same time. I know that might be hard to believe based on what you've experienced. Over time, you'll see how I operate. Can we start with you telling me what would actually help you succeed?"

Galatea looked surprised by the direct acknowledgment. She tentatively began describing her pain management challenges and fears about accessing healthcare legally. The officer listened, asked clarifying questions, and began exploring options for legitimate pain treatment.

Outcome

Over subsequent months, Galatea gradually developed trust in the relationship. She disclosed a relapse honestly rather than concealing it, allowing early intervention rather than escalation. When the officer did have to report a technical violation, Galatea accepted it without feeling betrayed because the possibility had been honestly communicated from the beginning.

Teaching Points

- Transparent acknowledgment of the dual role increases rather than decreases trust
- Supervisees with negative past experiences require consistent demonstration of the stated approach
- Early establishment of honest ground rules makes later difficult conversations easier

3.4 Sanctions Within MI Framework

The moment of greatest challenge for MI in criminal justice settings comes when the officer must deliver sanctions. A positive drug test, a missed treatment session, a new arrest: all may require responses that the supervisee will not welcome. Officers often assume that MI must be set aside during these moments, replaced by a more direct or authoritative approach. This assumption, while understandable, gives up the very tool most needed when rapport is at risk (Clark, 2006).

Delivering sanctions with MI spirit involves several principles. First, express regret rather than satisfaction. The officer who seems pleased to catch violations creates adversarial dynamics. The officer who expresses genuine disappointment that things did not go differently maintains relational connection. "I'm sorry this happened. I know this isn't what you wanted, and it's not what I wanted either."

Second, separate the sanction from the person's worth. The person made a mistake; they are not the mistake. "You tested positive, and there have to be consequences for that. What that doesn't change is that I still think you can do this." This separation allows the supervisee to accept accountability without feeling globally condemned.

Third, acknowledge the person's autonomy in how they respond to the sanction. "You didn't choose this consequence, but you do get to choose how you respond to it. Some people let this derail everything. Others use it as a turning point. Where do you want to go from here?"

Fourth, continue MI communication even while delivering the news. Resist the temptation to switch into lecture mode. Ask questions about what happened. Reflect what the supervisee says. Express confidence in their ability to move forward. The delivery of bad news does not require abandonment of good communication (Stinson & Clark, 2017).

The "feedback sandwich," sometimes recommended as a technique for delivering negative information, does not align well with MI. This approach surrounds criticism with praise, creating a formulaic structure that supervisees quickly recognize as manipulation. MI instead maintains a consistent authentic presence throughout difficult conversations.

3.5 Case Study: Handling a Violation

Background

Julius, a 38-year-old man on parole for burglary, had been doing well for six months. He maintained employment, attended programming, and developed a positive relationship with his parole officer. Then a random drug test came back positive for alcohol, a violation of his conditions.

Presentation

Julius appeared anxious when called in to discuss the test results. He immediately began explaining: "I know what you're going to say. My buddy had a birthday party and I had two beers. That's it. It's not like I went back to anything serious. Please don't send me back over this."

Analysis

The officer faced a choice point. Julius had genuinely made progress, and this was his first violation. The violation also represented a real breach of conditions that needed to be addressed. The officer wanted to maintain the positive relationship while also holding Julius accountable and creating an opportunity for learning.

Intervention

"I got the test results, and I can see you already know what they show. Before we talk about what happens next, I want to understand what happened. Not to judge you, but because understanding helps us figure out how to move forward. What was going on at that party?"

Julius, expecting immediate punishment, seemed uncertain how to respond. Slowly, he described feeling left out as his friends drank, social pressure, and the reasoning that "just a couple" would not matter. As he talked, he began identifying the thoughts and circumstances that led to his choice.

"It sounds like the thinking started before the party. 'It's just a couple, it won't matter, nobody will know.' I'm curious what you think about those thoughts now that you're sitting here."

Julius acknowledged that the thinking had been problematic and that he now saw how quickly he had abandoned his commitment. The officer then shifted to consequences.

"Here's where we are. I have to report this violation. That's not optional, and I want to be honest about it. What happens from there depends partly on what I recommend and partly on decisions others make. What I can tell you is that one violation, especially after six months of progress, is different from a pattern. What I need to see is that you've learned something and have a plan for handling these situations differently."

Outcome

Julius worked with his officer to develop specific strategies for social situations involving alcohol. The violation was reported with context, and Julius received increased substance abuse programming rather than revocation. The relationship remained intact, and Julius later cited this conversation as a turning point in his understanding of his own risk patterns.

Teaching Points

- Violations can be addressed using MI techniques without abandoning accountability
- Understanding the circumstances helps create genuine learning rather than just compliance
- Honest communication about consequences, paired with support, preserves relationship quality

3.6 When Authority Must Lead

Despite the value of MI in most situations, moments arise when enforcement must take clear priority. Immediate safety concerns, serious new criminal behavior, and threats of harm require direct intervention that may temporarily set aside MI engagement. Officers need to recognize these situations and respond appropriately, understanding that they can return to MI when the crisis has passed (Walters et al., 2007).

Safety situations include threats of violence toward others, credible suicidal statements, or discovery of weapons or contraband that pose immediate risk. In these moments, the officer's enforcement responsibility takes precedence. Clear directives, involvement of other authorities, and protective measures may be necessary regardless of their impact on the supervisory relationship.

The key is returning to MI after the safety response. An officer who discovers a supervisee with a weapon must respond to that danger. Once the immediate situation is resolved, the officer can return to MI: "That was a difficult situation, and I had to respond the way I did because safety had to come first. Now I want to understand what was going on for you and how we move forward from here."

Serious new criminal behavior presents a similar dynamic. If a supervisee reports or is discovered to have committed a significant new offense, the officer must respond appropriately to that offense. This response may include arrest, revocation proceedings, or other formal actions. Yet even in these circumstances, how the officer communicates matters. Treating the supervisee with respect even while taking enforcement action maintains the possibility of future engagement, whether on this case or with other supervisees who observe the interaction (Trotter, 2015).

Some officers worry that returning to MI after enforcement actions will seem insincere. Experience suggests the opposite. Supervisees who have experienced both enforcement and support from the same officer often develop deeper respect for that officer's integrity. They recognize that the officer fulfilled their duty while also demonstrating care. This combination builds credibility that pure support or pure enforcement cannot achieve alone.

3.7 Case Study: Safety First, Then MI

Background

Cyril, a 45-year-old man on probation for assault, had been making progress in anger management programming. During a routine visit, he arrived agitated and began making statements about wanting to hurt his former girlfriend's new partner. He described owning a gun and knowing where the new partner worked.

Presentation

Cyril's statements escalated in intensity as he spoke. He seemed to be seeking validation for his anger rather than expressing an immediate intent to act. The officer had to assess whether the situation required immediate protective intervention while also trying to understand what had precipitated this crisis.

Analysis

This situation required prioritizing safety while maintaining as much of the MI approach as possible. The officer needed to gather information to assess risk level, potentially notify potential victims and authorities, and interrupt escalation if possible. At the same time, alienating Cyril completely could decrease the likelihood of his cooperation with safety measures.

Intervention

"Cyril, I need you to slow down with me for a minute. I can hear you're furious, and something happened that brought you here feeling this way. Before we go any further, I need to understand more about what you're thinking of doing."

Through careful questioning, the officer determined that while Cyril was genuinely angry, he had not taken concrete steps toward action and was expressing fantasy rather than immediate intent. The officer acknowledged Cyril's anger while also being direct about concerns.

"I hear how angry you are, and anger like that is real and powerful. I also have to be honest that when you talk about hurting someone, I have obligations. Let's figure out how to help you deal with this anger in a way that doesn't end with you back in prison or someone getting hurt."

The officer facilitated an immediate connection with mental health crisis services and notified relevant parties about the threat. Throughout, the officer maintained a supportive stance while being clear about the required responses.

Outcome

Cyril engaged with crisis services and subsequently increased his involvement in treatment. He later acknowledged that the officer's response, taking his statements seriously while also maintaining support, had helped him recognize how close he had come to destroying his life. The relationship continued, with enhanced attention to anger management.

Teaching Points

- Safety concerns require direct response that may temporarily override MI techniques
- Even in crisis situations, how the officer communicates affects subsequent engagement
- Returning to MI after enforcement response preserves the possibility of ongoing work

3.8 Maintaining MI Long Term

The dual role challenge does not resolve itself after initial conversations. Officers must continually navigate the tension between support and enforcement throughout the supervision period. Several practices help maintain this balance over time.

Regular relationship check-ins help identify and address emerging tensions. An officer might occasionally ask: "How do you feel things are going between us? Are there things I could do differently that would help?" These questions, asked genuinely rather than formulaically, demonstrate ongoing commitment to the relationship and surface concerns before they escalate.

Consistency builds trust. When officers communicate transparently about their role and then act consistently with that communication, supervisees learn what to expect. Inconsistency, where officers sometimes overlook violations and sometimes respond harshly, creates anxiety and mistrust. Predictable responses, even if unwelcome, feel fairer than unpredictable ones (Kennealy et al., 2012).

Self-reflection helps officers notice when they are drifting toward one role at the expense of the other. Officers under pressure may become increasingly punitive, using enforcement as a stress release rather than a measured response. Others may become avoidant, overlooking problems to preserve relationships. Regular supervision and consultation provide external perspectives on whether officers are maintaining appropriate balance.

Finally, remembering the purpose of both roles helps integrate them. Enforcement exists not to punish but to maintain accountability that supports change. Support exists not to be nice but to create conditions where change becomes possible. Both roles ultimately serve the same goal: helping supervisees build lives that do not involve criminal behavior. This shared purpose unifies what might otherwise seem like contradictory functions.

3.9 Chapter Summary

The dual role of community corrections officers creates genuine tension that cannot be eliminated but can be managed effectively. Rather than choosing between support and enforcement, skilled officers integrate both functions in ways that enhance each. Transparency from the first contact establishes honest ground rules that make later difficult conversations possible.

Sanctions can be delivered within an MI framework by expressing regret, separating the behavior from the person's worth, acknowledging autonomy in response, and maintaining MI communication even when delivering unwelcome news. The feedback sandwich approach does not align with MI; consistent authentic presence works better than formulaic structures.

Safety situations require direct intervention that temporarily takes precedence over MI engagement. The key is returning to MI after the immediate crisis has passed, demonstrating that enforcement and support can come from the same relationship. This combination builds credibility and trust over time.

The following chapters build specific MI skills that work within this dual role context. Each skill needs to be understood not just technically but in relation to the unique position community corrections officers occupy.

PART II: CORE SKILLS FOR THE FIELD

Chapter 4.0: The Fundamental OARS Skills

A probation officer sits down for a routine check-in with someone who has been on her caseload for three months. She glances at her notes, then asks: "Have you been attending your treatment sessions?" The supervisee answers yes. "Any drug use since we last met?" No. "Are you employed?" Yes. The entire interaction takes four minutes. Both parties leave having exchanged information, but nothing meaningful has happened. The supervisee feels interrogated, the officer feels she did her job, and the opportunity for genuine engagement vanishes entirely. This scene plays out thousands of times daily across probation and parole offices nationwide.

This chapter introduces the four foundational skills of motivational interviewing, collectively known by the acronym **OARS**: Open questions, Affirmations, Reflections, and Summaries. These skills form the building blocks upon which all MI conversations rest. You will learn:

- How to ask questions that invite meaningful conversation rather than one-word answers
- The difference between genuine affirmations and empty praise
- Why reflections constitute the most important MI skill
- How to use summaries to consolidate progress and guide direction

4.1 Open Questions Explained

The questions officers ask shape the conversations they have. **Closed questions** can be answered with a single word or short phrase, typically yes, no, or a specific piece of information. **Open questions** invite elaboration, exploration, and extended response (Miller & Rollnick, 2013). The difference between these question types fundamentally determines whether a conversation becomes an interrogation or a dialogue.

Consider the contrast. "Did you go to treatment this week?" is closed. The answer provides a data point but nothing else. "What was treatment like for you this week?" is open. This version invites the supervisee to describe their experience, share reactions, and reveal information that would never emerge from a yes/no response. The open question takes no more time to ask but yields substantially richer information.

Research on probation officer communication patterns reveals that officers typically ask far more closed than open questions. In one observational study, officers asked an average of 4.7 questions per supervision contact, and the vast majority were closed compliance checks (Walters et al., 2010). This pattern makes sense given the administrative nature of supervision. Officers need to verify compliance with conditions. The problem is that compliance checks alone do not produce behavior change.

Open questions serve multiple purposes in MI conversations. They gather information more efficiently than closed questions because they encourage the supervisee to share context, explanations, and connections that closed questions would miss. They communicate respect by treating the supervisee as someone with thoughts worth hearing rather than a source of data to be extracted. And they create opportunities for **change talk**, statements from the supervisee that favor movement toward positive change, which we will examine in detail in Chapter 5.0 (Moyers et al., 2009).

Certain open questions prove particularly useful in criminal justice settings. "What brings you in today?" opens space for the supervisee to frame the conversation. "How has the past week been for you?" invites narrative rather than checklist responses. "What would you like to be different about your situation?" connects to the person's own desires for change. "Help me understand what happened" after a violation creates space for explanation without creating the defensive pressure of interrogation.

Some questions masquerade as open but function as closed. "Don't you think you should get a job?" appears to invite discussion but actually communicates a predetermined answer. "Wouldn't it be better if you stopped using drugs?" similarly closes down rather than opens up conversation. These **leading questions** trigger reactance because they tell the supervisee what they should think rather than inviting their genuine perspective (Moyers & Martin, 2006).

Officers sometimes worry that open questions will take too much time. The opposite often proves true. When supervisees feel genuinely heard, they provide information more efficiently than when they sense the officer is simply checking boxes. A single well-placed open question can yield information that would require numerous closed questions to obtain. The issue is not time but skill in asking questions that matter.

4.2 Affirmations That Work

Affirmations are statements that recognize and acknowledge something positive about the supervisee, including their strengths, efforts, intentions, or values (Miller & Rollnick, 2013). Affirmations build rapport, strengthen the working alliance, and help supervisees see themselves as capable of positive change. They also represent one of the most frequently misunderstood MI skills.

The most common mistake involves confusing affirmations with praise. Praise evaluates performance: "Good job on staying clean this week." This statement positions the officer as judge, determining what counts as good and implicitly suggesting that bad performance would receive different treatment. Affirmations, by contrast, recognize without evaluating: "You've put real effort into staying clean this week." The focus shifts from judgment to acknowledgment.

Effective affirmations share several characteristics. They are specific rather than generic. "That took courage" refers to something particular the person did or said. They focus on effort and process rather than outcomes alone. "You kept trying even when it got difficult" acknowledges persistence regardless of whether the ultimate goal was achieved. They connect to the person's values or identity: "That tells me something about how much your family matters to you" (Stinson & Clark, 2017).

Criminal justice settings present unique challenges for affirmation. Officers work with individuals who have caused harm, sometimes serious harm. Finding something genuine to affirm can feel difficult or even inappropriate. The key lies in recognizing that affirming a person's positive qualities does not mean approving of their negative behavior. A person who committed burglary can still demonstrate dedication to their children. Someone convicted of assault can still show genuine remorse. Affirming these positive elements does not minimize the harm caused; it acknowledges the complexity of human beings.

Affirmations also risk sounding patronizing, especially when the power differential between officer and supervisee is pronounced. "I'm so proud of you for going to treatment" can feel condescending to an adult who did not ask for the officer's pride. The solution involves affirming in ways that respect the supervisee's autonomy: "You made the decision to follow through with treatment" keeps the agency with the supervisee rather than making the officer the source of approval.

Timing matters for affirmations. An affirmation that follows immediately after the supervisee reveals something positive feels responsive and natural. An affirmation inserted randomly into conversation feels forced. Officers should listen for opportunities to affirm and respond to them in the moment rather than manufacturing affirmations to fill a quota (Moyers et al., 2016).

4.3 Reflections as Core Skill

If any single skill defines motivational interviewing, it is **reflection**. A reflection is a statement (not a question) that captures and returns something the supervisee has said, thought, or felt (Miller & Rollnick, 2013). Reflections demonstrate listening, deepen understanding, and guide the direction of conversation. Research consistently shows that reflection use distinguishes skilled MI practitioners from less skilled ones (Moyers et al., 2009).

At its simplest, reflection involves repeating or slightly rephrasing what the supervisee said. The supervisee says, "I've been stressed out lately." The officer reflects, "You've been under a lot of stress." This **simple reflection** confirms that the officer heard and encourages the supervisee to continue. Simple reflections have their place, but overuse makes conversation feel mechanical, like talking to someone who merely echoes everything back.

Complex reflections add value by going beyond what was explicitly stated. They might reflect the underlying meaning: "It sounds like you're feeling overwhelmed by everything you're dealing with." They might connect to emotion: "That frustration comes through when you talk about it." They might make an inference about what the person might be thinking but did not say: "Part of you wonders if all this effort is worth it." Complex reflections demonstrate deeper understanding and often help supervisees recognize things about themselves they had not fully articulated (Miller & Rollnick, 2013).

The **reflection-to-question ratio** provides a useful metric for MI practice. Skilled MI practitioners typically offer more reflections than questions. A ratio of approximately two reflections for every question indicates proficient practice (Moyers et al., 2016). Officers new to MI often show inverted ratios, asking many questions and offering few reflections. Tracking this ratio during practice helps identify patterns and guide improvement.

Reflections function strategically in MI. Because officers can choose what to reflect, they can selectively amplify certain elements of what the supervisee says. When a supervisee offers change talk, reflecting it strengthens and extends that language. When sustain talk appears, the officer can acknowledge it briefly without extensive reflection that might reinforce it. This selective attention does not involve manipulation; it involves helping the supervisee explore the part of their ambivalence that points toward positive change (Moyers & Martin, 2006).

One challenge involves knowing what to reflect when the supervisee has said many things. The solution is to reflect strategically. What element of the statement is most connected to change? What feeling seems most present? What underlying meaning might warrant exploration? Not everything requires reflection, and choosing what to reflect shapes the conversation's direction.

4.4 Case Study: Questions and Reflections

Background

Osric, a 28-year-old man on probation for possession with intent to distribute, attended his monthly supervision meeting. Previous sessions had been brief compliance checks with minimal engagement. His officer had recently completed MI training and decided to try a different approach.

Presentation

Osric arrived expecting the usual routine: verify address, verify employment, confirm treatment attendance, schedule next appointment. When his officer began with "What's been happening for you since we last met?" Osric paused, uncertain how to respond to a question that invited more than a one-word answer.

Analysis

This case illustrates the transition from closed questioning patterns to open inquiry. The officer's question signaled a different kind of conversation. Osric's initial uncertainty reflected unfamiliarity with being asked to share his perspective during supervision. The challenge for the officer was to continue using skills that invited engagement while Osric adjusted to this new dynamic.

Intervention

When Osric offered a brief "Not much," the officer responded with a reflection rather than moving to the next checklist item: "Things have been pretty routine." Osric nodded. The officer followed with another open question: "What's been the hardest part of being on probation?" Osric began talking about difficulty finding work with his record. The officer reflected: "You're trying to move forward, but your past keeps getting in the way." Osric agreed and expanded, describing specific rejections and his growing discouragement.

Outcome

The conversation lasted only ten minutes longer than typical sessions but yielded substantially more information. The officer learned about Osric's employment struggles, his living situation stressors, and his genuine desire to build a legitimate life. Osric later reported that this was the first time he felt his probation officer actually wanted to know what was happening with him rather than just checking boxes.

Teaching Points

- Transitioning from closed to open questions may initially create uncertainty that requires patience to navigate

- Reflecting brief responses encourages elaboration more effectively than asking additional questions
- Even modest increases in session length can yield substantial improvements in engagement quality

4.5 Summaries in Practice

Summaries collect and return multiple elements that have emerged during conversation (Miller & Rollnick, 2013). Unlike reflections, which capture single statements or themes, summaries gather several points together. Skilled use of summaries demonstrates comprehensive listening, helps supervisees see connections between scattered comments, and creates transition points in conversation.

Three types of summaries serve different purposes. **Collecting summaries** gather what has been said so far: "Let me see if I've got this. You've been struggling with finding work because of your record. You're living with your mother, which is creating tension. And you're worried about how you're going to pay the restitution you owe." This type confirms understanding and gives the supervisee opportunity to correct or add information.

Linking summaries connect related themes that the supervisee may not have explicitly connected: "You mentioned earlier that you want to be a better father to your daughter. And you've talked about how the drug use was taking you away from that. It sounds like being present for her is connected to staying clean." This type helps supervisees see relationships between different aspects of their situation.

Transitional summaries mark the end of one topic and the beginning of another: "So we've talked about how the first few weeks have gone and some of the challenges you're facing. What I'd like to do now is talk about what you want to focus on going forward." This type provides structure and signals movement in the conversation (Miller & Rollnick, 2013).

Summaries can strategically emphasize change talk while acknowledging ambivalence. If a supervisee has expressed both reasons for change and reasons to stay the same, the summary might acknowledge both but end with the change-oriented material: "So part of you thinks the old way was working fine and wonders why you should change. And part of you sees that the consequences keep piling up and you're ready for something different." Ending with change talk leaves that material most active in the conversation (Stinson & Clark, 2017).

Beginning summaries with phrases like "Let me see if I understand" or "So, what I'm hearing is" signals that the officer is checking their understanding rather than telling the supervisee what they think. Ending with an open question like "What else?" or "What am I missing?" invites the supervisee to correct, expand, or redirect.

4.6 Case Study: Affirmation and Summary

Background

Clotilde, a 42-year-old woman on parole for fraud, had a history of financial manipulation and had cycled through the system multiple times. She presented as defensive and distrustful, expecting to be treated as a criminal rather than a person.

Presentation

During her first month of supervision, Clotilde minimized her offense, blamed others, and seemed focused on getting through supervision with minimal engagement. Her parole officer noticed that despite this presentation, Clotilde always arrived on time, dressed professionally, and showed genuine warmth when discussing her grandchildren.

Analysis

Clotilde's defensive presentation likely protected against expected judgment and reflected experiences with a system that had not treated her as someone capable of change. The challenge was finding genuine points of affirmation that might open space for engagement without minimizing the seriousness of her offense history.

Intervention

The officer began affirming specific observations: "You're here on time every visit. That tells me you take this seriously." Clotilde seemed surprised to have this acknowledged. The officer later observed: "When you talk about your grandchildren, something shifts. That relationship clearly matters to you." Clotilde agreed, becoming emotional. Near the end of one session, the officer offered a summary: "You've been through this system before, and it sounds like those experiences weren't helpful. You're skeptical that this time will be different. And at the same time, you want to be present for those grandchildren in a way your past has prevented. Both of those things seem true."

Outcome

Over subsequent visits, Clotilde's defensiveness gradually decreased. She began discussing her offense pattern more honestly, connecting it to financial stress and a belief that legitimate options were not available to her. The affirmations and summaries had created enough safety for her to engage more authentically.

Teaching Points

- Affirmations that recognize specific behaviors (punctuality, presentation) can open relationships even when overall presentation is defensive
- Connecting observations to the person's values (grandchildren) builds rapport more effectively than generic encouragement
- Summaries that acknowledge both resistance and desire for change validate the supervisee's full experience

4.7 Putting Skills Together

Individual OARS skills gain power when combined fluidly. A typical MI sequence might begin with an open question, follow with reflections that deepen the response, offer an affirmation when appropriate, and periodically provide summaries that collect what has emerged. This cycling through skills creates a conversation rhythm that feels natural rather than mechanical (Miller & Rollnick, 2013).

The balance among skills shifts depending on where the conversation is. Early in a relationship, more open questions help the officer learn about the supervisee's situation. As understanding develops, reflections predominate because they demonstrate that learning and encourage continued exploration. Affirmations appear when genuine opportunities arise. Summaries mark transitions and consolidate progress.

Common patterns suggest areas for improvement. Officers who ask many questions but offer few reflections may be gathering information without demonstrating understanding. Those who reflect but never summarize may lose the thread of conversation. Those who avoid affirmation may miss opportunities to strengthen rapport and recognize strengths. Tracking skill use through audio recording and review provides concrete data for improvement (Moyers et al., 2016).

OARS skills work within the spirit of MI described in Chapter 2.0. Technically correct open questions, reflections, affirmations, and summaries can still feel hollow if delivered without genuine partnership, acceptance, compassion, and evocation. The skills are not formulas to be applied mechanically but tools that express the underlying MI approach. When spirit and skills align, conversations take on a quality that supervisees recognize as different from typical interactions.

4.8 Chapter Summary

The OARS skills provide the foundation for all MI conversations. Open questions invite exploration and yield richer information than closed compliance checks. Affirmations recognize strengths and efforts without judging or patronizing. Reflections, the heart of MI, demonstrate listening and strategically guide conversation direction. Summaries gather multiple elements and create structure within the conversation.

These skills operate best in combination, cycling fluidly as conversation evolves. The reflection-to-question ratio provides a useful metric for practice, with skilled practitioners offering approximately two reflections for every question. Individual skill improvement comes through deliberate practice, audio review, and attention to patterns.

Chapter 5.0 builds on these foundational skills by examining how to recognize and respond to change talk, the language that signals movement toward positive change.

Chapter 5.0: Recognizing Change Talk

A supervisee sits across from his probation officer, describing his struggle with alcohol. "I know I should probably cut back," he says, "but it's hard when all my friends drink. Still, I can't keep waking up feeling like garbage every morning. My daughter asked me why I smell bad, and that really got to me." In these few sentences, multiple signals appear that indicate movement toward change. The skilled officer recognizes each one and responds in ways that strengthen them. The unskilled officer hears only the ambivalence and responds to the wrong parts. This difference determines whether the conversation moves toward or away from change.

This chapter examines change talk, the language that signals a person's movement toward behavior change. Building on the OARS skills from Chapter 4.0, you will learn:

- The seven types of change talk organized in the DARN-CAT framework
- How to hear change talk in criminal justice contexts, including subtle forms
- Strategies for evoking change talk when it does not emerge naturally
- How to respond to change talk in ways that strengthen and extend it

5.1 The DARN CAT Framework

Change talk refers to any self-expressed language that favors movement toward a change target (Miller & Rollnick, 2013). When supervisees argue for change themselves, they are more likely to actually change than when officers argue for it. This phenomenon has been demonstrated across numerous studies showing that client language during sessions predicts subsequent behavior change (Amrhein, Miller, Yahne, Palmer, & Fulcher, 2003).

The acronym **DARN-CAT** organizes the seven types of change talk into two categories: preparatory change talk (DARN) and mobilizing change talk (CAT). Understanding this framework helps officers recognize change talk when it appears and understand its significance.

Desire statements express wanting, wishing, or preferring change: "I want to stop getting in trouble." "I wish things were different." "I'd like to be able to see my kids again." Desire reflects motivation but does not yet indicate ability or commitment.

Ability statements indicate capability or confidence about change: "I could probably cut back if I really tried." "I've quit before, so I know I can do it." "I think

I could find a job if I had some help." Ability reflects perceived capacity but does not yet indicate decision or action.

Reasons statements explain why change would be beneficial: "Because I'm tired of this life." "It would make things better with my family." "So I don't end up back in prison." Reasons provide rationale for change but do not yet indicate commitment to pursue it.

Need statements express necessity or urgency: "I have to do something different." "Things can't keep going this way." "I need to get my life together." Need reflects imperative but does not yet specify what change will occur (Miller & Rollnick, 2013).

These four types comprise preparatory change talk. They indicate movement in the direction of change but stop short of indicating that change will actually happen. Preparatory change talk matters because it creates the foundation for stronger commitment language.

Commitment statements indicate intention or decision: "I will go to treatment." "I'm going to stop hanging out with those people." "I promise I'll follow through this time." Commitment language predicts behavior more strongly than preparatory language (Amrhein et al., 2003).

Activation statements indicate readiness without full commitment: "I'm ready to make some changes." "I'm willing to try." "I'm prepared to do what it takes." Activation reflects movement toward commitment but remains somewhat conditional.

Taking steps statements describe actions already underway: "I've already started looking for jobs." "I called the treatment center yesterday." "I've been avoiding the places where I used to get in trouble." Taking steps language indicates that change has already begun.

Together, these seven types form a rough progression from early movement toward change (desire, ability, reasons, need) through mobilization (commitment, activation, taking steps). However, change talk does not always appear in this sequence, and supervisees may express different types simultaneously (Miller & Rollnick, 2013).

5.2 Hearing Change Talk

Recognizing change talk requires attentive listening. In the flow of conversation, change talk can pass quickly, especially when mixed with sustain talk (arguments for not changing) or general discussion. Officers who develop sensitivity to change talk hear opportunities that less attuned listeners miss.

Consider this statement: "I know I need to do something, but it's not like I'm some addict." This brief comment contains both change talk ("I know I need to do something") and sustain talk ("it's not like I'm some addict"). The unskilled response might address the minimization. The skilled response recognizes and reflects the change talk: "You're seeing that something needs to change."

Change talk in criminal justice settings often appears in muted forms. A supervisee might say: "I guess I probably shouldn't have done that." The words "guess" and "probably" indicate ambivalence, but the underlying message still points toward recognizing problematic behavior. Another might say: "My mother keeps telling me I need to get my act together." This statement attributes the message to someone else, but the supervisee chose to report it, suggesting it resonates at some level (Stinson & Clark, 2017).

Some common forms of change talk from probationers and parolees include:

- References to wanting a different life: "I'm sick of living like this."
- Mentions of family motivation: "I want to be there for my kids."
- Recognition of consequences: "If I keep going this way, I'll end up dead or back inside."
- Expressions of capability: "I stayed clean before when I had a reason to."
- Statements of intention: "I'm done with that crowd."

Officers must distinguish change talk from **compliance talk**, statements that appear positive but reflect only what the supervisee thinks the officer wants to hear. "I'll do whatever you say" differs from "I've decided I need to make some changes." The first indicates submission to authority; the second indicates internal motivation. Compliance talk tends to sound formulaic and disconnected from emotion, while genuine change talk often carries affect and personal significance (Moyers et al., 2009).

The context surrounding statements helps clarify their meaning. "I'll go to treatment" might represent commitment or compliance depending on how it emerges. If the officer has been pressuring the supervisee and the statement comes grudgingly, it likely represents compliance. If it emerges after the supervisee has been exploring their situation and its consequences, it more likely represents genuine commitment.

5.3 Case Study: Recognizing Subtle Forms

Background

Simeon, a 33-year-old man on probation for theft, presented as resistant during initial supervision contacts. He minimized his offense, blamed economic circumstances, and seemed disengaged from the supervision process. His officer assumed he was not motivated to change.

Presentation

During one session, Simeon was describing why his theft conviction was unfair. In the middle of his explanation, he said: "I mean, I know stealing is wrong. I'm not stupid. But what else was I supposed to do when I couldn't pay my rent?" He then continued justifying his behavior.

Analysis

The statement "I know stealing is wrong" represents change talk, specifically a recognition that the behavior violated his own values. It appeared briefly within a longer statement of justification and could easily be missed. The officer's task was to recognize this moment and respond to it rather than to the surrounding minimization.

Intervention

The officer reflected: "Part of you knows this isn't who you want to be." Simeon paused, then nodded. The officer followed with an open question: "What kind of person do you want to be?" Simeon began talking about his grandfather, who had worked hard his whole life and never took anything that wasn't his. This values exploration revealed motivation that had been obscured by defensive justification.

Outcome

By attending to subtle change talk rather than confronting the more prominent minimization, the officer opened a conversation about Simeon's values and identity. Subsequent sessions explored the gap between who Simeon wanted to be and the path his behavior was taking him down. This approach proved far more effective than attempting to argue against his justifications.

Teaching Points

- Change talk often appears briefly within longer statements of sustain talk or minimization

- Responding to change talk rather than sustain talk moves conversation in a productive direction
- Values-based exploration can reveal motivation that defensive presentations obscure

5.4 Evoking Change Talk

Change talk does not always emerge spontaneously. When supervisees express only sustain talk or remain silent about their situation, officers can use specific strategies to evoke change talk while respecting autonomy (Miller & Rollnick, 2013).

Importance and confidence rulers provide a structured approach. The officer asks: "On a scale of zero to ten, where zero is not at all important and ten is extremely important, how important is it to you to [target behavior]?" After the supervisee responds, the officer asks: "Why did you pick that number and not a lower one?" This second question invites the supervisee to argue for the importance of change, generating their own reasons rather than hearing the officer's (Stinson & Clark, 2017).

Similarly, confidence rulers ask: "On a scale of zero to ten, how confident are you that you could [target behavior] if you decided to?" Following up with "Why not lower?" evokes ability change talk. Even low numbers (three or four) indicate some belief in capability that can be explored and strengthened.

Looking forward invites the supervisee to imagine a changed future: "If you were to make this change, what would be different in your life?" "Where would you like to be in five years?" "What would your life look like if you weren't dealing with these problems?" These questions help supervisees articulate positive visions that can motivate change.

Looking back connects to times before the problem developed or to previous successful changes: "What was different when things were going better?" "Tell me about a time when you were able to make a change you wanted to make." "How did you manage to stop before?" These questions remind supervisees of their capacity and of life without the problem (Miller & Rollnick, 2013).

Exploring values connects behavior to what matters most: "What are the most important things in your life right now?" "How does your current situation fit with what you value?" "If your children were watching your life, what would you want them to see?" Values questions often generate powerful change talk because they connect behavior to identity and meaning.

Querying extremes asks about the potential worst outcomes: "What concerns you most about continuing this way?" "What's the worst thing that could happen if nothing changes?" These questions evoke need statements and can help supervisees confront consequences they have been avoiding. However, they should be used sparingly to avoid creating excessive distress.

5.5 Responding to Strengthen

Recognizing and evoking change talk accomplishes nothing if officers do not respond effectively. The response to change talk either strengthens it or allows it to dissipate. Four strategies, forming the acronym EARS, guide effective responses (Miller & Rollnick, 2013).

Elaboration invites the supervisee to say more: "Tell me more about that." "What else?" "In what way?" When a supervisee offers change talk, asking for elaboration helps them develop and deepen the statement. Each additional detail strengthens the change talk's presence in the conversation.

Affirmation acknowledges the significance of what was said: "That took courage to say." "It sounds like you've been doing a lot of thinking about this." "That tells me something important about what matters to you." Affirmation, as discussed in section 4.2, recognizes the person's movement toward change without praising or evaluating.

Reflection mirrors and extends the change talk: The supervisee says, "I don't want to keep living like this." The officer reflects, "You're ready for something different." This reflection slightly amplifies the original statement, strengthening it while checking understanding. Complex reflections that add underlying meaning prove particularly effective.

Summary collects multiple pieces of change talk: "So let me see if I've captured this. You want to be present for your daughter. You're tired of the chaos that comes with using. You've managed to stay clean before when you had a good reason. And you're starting to wonder if now might be the time to make a real change." This summary reinforces change talk by returning it to the supervisee in concentrated form (Moyers & Martin, 2006).

The strategic use of these responses shapes conversation direction. When officers consistently elaborate, affirm, reflect, and summarize change talk while only briefly acknowledging sustain talk, the balance of conversation shifts toward change. This differential attention does not involve ignoring what the supervisee says; it involves choosing where to focus exploration and emphasis.

5.6 Case Study: Evoking and Responding

Background

Eudora, a 26-year-old woman on probation for drug-related offenses, attended supervision meetings but offered little engagement. She answered questions minimally and seemed to be waiting out her supervision term. Her officer had heard no change talk across several months of contact.

Presentation

When asked open questions about her situation, Eudora typically responded with shrugs or brief statements indicating that things were fine. She denied any desire to change, stating that she had her drug use under control and that the arrest was a one-time mistake. Traditional approaches had produced no movement.

Analysis

Eudora's presentation suggested either genuine absence of motivation or motivation that remained unexpressed due to lack of safety or relevance in the supervision relationship. The officer decided to try evoking strategies rather than continuing to ask questions that were not producing meaningful responses.

Intervention

The officer used a values exploration approach: "Setting aside probation for a moment, what matters most to you in your life right now?" Eudora, after a pause, mentioned her younger brother, for whom she felt responsible after their mother's death. The officer explored this: "What would you want for him?" Eudora began describing hopes that he would avoid her mistakes. The officer reflected: "You want something different for him than what you've experienced." Eudora agreed, becoming emotional.

The officer then connected this to Eudora's own situation: "On a scale of zero to ten, how important is it to you to be a good influence for your brother?" Eudora said eight. "Why eight and not lower?" Eudora began articulating reasons why being a positive influence mattered, essentially arguing for change in her own life.

Outcome

By finding a personally meaningful entry point, the officer evoked change talk that had not appeared in months of standard supervision contacts. Subsequent conversations explored how Eudora's current patterns might affect her brother and what kind of example she wanted to set. Her engagement increased substantially as supervision became connected to something she genuinely cared about.

Teaching Points

- Absence of change talk may indicate need for different evocation strategies rather than absence of motivation
- Values exploration often reveals motivation that direct questions about the problem behavior do not reach
- Importance rulers followed by "why not lower" reliably generate change talk from supervisees at any point on the scale

5.7 Context in Criminal Justice

Change talk in criminal justice settings carries particular features that deserve attention. Supervisees may express change-oriented language for different reasons, and distinguishing genuine motivation from strategic performance matters for effective practice.

Motivation sources in mandated settings often include external pressures: avoiding incarceration, satisfying court requirements, regaining custody of children, or removing supervision restrictions. These external motivations are not inherently problematic. Research suggests that external pressures can catalyze genuine internal motivation when addressed skillfully (Wild, Cunningham, & Ryan, 2006). The key is whether external pressure connects to internal values or remains purely instrumental compliance.

Testing language sometimes appears as supervisees gauge whether change talk will be met with support or skepticism. A supervisee might tentatively say, "I've been thinking about maybe getting some help," while watching the officer's response. If met with enthusiasm that feels pushy, the supervisee may retreat. If met with reflective interest that respects autonomy, the supervisee may elaborate.

Stage-appropriate expectations recognize that change talk develops over time. Early in supervision, preparatory change talk (desire, ability, reasons, need) represents meaningful progress even if commitment has not yet appeared. Expecting commitment language too early can pressure supervisees in ways that trigger reactance. Later in supervision, the presence of only preparatory change talk without movement toward commitment may indicate stuckness that warrants exploration (Prochaska & DiClemente, 1983).

Officers should also attend to the **trajectory** of change talk across sessions. Is change talk increasing, decreasing, or remaining stable? Increasing change talk over time suggests growing motivation. Decreasing change talk may indicate setbacks, discouragement, or issues in the supervisory relationship. Stable change talk without movement toward commitment may suggest ambivalence that requires further exploration.

5.8 Core Concepts Recap

Change talk represents the language of motivation, and recognizing it proves essential for effective MI practice. The DARN-CAT framework organizes seven types: Desire, Ability, Reasons, and Need comprise preparatory change talk, while Commitment, Activation, and Taking Steps comprise mobilizing change talk. Each type signals movement toward change at different levels of intensity.

Hearing change talk requires attentive listening, especially for subtle forms embedded within sustain talk or minimization. Officers must distinguish genuine change talk from compliance talk that reflects only what supervisees think they should say. Context, affect, and spontaneity help make this distinction.

When change talk does not emerge naturally, evocation strategies including importance and confidence rulers, looking forward and backward, values exploration, and querying extremes can draw it out while respecting autonomy. Once change talk appears, responding with elaboration, affirmation, reflection, and summary strengthens it and shifts the conversation's balance toward change.

Chapter 6.0 addresses the other side of ambivalence: sustain talk and discord, and how to respond when supervisees argue against change or push back against the officer.

Chapter 6.0: Sustain Talk and Discord

The probation officer explains the consequences of continued drug use. The supervisee responds: "Look, I've been using for twenty years. It's not hurting anyone. I work, I pay my bills, I don't bother people. You think some classes are going to change that?" The officer feels the familiar pull to argue, to present evidence, to explain why the supervisee is wrong. This pull is powerful, nearly automatic. And acting on it would make everything worse. Understanding why, and knowing what to do instead, separates effective MI practice from well-intentioned failure.

This chapter addresses the challenging moments when supervisees argue against change or push back against the officer. Building on the change talk concepts from Chapter 5.0, you will learn:

- The distinction between sustain talk and discord
- Strategies for responding to sustain talk without amplifying it
- Techniques for reducing discord when the relationship becomes strained
- How to recognize and resist the righting reflex

6.1 Sustain Talk Versus Discord

Sustain talk represents the opposite side of ambivalence from change talk. Where change talk favors movement toward change, sustain talk favors the status quo. Sustain talk includes statements expressing desire not to change ("I don't want to quit"), inability ("I can't imagine living without it"), reasons against change ("It helps me relax"), and need to continue ("I have to have something to take the edge off") (Miller & Rollnick, 2013).

Sustain talk is normal and expected. Ambivalence by definition involves both change talk and sustain talk. If supervisees only expressed change talk, they would already be changing. The presence of sustain talk does not indicate failure or resistance; it indicates that the person is human and conflicted about change.

Discord is different from sustain talk. Discord reflects friction in the relationship between officer and supervisee rather than the supervisee's arguments about the target behavior. Signs of discord include arguing against the officer ("You don't understand my life"), interrupting, becoming defensive, dismissing ("Whatever you say"), and disengaging (going silent, changing the subject, looking away). Discord signals that something has gone wrong in the interaction itself (Miller & Rollnick, 2013).

The distinction matters because sustain talk and discord require different responses. Sustain talk is about the behavior; discord is about the relationship. An officer who treats discord as sustain talk (trying to address arguments about the behavior) misses the real problem: the supervisee is pushing back against the officer, not just against change.

Discord often arises when officers trigger psychological reactance, the motivational response to perceived threats to freedom discussed in Chapter 1.0. When supervisees feel pressured, judged, or not listened to, they may resist the officer regardless of their actual feelings about the behavior in question. Reducing discord requires addressing the relationship rupture rather than continuing to argue about the behavior (Moyers & Martin, 2006).

6.2 Responding to Sustain Talk

The natural response to sustain talk is to argue against it. When a supervisee says "Using helps me relax," the officer wants to explain why this is wrong, to point out the negative consequences, to provide evidence that the coping mechanism is maladaptive. This natural response represents the **righting reflex**: the desire to fix things, correct errors, and set people straight (Miller & Rollnick, 2013).

The problem is that arguing against sustain talk typically produces more sustain talk. When the officer says "But drugs are destroying your life," the supervisee responds with more arguments defending drug use. Each argument generates counterargument. The conversation becomes a debate that the officer cannot win because the supervisee will always know their own situation better and have more investment in their own perspective.

Instead of arguing, effective responses acknowledge sustain talk without amplifying it, then guide conversation toward change talk. Several strategies accomplish this goal.

Simple reflection acknowledges the sustain talk directly: "You're not convinced that change is necessary right now." This response demonstrates that the officer heard and does not intend to argue. It often allows the supervisee to move on rather than needing to repeat or escalate their position. The reflection should not be sarcastic or dismissive; it should convey genuine acknowledgment.

Amplified reflection returns the sustain talk with slight exaggeration: The supervisee says, "I can cut back anytime I want." The officer reflects, "You have complete control over your use, and it's not really a problem at all." This response can prompt the supervisee to moderate their position ("Well, I wouldn't say it's not a problem at all..."), potentially eliciting change talk. However, amplified reflection must be delivered without sarcasm, which would create discord. It requires skillful tone and is not appropriate for all situations (Stinson & Clark, 2017).

Double-sided reflection acknowledges both sustain talk and any change talk that has appeared: "On one hand, using helps you cope with stress. On the other hand, you mentioned that your daughter is starting to notice your drinking." This response validates the ambivalence without taking sides. Importantly, the change talk side should come second, as the final element tends to be most memorable.

Shifting focus moves the conversation away from the contested topic: "We seem to be stuck on this point. Let me ask you about something different. What matters most to you right now in your life?" This strategy works when continuing to discuss the target behavior is producing only sustain talk and discord. Sometimes the path to change talk lies through different territory than direct discussion of the problem (Miller & Rollnick, 2013).

6.3 Case Study: Sustain Talk Response

Background

Gawain, a 45-year-old man on probation for his third DWI, had been mandated to complete alcohol treatment. He arrived at his supervision meeting angry about the treatment requirement, viewing it as unnecessary punishment.

Presentation

Gawain launched into an extended argument: "This is ridiculous. I'm not an alcoholic. I had a couple beers and drove. That's it. Now I have to sit in some room with real addicts and pretend I have a problem I don't have. I've been drinking the same way for thirty years, and it's never been an issue. The only issue is I got caught."

Analysis

Gawain's statement contained extensive sustain talk: denial of a problem, minimization, external attribution of the issue to getting caught rather than the behavior itself. The officer faced a choice: argue against each of these points or respond in a way that might move the conversation in a more productive direction.

Intervention

The officer resisted the urge to argue and instead offered a double-sided reflection: "So the way you see it, you're being punished for something that isn't really a problem. And at the same time, you've been arrested three times now for drinking and driving."

Gawain paused, then said, "Well, I mean, I know the law is the law. I just don't think I need to be in treatment with people who have real problems."

The officer reflected this shift: "You're making a distinction between people whose drinking is out of control and yourself." Gawain agreed. The officer then explored: "Help me understand how you see your own drinking. Not compared to others, but just in your own life."

Outcome

By not arguing against the sustain talk directly, the officer created space for Gawain to begin examining his own situation more honestly. Subsequent conversation revealed that Gawain's wife had been expressing concern about his drinking for years and that his relationship with his adult children had been affected. The sustain talk did not disappear, but the conversation's tone shifted from adversarial to exploratory.

Teaching Points

- Arguing against sustain talk typically produces more sustain talk and creates adversarial dynamics
- Double-sided reflections acknowledge both sides of ambivalence without requiring the officer to take a position
- Following reflections with open questions invites exploration rather than debate

6.4 Reducing Discord

When discord arises, the priority shifts from discussing the target behavior to repairing the relationship. Discord not addressed tends to worsen, damaging the working alliance that makes any productive conversation possible. Several strategies help reduce discord when it appears.

Apologizing can be appropriate when the officer has contributed to discord: "I think I came across as lecturing you. That wasn't my intention, and I'm sorry." This response takes responsibility without being excessive. It demonstrates that the officer notices relational dynamics and cares about maintaining a respectful interaction. Apology does not require admitting fault for something the officer did not do; it acknowledges impact regardless of intent.

Affirming autonomy explicitly acknowledges the supervisee's right to make their own choices: "Ultimately, what you do is up to you. I can't make you change, and I wouldn't try to. What I can do is help you figure out what you want and how to get there." This response reduces the sense of pressure that often generates discord. It paradoxically often increases openness to change by removing the reactance-triggering perception of coercion (Deci & Ryan, 2000).

Emphasizing personal choice reframes the conversation from compliance to autonomy: "You're the expert on your own life. You know what's worked and what hasn't better than anyone. What do you think makes sense here?" This response positions the supervisee as the decision-maker rather than the recipient of directives.

Coming alongside involves shifting from opposition to collaboration: "It sounds like we've gotten into an argument here, and that's not really where I want to be. Can we start over? I'm genuinely trying to understand your situation." This response explicitly names the discord and invites a reset. It demonstrates that the officer values the relationship above winning any particular point (Miller & Rollnick, 2013).

When discord persists despite these efforts, the officer should consider whether deeper issues exist. Sometimes discord reflects experiences with past officers or with the system generally. Sometimes it reflects the supervisee's personal style or mental health factors. Sometimes it signals a poor match that might benefit from reassignment to a different officer. Not all discord is repairable within a given conversation, and recognizing limits prevents futile escalation.

6.5 Case Study: Discord Repair

Background

Honora, a 31-year-old woman on parole for assault, had developed a contentious relationship with her parole officer. She frequently arrived late, answered questions sarcastically, and seemed to view each contact as a battle to endure.

Presentation

During one particularly difficult session, Honora responded to a routine question about employment with: "Why do you care? You're just going to violate me for something anyway. That's what all of you do." Her tone communicated contempt, and her body language (arms crossed, looking away) signaled complete disengagement.

Analysis

Honora's statement reflected discord rather than sustain talk about any particular behavior. She was pushing back against the officer and the system, not arguing for or against change in her own conduct. The relationship itself had become the obstacle. Addressing this required stepping out of the routine supervision script entirely.

Intervention

The officer set aside her usual agenda and said: "You sound really frustrated. Not just today, but generally. What's been your experience with parole officers?" Honora, surprised by the question, began describing previous experiences where she felt judged, disrespected, and set up to fail.

The officer listened, reflected, and then said: "It sounds like you've learned to expect that from people in my position. I can see why you'd come in here ready to fight. I want you to know that I'm not trying to catch you failing. I'd much rather see you succeed and never have to see me again."

Outcome

This single conversation did not resolve all discord, but it marked a turning point. Honora began arriving on time and engaging more cooperatively. When frustrations arose, she was more willing to voice them directly rather than through sarcasm and withdrawal. The officer had validated her past experiences while differentiating the current relationship.

Teaching Points

- Discord often reflects accumulated experiences rather than the current interaction alone
- Stepping out of the routine supervision script to address relationship issues directly can create breakthrough moments
- Validating negative experiences with the system can paradoxically increase engagement with the current officer

6.6 The Righting Reflex

The **righting reflex** refers to the natural desire of helping professionals to fix problems, correct misconceptions, and guide people toward better choices (Miller & Rollnick, 2013). Officers see clearly what their supervisees should do: stop using drugs, get a job, avoid criminal associates, comply with conditions. The temptation to simply tell them these things feels almost irresistible.

The righting reflex emerges from good intentions. Officers genuinely want their supervisees to succeed. They can see paths forward that the supervisee might miss. They possess expertise that could benefit the supervisee if only it would be accepted. The problem is not the motivation behind the righting reflex but its effects when enacted.

When officers argue for change, supervisees often argue against it. This pattern emerges from psychological reactance (discussed in Chapter 1.0) and from the interpersonal dynamics of persuasion. Being told what to do triggers resistance; exploring one's own situation leads to self-generated motivation. The righting reflex puts the officer in the position of arguing for change while the supervisee argues against it, exactly the reverse of what produces actual change (Miller, Benefield, & Tonigan, 1993).

Recognizing the righting reflex in oneself requires honest self-observation. Common signs include:

- Asking questions to which you already know the "right" answer
- Finishing supervisees' sentences or cutting them off to make points
- Feeling frustrated that they don't see what seems obvious
- Arguing, debating, or trying to convince
- Providing unsolicited advice or suggestions
- Feeling like the conversation is a battle to be won

The antidote to the righting reflex involves redirecting the energy toward evoking rather than imposing. Instead of telling supervisees what they should think, officers ask questions that help supervisees discover their own thoughts. Instead of providing reasons for change, officers help supervisees articulate their own reasons. The goal shifts from "getting them to see" to "helping them explore" (Miller & Rollnick, 2013).

6.7 Case Study: Resisting the Reflex

Background

Benedictus, a 24-year-old man on probation for burglary, spent his third supervision session describing his plans to continue associating with friends who were involved in criminal activity. His officer knew that antisocial associates represented a primary risk factor for recidivism.

Presentation

Benedictus explained: "These are my boys. I've known them since I was little. They had my back when nobody else did. You can't just throw people away because they got in trouble. That's not loyalty."

The officer felt the righting reflex powerfully. She wanted to explain how these associations increased his risk, how loyalty should not extend to enabling criminal behavior, how he needed new friends if he wanted to stay out of prison. All of this seemed obviously true and important.

Analysis

The officer recognized that arguing these points would trigger Benedictus to defend his friends more vigorously. The more she pushed against the associations, the more he would push back. Instead, she needed to help him explore the situation himself without abandoning her genuine concern about his risk.

Intervention

Rather than lecturing, the officer explored: "Tell me about these friendships. What makes them important to you?" Benedictus described shared history, mutual support, and a sense of belonging. The officer reflected: "They've been your family in a lot of ways." Benedictus agreed.

The officer then asked: "Where do you see these friendships going over the next few years? If everyone stays on their current path?" Benedictus became quiet. Eventually he said, "Probably prison. Or worse." The officer reflected: "You see where this road leads." Benedictus nodded.

Outcome

By resisting the righting reflex, the officer helped Benedictus arrive at recognition that she could not have imposed through argument. The conversation continued to explore how he might maintain loyalty while also building toward a different future. The change emerged from his own exploration rather than from the officer's persuasion.

Teaching Points

- The righting reflex emerges from genuine concern but produces counterproductive effects when enacted

- Exploring the supervisee's perspective often leads them to conclusions the officer wanted to impose
- Questions that invite the supervisee to consider futures and consequences can evoke change talk without lecturing

6.8 Essential Points Recap

Sustain talk and discord represent distinct challenges requiring different responses. Sustain talk reflects arguments against change and is a normal part of ambivalence. Discord reflects relationship friction and signals that something has gone wrong in the interaction itself. Effective officers distinguish between these and respond appropriately.

Responding to sustain talk involves acknowledging without amplifying, using simple reflections, amplified reflections, double-sided reflections, or shifting focus. The goal is not to argue against sustain talk but to create space for change talk to emerge. Arguing against sustain talk typically produces more sustain talk and risks generating discord.

Reducing discord requires attending to the relationship. Strategies include apologizing appropriately, affirming autonomy, emphasizing personal choice, and coming alongside the supervisee. When discord persists, deeper exploration of its sources may be needed.

The righting reflex represents a consistent threat to MI practice. Recognizing it in oneself and redirecting energy from imposing to evoking helps maintain MI spirit and effectiveness. Chapter 7.0 applies all skills learned thus far across the full supervision cycle, from intake to discharge.

Chapter 7.0: MI Throughout Supervision

The supervision cycle spans months or years, beginning when someone first appears in the probation or parole office and ending when they successfully complete their term or transfer out of the system. Across this span, the same supervisee presents differently at different times: anxious and guarded at intake, frustrated after a violation, hopeful when things go well, discouraged when setbacks occur. Each phase of supervision presents distinct opportunities and challenges for MI application. The officer who uses MI only during crisis moments misses countless opportunities; the officer who adapts MI to each phase maximizes its impact.

This chapter traces MI application across the supervision cycle. Building on skills from Chapters 4.0 through 6.0, you will learn:

- How to establish an MI-informed relationship from the first meeting
- Strategies for collaborative case planning that generates genuine buy-in
- Brief MI techniques for time-limited routine contacts
- How to handle post-violation conversations while maintaining alliance
- The termination conversation and its importance for sustained change

7.1 The Initial Interview

First impressions carry disproportionate weight in shaping relationships. Research on impression formation demonstrates that early interactions establish frameworks through which subsequent information is interpreted (Asch, 1946). The supervisee who experiences their first supervision contact as respectful and collaborative develops expectations that color all future interactions. Conversely, the supervisee whose first experience confirms expectations of judgment and coercion may resist engagement for months or years.

The initial interview serves multiple purposes: gathering required information, explaining conditions and expectations, completing paperwork, and establishing the supervisory relationship. Traditional approaches treat the first three purposes as primary and the fourth as incidental or irrelevant. MI-informed practice recognizes that how the first three purposes are accomplished either builds or damages the fourth.

Opening the initial interview with a direct question like "Tell me why you're here" invites the supervisee to engage from the start. This question may elicit a recitation of charges, an explanation of circumstances, or a complaint about the justice system. Whatever emerges provides useful information about the person's current state while communicating that their perspective matters.

After initial exploration, the officer can set an agenda collaboratively: "We have some things we need to cover today, including your conditions of supervision and some background information. I also want to learn about your situation and what you're hoping to accomplish while we're working together. Where would you like to start?"

Conditions and requirements can be presented factually without lecturing: "The court has required that you complete substance abuse treatment, maintain employment, and check in with me twice monthly. These aren't negotiable, but how you approach them has some flexibility. What questions do you have about these?" This framing acknowledges the reality of mandated conditions while preserving the supervisee's sense of agency.

Throughout the intake process, opportunities for OARS skills arise naturally. Open questions gather required information while inviting elaboration. Reflections demonstrate that the officer is listening, not just filling out forms. Affirmations recognize what the supervisee brings: "You've held jobs before, and that experience will help." Summaries collect what has been learned and signal movement between topics.

7.2 Collaborative Case Planning

Case planning typically involves identifying goals, specifying interventions, and establishing timelines. Traditional case planning proceeds as the officer identifying problems, determining what needs to happen, and presenting the plan to the supervisee for compliance. MI-informed case planning involves the supervisee as an active participant in developing a plan they can genuinely own (Stinson & Clark, 2017).

The foundation for collaborative case planning lies in the assessment process. Rather than assessment happening to the supervisee, it can happen with them. Risk and needs instruments generate discussion points: "This assessment suggests that substance use has been connected to your legal problems. How does that fit with your own understanding?" Information from assessment becomes material for exploration rather than conclusions imposed from above.

Goal-setting in MI-informed practice starts with the supervisee's priorities: "Setting aside what the court requires, what would you most like to see change in your life?" This question often reveals motivations that would not emerge from compliance-focused conversation. A supervisee might mention wanting to repair a relationship with their children, regain self-respect, or build a stable life. These goals can then be connected to required interventions: "It sounds like being present for your kids is really important to you. How do you think the substance abuse treatment might relate to that goal?"

Conditions of supervision become means to ends rather than ends in themselves. Employment conditions connect to goals of financial stability and self-sufficiency. Treatment requirements connect to goals of improved health and functioning. Community service connects to goals of making amends or giving back. When supervisees understand how conditions serve their own goals, compliance shifts from external imposition to internal commitment.

The case plan document should reflect this collaborative process. Language shifts from "Supervisee will" to "We agreed that" or "Supervisee has decided to." Goals stated in the supervisee's own words carry more weight than generic statements. Timelines negotiated together prove more realistic than timelines imposed unilaterally.

Prioritization emerges from dialogue rather than dictation. When multiple needs exist, the officer can present them as options: "We've identified concerns about substance use, employment, and housing. All of these need attention eventually. If you had to pick one to focus on first, what would it be?" This approach respects that supervisees understand their own situations and may sequence interventions differently than officers would.

7.3 Case Study: Intake and Planning

Background

Melisande, a 39-year-old woman, arrived for her initial probation appointment following conviction for embezzlement from her employer. She had no prior criminal history and presented as ashamed, anxious, and uncertain about what to expect from supervision.

Presentation

Melisande sat stiffly, answered questions minimally, and apologized repeatedly for being there. She seemed to expect judgment and appeared to be bracing for a lecture about her wrongdoing. Her posture communicated a desire to get through the appointment with minimal engagement.

Analysis

Melisande's presentation suggested someone for whom criminal justice involvement was foreign and shameful. Traditional intake approaches might confirm her worst expectations and establish an adversarial dynamic. An MI-informed approach could help her engage more authentically and establish a collaborative relationship.

Intervention

The officer began: "You seem uncomfortable. I imagine being here isn't something you ever expected." Melisande agreed, her eyes welling. The officer continued: "Before we get into the paperwork, I'm curious what's on your mind. What are you most worried about?"

Melisande described fears about her career, her marriage, and her reputation in the community. The officer listened, reflected, and affirmed: "You're dealing with a lot of consequences, and you're facing them rather than running from them."

When moving to case planning, the officer asked: "Given everything you're dealing with, what feels most important to address? The court has certain requirements, but within those, you have some say in how we approach things." Melisande identified financial counseling as a priority, having realized that her offense emerged from financial pressure and poor coping. This became the first focus of the case plan.

Outcome

Melisande's engagement increased substantially after this first meeting. She completed supervision requirements ahead of schedule and later reported that feeling respected rather than judged during intake made her willing to invest in the process rather than merely endure it.

Teaching Points

- First impressions powerfully shape supervisory relationships and subsequent engagement
- Asking about concerns and priorities invites collaboration rather than compliance
- Connecting required conditions to the supervisee's identified goals increases buy-in

7.4 Routine Supervision Visits

Most supervision contacts occur during routine visits: the check-ins between crises, the standard appointments that comprise the majority of officer-supervisee interaction. These contacts often become perfunctory, focused on verifying compliance without meaningful engagement. MI principles can transform routine visits into opportunities for ongoing motivation enhancement.

Time constraints present a genuine challenge. Officers with large caseloads may have only 15 or 20 minutes per visit. This limitation requires efficiency but does not preclude MI. Brief MI techniques, adapted from healthcare settings where time pressure is also substantial, demonstrate effectiveness even in contacts lasting less than 15 minutes (Rollnick, Miller, & Butler, 2008).

A routine visit might begin with an open question: "What's been happening since we last met?" This opening invites the supervisee to share what seems most relevant rather than responding to a checklist. Within the response, the officer listens for change talk or sustain talk and responds accordingly.

Compliance checks can be conducted using MI spirit. Instead of "Did you go to treatment this week?" the officer might ask "How has treatment been going?" The latter invites process information, not just attendance verification. Instead of "Have you been using?" the officer might ask "What's been happening with the substance use?" This phrasing assumes complexity rather than simple yes/no compliance.

Progress tracking through MI involves more than noting whether conditions are met. The officer explores what the supervisee has learned, how confidence has changed, what obstacles have appeared, and how the person feels about their progress. A brief scaling question ("On a scale of zero to ten, how confident are you that you'll stay on track this month?") can yield useful information and potential change talk in under a minute.

Routine visits also provide opportunities to maintain and strengthen the relationship. Brief affirmations recognize ongoing effort: "You've kept all your appointments. That consistency says something." Reflections on changes observed: "You seem more settled than you did a few months ago." These moments take only seconds but communicate continued attention and care.

7.5 Post Violation Conversations

Violations occur. Despite best efforts, supervisees sometimes fail drug tests, miss appointments, fail to complete requirements, or incur new charges. Post-violation conversations represent critical moments for the supervisory relationship. How officers handle violations either maintains alliance while enforcing accountability or destroys trust and generates lasting discord.

Chapter 3.0 addressed the dual role challenge and delivering sanctions within MI spirit. Post-violation conversations apply those principles in specific situations. The key lies in separating the enforcement response (which may be required regardless of how the conversation goes) from the conversation itself (which should explore what happened and where to go from here).

Opening with accusation or disappointment triggers defensiveness. "You tested positive for cocaine" as an opening statement positions the officer as judge and the supervisee as defendant. An alternative: "Something came up in your test results that we need to talk about. What happened?" This opening still addresses the issue but invites explanation rather than defense.

Exploring the violation without interrogating involves genuine curiosity about circumstances. "Walk me through what happened" differs from "Why did you use?" The first requests narrative; the second demands justification. Most violations have contexts that supervisees will share if given space to do so without feeling attacked.

When supervisees take responsibility, affirmation is appropriate: "Thank you for being honest about what happened. That takes some courage." When they minimize or blame others, reflection without argument works better: "You see this as more about the situation than about your choices." Arguing against minimization produces more minimization; reflection creates space for the supervisee to reconsider.

Finding motivation to continue after a violation involves looking forward rather than dwelling on the past. "Given what happened, what do you want to do now?" places the supervisee in the driver's seat. "What would help prevent this from happening again?" invites problem-solving. "Where does this leave you in terms of your goals?" reconnects the violation to the broader context of the person's life and aspirations.

7.6 Case Study: After Violation

Background

Quirin, a 30-year-old man on parole for drug distribution, had been doing well for eight months: employed, clean drug tests, regular attendance. Then he missed two appointments and a positive drug test followed. His parole officer called him in for what Quirin expected to be a hostile confrontation.

Presentation

Quirin arrived defensively, arms crossed, explaining before the officer could speak: "I know what you're going to say. I messed up. Just do what you have to do." His tone suggested resignation and expectation of punishment.

Analysis

Quirin's eight months of success indicated genuine motivation and capability. The violation, while serious, represented a departure from his established pattern. The officer faced a choice: treat this as confirmation of expected failure or as a setback within an overall trajectory of change.

Intervention

The officer said: "I noticed you jumped right to 'do what you have to do.' Before we talk about consequences, I'd like to understand what happened. You were doing really well for a long time. Something changed. What was it?"

Quirin, surprised not to be immediately sanctioned, began describing a series of stressors: a family member's illness, job pressure, feeling isolated and overwhelmed. He had reconnected with old friends as a coping mechanism, and one thing led to another. The officer reflected: "You were dealing with a lot, and you went back to what used to work for managing stress." Quirin agreed.

The officer then addressed consequences honestly: "I have to report the positive test and the missed appointments. What happens from there involves decisions above my level. What I can tell you is that eight months of good progress matters, and I'll include that context in my report. What I'm more interested in is what happens next for you. You know this road. Do you want to go down it again, or do you want to find a different way forward?"

Outcome

Quirin engaged in developing a relapse prevention plan, identifying warning signs and alternative coping strategies. He received a sanction (increased supervision frequency) but not revocation. More importantly, the violation became an opportunity for learning rather than confirmation of failure.

Teaching Points

- Post-violation conversations can maintain alliance while still enforcing accountability
- Exploring circumstances demonstrates interest in the person, not just the violation

- Connecting violations to patterns and coping helps supervisees understand and prevent future occurrences

7.7 Successful Termination

Termination represents the end of formal supervision, and how it occurs affects the durability of changes made during the supervision period. Traditional termination often consists of paperwork completion and congratulations. MI-informed termination consolidates gains, prepares for future challenges, and strengthens the supervisee's confidence in maintaining change independently.

The termination conversation should acknowledge accomplishment: "You've completed everything required of you and then some. Looking back over the past year, what are you most proud of?" This question invites the supervisee to articulate their own achievements, strengthening self-efficacy for maintaining those achievements.

Reviewing the journey helps supervisees recognize how far they have come: "Think back to when you first walked in here. What's different now?" The contrast between starting point and ending point often reveals change that gradual progress obscured. Supervisees who recognize their own transformation are better equipped to maintain it.

Anticipating challenges prepares supervisees for the reality that change maintenance requires ongoing effort. "Now that supervision is ending, what might make it harder to keep going the direction you've been going?" This question invites realistic planning rather than unrealistic optimism. Identified risks can be addressed with specific strategies.

Building confidence for independence involves affirming capability while acknowledging limits: "You've done this work. I've watched you handle setbacks and keep going. You've learned things about yourself and developed skills you didn't have before. Those don't go away when supervision ends." This affirmation attributes success to the supervisee rather than to the officer or the system.

The officer can offer appropriate ongoing support while maintaining boundaries: "Supervision is ending, but if you ever find yourself struggling and want to talk to someone who knows your situation, you can reach out." This offer acknowledges the relationship that has developed without creating inappropriate dependency.

7.8 Case Study: Termination Conversation

Background

Theodora (introduced in Chapter 1.0) had cycled through the system six times before an MI-informed approach produced different results. After two years of successful supervision, her probation was ending.

Presentation

Theodora arrived for her final appointment appearing confident but somewhat emotional. She acknowledged feeling nervous about no longer having supervision as an external structure.

Analysis

Theodora's history made this termination particularly significant. Her nervousness about ending supervision suggested appropriate awareness of her own patterns and risks. The termination conversation needed to consolidate her gains while preparing her for independence.

Intervention

The officer began: "This is our last official meeting. Before we do the paperwork, I'd like to take some time to look back. When you first came in two years ago, where were you?" Theodora described her cynicism, her pattern of failure, and her belief that she was incapable of change.

"And now?" Theodora described her employment, her apartment, her restored relationship with her daughter, and her new understanding of herself. The officer reflected: "You've built a different life than the one you had before."

The officer then asked: "What did you learn about yourself through this process that you didn't know before?" Theodora talked about recognizing her patterns, understanding her triggers, and believing she could make different choices. The officer affirmed: "That knowledge doesn't go away. You carry that with you."

Finally: "What worries you about supervision ending?" Theodora identified the loss of external accountability and fear of slipping into old patterns. Together, they developed a plan involving continued peer support attendance and checking in with herself regularly using questions similar to those the officer had asked throughout supervision.

Outcome

Theodora successfully transitioned off supervision and has not returned to the system. She later credited the termination conversation as helping her believe she could succeed without external oversight.

Teaching Points

- Termination conversations consolidate gains by helping supervisees articulate their own growth
- Acknowledging nervousness about ending is appropriate and allows for planning
- Transferring external accountability to internal self-monitoring prepares supervisees for independence

7.9 Bringing It Together

MI application across the supervision cycle requires adapting skills to different phases and purposes while maintaining consistent spirit. The initial interview establishes the relationship and sets expectations for collaboration. Case planning involves supervisees as active participants in developing plans they can own. Routine visits maintain engagement and track progress using brief MI techniques. Post-violation conversations balance accountability with continued alliance. Termination consolidates gains and prepares for independence.

Throughout all phases, the OARS skills from Chapter 4.0 apply. Open questions invite exploration at every stage. Affirmations recognize effort and progress regardless of phase. Reflections demonstrate ongoing listening and guide conversation direction. Summaries collect and organize what emerges.

Change talk recognition from Chapter 5.0 remains relevant across phases. Intake may reveal surprising motivation. Routine visits track whether change talk is increasing or decreasing. Violations provide opportunities for renewed commitment. Termination elicits commitment to maintenance.

Sustain talk and discord from Chapter 6.0 can appear at any phase. Officers must continually resist the righting reflex and respond to resistance without escalation. The relationship established at intake and maintained through routine contacts provides resilience when difficult moments arise.

The cumulative effect of consistent MI application across the supervision cycle transforms not only individual interactions but the overall supervision experience. Supervisees who experience their officer as genuinely interested in their success, respectful of their autonomy, and skilled in conversation develop qualitatively different relationships than those who experience supervision as mere surveillance and control.

PART III: SPECIAL POPULATIONS & CRIME-SPECIFIC APPLICATIONS

Chapter 8.0: Substance Use and MI

A probation officer reviews her caseload for the day and notices that seven of her ten scheduled appointments involve individuals with substance use conditions as their primary criminogenic need. She has attended trainings on drug testing procedures, learned about the signs of intoxication, and memorized the names of various treatment programs in her jurisdiction. Yet she feels unprepared for the conversations themselves. How do you talk to someone about their drug use in a way that actually helps? How do you respond when they deny having a problem? What do you say when they relapse for the third time? These questions matter because substance use drives a substantial portion of criminal justice involvement, and how officers address it determines outcomes.

This chapter examines the application of motivational interviewing to substance use concerns, the very population for which MI was originally developed. You will learn:

- Why MI proves particularly effective for addiction-related issues
- How to have productive conversations about substance use beyond compliance checking
- Strategies for responding to relapse while maintaining therapeutic alliance
- Methods for coordinating effectively with treatment providers

8.1 MI Origins in Addiction

Motivational interviewing emerged directly from addiction treatment. William Miller developed the approach in the early 1980s while working with problem drinkers in New Mexico (Miller, 1983). He noticed that certain counselor behaviors predicted client outcomes more strongly than client characteristics did. When counselors listened empathically and avoided argumentation, clients changed more than when counselors confronted and directed. This observation led to the systematic development of what became MI.

The connection between MI and addiction treatment runs deeper than historical accident. **Ambivalence** represents the central psychological feature of addictive behavior (Miller & Rollnick, 2013). People with substance use disorders simultaneously want to use and want to stop. They experience genuine conflict between the immediate rewards of substances and the longer-term consequences. Traditional approaches that demanded commitment to abstinence before treatment could begin failed to recognize this ambivalence as normal rather than pathological.

The **Transtheoretical Model of Change**, developed by Prochaska and DiClemente (1983), provided theoretical grounding for MI's approach to addiction. This model identifies stages through which people move when changing behavior: precontemplation (not considering change), contemplation (considering change but ambivalent), preparation (planning to change), action (actively changing), and maintenance (sustaining change). The model demonstrated that people at different stages need different interventions. Pushing action strategies on someone in precontemplation produces resistance, not change.

Research consistently shows MI effectiveness for substance use disorders. A meta-analysis of 119 studies found that MI produced a significant effect on substance use outcomes, with effects appearing even after brief interventions (Lundahl et al., 2010). Studies specifically examining MI in criminal justice settings show similar results. Probationers who receive MI demonstrate higher rates of treatment initiation, better treatment retention, and reduced substance use compared to those receiving standard supervision (Walters et al., 2010).

The match between MI and addiction reflects the nature of the problem. Substance use involves deeply personal choices about pleasure, coping, identity, and lifestyle. External pressure alone rarely produces lasting change in such personal domains. MI works because it engages the person's own values and motivations rather than relying solely on external consequences (Miller & Rollnick, 2013).

8.2 Substance Use Conversations

Standard probation practice often reduces substance use conversations to compliance verification. "Have you used since we last met?" "Are you attending treatment?" "Did your drug test come back clean?" These questions gather data but do not facilitate change. Moving beyond compliance checking requires different questions and different ways of responding to answers.

Open questions invite exploration rather than yes/no responses. Instead of "Are you still using?" an officer might ask "What's been happening with your substance use lately?" Instead of "Did you go to your AA meeting?" the question becomes "How has the recovery program been working for you?" These phrasings invite narrative responses that reveal context, meaning, and motivation that closed questions miss (Miller & Rollnick, 2013).

When supervisees disclose ongoing use, the response matters enormously. A judgmental or alarmed reaction trains them not to disclose in the future. A reflective, curious response creates safety for honest conversation. "So you used twice this week. Tell me about what was happening for you when that occurred." This response neither approves nor condemns; it explores.

Discussing **treatment readiness** involves assessing where the person falls on the stages of change continuum. Someone in precontemplation who sees no problem with their use needs different engagement than someone in contemplation who recognizes problems but feels stuck. Scaling questions help assess readiness: "On a scale of zero to ten, how ready are you to make changes in your substance use?" Following up with "What would need to happen for that number to increase?" identifies barriers and potentially evokes change talk (Stinson & Clark, 2017).

A critical distinction exists between **denial** and **ambivalence**. Denial involves active rejection of reality, often as a defense mechanism. Ambivalence involves genuine conflict between competing desires. Officers frequently mislabel ambivalence as denial, leading to confrontational approaches that worsen outcomes. True denial is relatively rare; most supervisees who minimize or deflect are actually expressing one side of their ambivalence. Responding to the change-oriented side, however faintly expressed, proves more effective than attacking the minimization (Miller & Rollnick, 2013).

Sample conversation for exploring treatment entry:

Officer: "What are your thoughts about the treatment requirement?"

Supervisee: "I don't think I need it. I'm not like those people in rehab."

Officer: "You see yourself as different from people who go to treatment programs."

Supervisee: "Yeah. I mean, I use sometimes, but I can control it."

Officer: "You have some control over your use. And yet it's brought you here, to probation. Help me understand how you see those two things fitting together."

This exchange avoids argument while inviting the supervisee to examine their situation. The officer reflects without agreeing or disagreeing, then asks a question that highlights discrepancy without confrontation.

8.3 Case Study: Treatment Resistance

Background

Darian, a 29-year-old man, was placed on probation for possession of methamphetamine. His conditions included completing substance abuse treatment, but he had failed to enroll after three months of supervision. His officer had reminded him repeatedly about the requirement, and Darian always agreed to "look into it" but never followed through.

Presentation

When his officer raised the treatment issue again, Darian said: "I told you, I'll get to it. I'm busy with work. Besides, I don't even use that much anymore. The arrest scared me straight. I don't need some group where people talk about their feelings." His tone conveyed frustration with what he perceived as nagging.

Analysis

Darian's presentation suggested precontemplation regarding treatment, though his comment about the arrest "scaring him straight" contained a hint of change talk. His resistance likely reflected ambivalence about the treatment process itself rather than complete denial of any substance issue. Previous approaches had focused on the requirement rather than his experience, generating reactance without movement.

Intervention

The officer tried a different approach: "You've mentioned the arrest scared you, and you've cut back on your own. That took some effort. I'm curious what made you able to do that." Darian described specific changes he had made. The officer reflected: "So you've already made some changes without treatment. What worries you about going to a program?"

Darian revealed concerns about missing work, being labeled as an addict, and having to share personal information with strangers. The officer explored each concern, validating them while also providing information about program options that might address them. Using an importance ruler, the officer asked: "How important is it to you to stay on the path you've started since the arrest?" Darian rated it highly. "What do you think would help you stay on that path?"

Outcome

The conversation shifted from compliance pressure to exploring Darian's own goals and concerns. He eventually enrolled in an evening intensive outpatient program that accommodated his work schedule. By connecting treatment to his own stated goals rather than framing it purely as a requirement, the officer helped Darian find motivation to engage.

Teaching Points

- Repeated reminders about requirements often generate reactance rather than compliance
- Exploring concerns about treatment creates opportunities to address barriers

- Connecting treatment to the person's own goals increases genuine engagement

8.4 Responding to Relapse

Relapse occurs frequently in substance use disorders. Research indicates that relapse rates for addiction are similar to those for other chronic conditions like hypertension and diabetes, approximately 40-60% (McLellan et al., 2000). This comparison helps reframe relapse as an expected part of recovery rather than evidence of failure or moral weakness.

The moment of relapse disclosure represents a critical juncture. How officers respond shapes whether the supervisee continues honest communication or learns to conceal future use. A punitive response may be emotionally satisfying but typically produces hiding rather than help-seeking. An MI-informed response explores what happened while maintaining support.

Effective relapse response involves several elements. Normalizing without minimizing acknowledges that setbacks occur without suggesting they do not matter: "Slips happen in recovery. They're disappointing, and they're also opportunities to learn something." Exploring the relapse helps identify triggers and patterns: "Walk me through what happened. What was going on before you used?" Finding motivation to recommit involves evoking change talk about returning to recovery: "Where does this leave you in terms of your goals?" (Stinson & Clark, 2017).

When relapse requires official action, officers can maintain MI spirit while enforcing consequences. As discussed in Chapter 3.0, sanctions and support are not mutually exclusive. An officer might say: "I have to report this positive test. That's part of my job, and I want to be straight with you about it. What I'm more concerned about is what happens next for you. One slip doesn't erase six months of progress unless we let it."

The goal is helping supervisees develop their own **relapse prevention** awareness rather than imposing external monitoring as the only safeguard. Questions that build this awareness include: "What warning signs did you notice before you used?" "What would you do differently if you found yourself in a similar situation?" "Who could you reach out to when you're feeling that way?"

8.5 Case Study: After Relapse

Background

Ianthe, a 38-year-old woman on probation for theft related to her heroin use, had maintained six months of sobriety while in treatment. She had rebuilt her relationship with her teenage daughter and found stable employment. Then she used once, disclosed it to her officer, and arrived at her next appointment expecting punishment.

Presentation

Ianthe was tearful and defeated: "I ruined everything. Six months down the drain. You're going to violate me now, right? I might as well have never tried." She had not used again since the single incident but seemed to have given up on her recovery.

Analysis

Ianthe's response illustrated the "abstinence violation effect," where a single slip leads to catastrophic thinking and abandonment of recovery efforts (Marlatt & Gordon, 1985). Her progress was genuine and substantial. The critical task was helping her see that one use did not erase six months of growth and that continuation, not perfection, defined recovery success.

Intervention

The officer said: "Six months ago, you were using daily. You'd lost custody of your daughter. You couldn't hold a job. Today, you've had one use in six months. Your daughter is living with you. You're employed. Help me understand how all of that is 'ruined.'"

Ianthe looked surprised at this framing. The officer continued: "I'm not saying the use doesn't matter. It does, and we'll talk about what happened and what to do about it. But I'm not going to let you throw away everything you've built because of one mistake."

They explored the circumstances of the relapse together, identified triggers and warning signs, and developed specific strategies for preventing recurrence. The officer explained the reporting requirement honestly while emphasizing that reporting did not mean recommending revocation given the context of overall progress.

Outcome

Ianthe's treatment provider was informed, and she increased her meeting attendance temporarily. The violation was reported with context, and she was not revoked.

More importantly, she did not abandon her recovery. At her next appointment, she said the officer's response had been a turning point: "I expected you to give up on me. When you didn't, it made me not want to give up on myself."

Teaching Points

- The abstinence violation effect can cause more damage than the relapse itself if not addressed
- Putting lapses in context of overall progress prevents all-or-nothing thinking
- Honest reporting combined with supportive response maintains both accountability and alliance

8.6 Treatment Provider Coordination

Effective supervision of individuals with substance use disorders requires coordination with treatment providers. When probation officers and counselors work at cross purposes, supervisees suffer. When they work together, the combined effect exceeds what either could achieve alone.

MI alignment across systems means that treatment providers and supervision officers share a common approach to motivation and change. If a counselor uses MI while an officer uses confrontation, the supervisee receives mixed messages and may play one against the other. If both use MI, the consistent approach reinforces change-oriented communication regardless of setting (Walters et al., 2007).

Communication between officer and treatment provider should support treatment engagement, not merely verify attendance. Knowing that a supervisee attended sessions tells you little about their progress. Knowing that they are struggling with a particular issue in treatment allows the officer to reinforce relevant themes during supervision contacts. Of course, confidentiality rules govern what information can be shared, and appropriate releases must be in place.

Officers can support treatment in several ways beyond monitoring attendance. Affirming treatment participation recognizes effort: "You've been going to group twice a week for two months. That takes commitment." Exploring treatment experience shows interest: "What have you been learning in your sessions?" Helping problem-solve barriers prevents dropout: "You mentioned transportation has been hard. What would help with that?"

When concerns arise about treatment quality or appropriateness, officers should address them through proper channels rather than undermining treatment in conversation with supervisees. Similarly, treatment providers who have concerns about supervision approaches should communicate directly with officers rather than expressing frustration to clients.

8.7 Core Principles Recap

Motivational interviewing originated in addiction treatment, making substance use disorders the population for which MI has the longest and strongest evidence base. Ambivalence represents the central feature of addiction, and MI addresses ambivalence more effectively than confrontational approaches that demand immediate commitment.

Productive conversations about substance use move beyond compliance verification to genuine exploration of the person's experience, goals, and concerns. Distinguishing ambivalence from denial helps officers respond to minimization without triggering additional resistance. Treatment readiness varies, and meeting people where they are produces better results than pushing action strategies on those not yet ready.

Relapse should be expected and addressed as a learning opportunity rather than evidence of hopelessness. The officer's response to relapse significantly influences whether supervisees continue honest disclosure or learn to conceal their use. Coordination with treatment providers strengthens the combined impact of supervision and treatment.

Chapter 9.0 addresses intimate partner violence, a population where MI must be adapted to address accountability while maintaining engagement.

Chapter 9.0: Intimate Partner Violence Cases

The probation officer reads the pre-sentence report describing an assault between a couple married for fifteen years. The defendant minimizes the incident, the victim has recanted, and both parties want the relationship to continue. The officer knows that intervention is necessary but wonders how to engage someone who denies having done anything seriously wrong. Standard batterer intervention programs report high dropout rates, and confrontational approaches often backfire. Yet accountability cannot be compromised when someone's safety is at stake. How do you balance MI's collaborative spirit with the need to address harmful behavior directly?

This chapter examines the specialized application of MI to intimate partner violence perpetrators, a population requiring careful adaptation of standard techniques. You will learn:

- What research shows about MI effectiveness with IPV offenders
- How to address accountability within MI's framework
- Approaches to common IPV supervision conversations
- When victim safety must override other considerations

9.1 Evidence for MI in IPV

Research on MI with intimate partner violence perpetrators shows promising results, particularly regarding treatment engagement. **Batterer intervention programs (BIPs)** typically experience high dropout rates, with studies reporting attrition between 40% and 60% (Eckhardt et al., 2013). Given that treatment completion correlates with reduced recidivism, anything that improves retention has practical significance.

Studies examining MI as a prelude to or adjunct to batterer intervention programs demonstrate improved engagement. Murphy, Linehan, Reyner, Musser, and Taft (2012) found that a two-session MI intervention preceding standard BIP participation produced significantly better treatment completion rates compared to control conditions. Participants who received MI showed 66% completion rates versus 33% for those who did not. This difference appeared particularly pronounced for men initially assessed as less ready to change.

A systematic review by Soleymani, Britt, and Wallace-Bell (2018) found that MI interventions improved session attendance, homework compliance, and overall engagement in batterer intervention programs. The authors noted that MI's emphasis on autonomy and collaborative relationship-building may counteract the defensive and resistant presentations common among IPV perpetrators who feel coerced into treatment.

However, evidence specifically examining whether MI reduces IPV recidivism remains limited. Most studies focus on engagement and process outcomes rather than reoffending. Some researchers caution that MI's non-confrontational stance might be interpreted by perpetrators as implicit permission or minimization of their behavior (Murphy & Meis, 2008). This concern requires careful attention to how MI is adapted for this population.

The key adaptation involves integrating MI with explicit attention to accountability. MI does not mean accepting the perpetrator's narrative uncritically. It means engaging with their perspective as a starting point while also introducing information about impact and working toward recognition of harm (Musser, Semiatin, Taft, & Murphy, 2008).

9.2 Accountability in MI Framework

The apparent tension between MI's non-judgmental stance and the need for perpetrator accountability represents the central challenge for this population. MI emphasizes meeting people where they are, reflecting their statements without argument, and avoiding the "righting reflex" that produces resistance. Yet IPV perpetrators frequently minimize, blame victims, and externalize responsibility. Simply reflecting these statements without challenge might reinforce harmful cognitions.

The resolution lies in understanding what MI actually prescribes. MI is non-judgmental about the person, not about behavior. Acceptance in MI means recognizing the person's inherent worth while still being honest about consequences and impacts. An officer can communicate genuine respect for a person while also communicating clearly that their behavior caused harm.

Exploring **impact** without lecturing involves asking questions that help the perpetrator consider consequences they may be avoiding. "What do you think it was like for her when that happened?" "How do you think your children were affected?" "When you look back at that night, what concerns you about what happened?" These questions invite reflection rather than demanding confession.

Evoking **recognition of harm** uses change talk principles adapted for this context. Just as officers listen for change talk about substance use, they can listen for acknowledgments of harm, however partial. "I know I shouldn't have grabbed her" contains both minimization (just grabbing) and acknowledgment (shouldn't have).

The skilled officer reflects the acknowledgment: "You're seeing that what happened wasn't okay."

When perpetrators express change-oriented statements about their relationship or their behavior, officers strengthen these through elaboration, affirmation, reflection, and summary (EARS), as discussed in section 5.5. "Tell me more about wanting to be different" invites elaboration. "It takes courage to look at your own role" offers affirmation. "You're recognizing the impact your actions have on people you care about" provides reflection.

9.3 Case Study: Minimization and Accountability

Background

Faramond, a 42-year-old man, was convicted of misdemeanor domestic battery after pushing his wife during an argument. He minimized the incident consistently: "I barely touched her. She fell over a chair and exaggerated the whole thing to police. If anyone was violent, it was her, screaming and throwing things at me first."

Presentation

At intake, Faramond was defensive and blamed the criminal justice system for overreacting to a "minor domestic dispute." He denied needing the court-ordered batterer intervention program. His wife supported his version of events and wanted charges dropped. Faramond saw himself as a victim of a system that unfairly targets men.

Analysis

Faramond's presentation typified IPV perpetrator minimization and victim-blaming. Confronting these distortions directly would likely produce more defensiveness. However, simply reflecting his perspective without challenge would implicitly validate harmful narrative. The officer needed to engage with Faramond's perspective while also introducing discrepant information that might prompt reflection.

Intervention

The officer began by exploring Faramond's experience: "This whole situation feels unfair to you." Faramond agreed emphatically. The officer asked: "Tell me about your marriage before this incident. What's it been like?" Faramond described a relationship with frequent arguments, escalating tension, and past separations.

The officer reflected: "So there's been a pattern of conflict and intensity in the relationship." Then: "When arguments get heated at your house, what does your daughter see?" This question introduced impact without lecturing. Faramond became quieter, acknowledging that their daughter had witnessed several arguments.

"What do you think that's been like for her?" Faramond admitted concern about his daughter's anxiety. The officer made a linking reflection: "So even if you see this particular incident differently than the police report describes, you're worried about the overall pattern's effect on your daughter."

Outcome

The conversation did not produce dramatic acknowledgment of wrongdoing, but it shifted Faramond from pure defensiveness to partial reflection. He attended the batterer intervention program initially for compliance reasons, but engagement increased as he recognized patterns in his relationship. The officer continued using MI throughout supervision, gradually building acknowledgment of responsibility over time.

Teaching Points

- Complete acknowledgment rarely occurs in a single conversation; progress may be incremental
- Questions about impact on children often access motivation that direct confrontation does not
- Reflecting partial acknowledgments without demanding full confession creates space for continued growth

9.4 Common IPV Conversations

Several scenarios arise frequently in IPV supervision, each requiring adapted MI approaches.

Discussing the incident involves exploring what happened without conducting interrogation. "Tell me what happened that night, from your perspective" opens the conversation. Officers listen for acknowledgments and concerns that can be reflected and explored. When significant distortions appear, officers can introduce information without arguing: "The police report describes it differently. I'm interested in understanding how you saw it."

Treatment engagement conversations for batterer intervention programs mirror those for substance abuse treatment. Exploring concerns about the program, connecting attendance to the person's own goals, and addressing barriers all apply. "What are your concerns about the program?" "What would make it useful rather than just something you have to get through?" "You mentioned wanting things to be different with your wife. How do you see the program connecting to that?"

Contact restrictions frequently generate resistance, particularly when couples want to reunite. MI approaches this by exploring the person's understanding of the restriction's purpose, acknowledging the difficulty, and helping them identify ways to manage the situation. "What do you understand about why the court imposed this no-contact order?" "What's been hardest about not having contact?" "How are you managing the separation?"

Relationship changes and co-parenting become relevant as cases progress. Officers can use MI to explore how the person thinks about their relationship moving forward, what changes they want to make, and how they plan to co-parent effectively. These conversations provide opportunities for change talk about becoming a different kind of partner or parent.

9.5 Victim Safety Priority

Throughout IPV supervision, **victim safety** remains the overriding priority. MI is a valuable tool for engaging perpetrators and supporting change, but it cannot supersede protection of those at risk. Officers must maintain clear boundaries about when MI approaches must be set aside for direct safety intervention.

Situations requiring direct action include: credible threats of harm, violation of protective orders, stalking behavior, escalating risk indicators, and any indication of imminent danger. In these circumstances, officers must respond decisively rather than continuing to explore motivation. Safety actions can be explained honestly: "I'm required to take this seriously because safety is my first responsibility. We can talk about your perspective after I've made sure everyone is protected."

Integrating MI with **safety planning** involves coordinating with victim advocates and protection services. Officers should not assume that maintaining good rapport with perpetrators means they fully understand the risk picture. Information from victim advocates and risk assessment tools provides context that perpetrator self-report cannot.

When victim advocates express safety concerns that conflict with the perpetrator's account, officers should treat the discrepancy seriously. This does not mean automatically disbelieving the perpetrator, but it does mean not relying solely on their perspective when making risk judgments.

After safety interventions, officers can return to MI approaches while remaining honest about what occurred: "I had to report those contacts because of the protective order. That's not negotiable, and I want to be straight about that. Now I'd like to understand what's happening for you that led to the contacts."

9.6 Chapter Synthesis

Motivational interviewing shows promise for improving engagement among intimate partner violence perpetrators, particularly as preparation for or adjunct to batterer intervention programs. High dropout rates from standard programs make any intervention that improves retention valuable. Evidence suggests MI can improve session attendance, compliance, and overall treatment engagement.

Adapting MI for IPV requires balancing collaborative engagement with accountability for harm. MI's non-judgmental stance applies to the person, not to behavior. Officers can explore perpetrators' perspectives while also introducing information about impact and working toward recognition of harm. Questions about effects on children and partners can access motivation that direct confrontation does not reach.

Common IPV scenarios, including discussing the incident, treatment engagement, contact restrictions, and relationship changes, each benefit from MI approaches. Throughout supervision, victim safety remains paramount. MI must be set aside when direct safety intervention is required, though officers can return to collaborative approaches afterward.

Chapter 10.0 addresses DUI/DWI offenders, a population where brief MI interventions have demonstrated particularly strong evidence of effectiveness.

Chapter 10.0: DUI and Impaired Driving

A 23-year-old college student appears for pre-sentence investigation following his second DUI arrest in eighteen months. He insists he doesn't have a drinking problem, that both arrests were "bad luck," and that he just needs to be more careful. A 55-year-old professional explains that her first DUI in thirty years of driving shouldn't require treatment because she "made one mistake." A 40-year-old man with three prior convictions says he knows he needs to change but hasn't figured out how. Each of these individuals requires a different approach, yet traditional DUI supervision often applies the same compliance-focused model to all. Research suggests that motivational interviewing, even in brief doses, can produce lasting changes in impaired driving behavior.

This chapter examines MI application to DUI/DWI offenders, a population where brief interventions demonstrate particularly strong evidence. You will learn:

- The research base for MI effectiveness with impaired driving offenders
- How to explore ambivalence about drinking and driving
- MI approaches for various points in DUI supervision
- Strategies for assessing who needs intensive treatment versus brief intervention

10.1 Evidence Base for DUI

Research on MI with DUI offenders provides some of the strongest evidence for brief motivational interventions in criminal justice settings. Randomized controlled trials demonstrate that even single-session MI interventions can reduce subsequent DUI arrests and dangerous driving behavior (Brown et al., 2015).

The study by Brown and colleagues (2015) followed DWI recidivists for nearly five years after receiving either a 30-minute brief motivational interviewing session or a control intervention involving information and advice. The brief MI session was more effective in delaying subsequent DWI arrests and other dangerous traffic violations. Effects were particularly pronounced for younger drivers and those with higher levels of problem drinking severity.

Miller, Sovereign, and Krege (1988) conducted an early study finding that a brief MI intervention for individuals convicted of DUI produced significantly better outcomes than standard education programming at a two-year follow-up. The MI group showed 50% fewer DUI recidivism events compared to the control group.

A systematic review by Gaume, Gmel, Faouzi, and Daeppen (2008) examined brief interventions for young adults with alcohol problems and found consistent evidence of effectiveness. DUI offenders represent a significant portion of the populations studied, and effects appear durable across follow-up periods extending to several years.

The effectiveness of brief MI with DUI offenders likely reflects the population's characteristics. Most DUI offenders do not have severe alcohol use disorders. Many are situational drinkers whose impaired driving results from poor decisions in specific circumstances rather than chronic alcohol dependence (Cavaiola, Strohmetz, & Abreo, 2007). For these individuals, a brief intervention that prompts reflection and increases awareness may be sufficient to change behavior. Those with more serious alcohol problems benefit from the motivation enhancement that MI provides, increasing their likelihood of engaging with intensive treatment.

10.2 Exploring Drinking and Driving

Conversations about drinking and driving with DUI offenders require distinguishing between two separate issues: the person's general relationship with alcohol and their specific behavior of driving after drinking. Some individuals drink moderately but made a poor decision about driving. Others have problematic drinking that makes impaired driving likely to recur. Still others may have minimal alcohol involvement but drove impaired due to prescription medication or other substances.

Most DUI offenders initially present with **minimization**. "I only had two beers." "I was barely over the limit." "I've driven like that a hundred times and nothing ever happened." These statements reflect cognitive patterns common after any arrest: the desire to reduce personal responsibility and consequences. Arguing against minimization typically produces more minimization; exploring the person's perspective creates opportunity for reflection.

Questions that invite exploration include: "Tell me about that night. What was happening?" "How does that night compare to your typical pattern?" "What surprised you about what happened?" "Looking back, what would you do differently?" These questions gather information while prompting the person to examine their own behavior.

Discussing consequences includes both what has already occurred and what could occur. "What's this arrest cost you so far?" identifies concrete impacts. "What concerns you about continuing as you have been?" explores future orientation. "What's the worst thing that could happen if nothing changes?" accesses fear-based motivation when appropriate, though this technique should be used judiciously.

The distinction between drinking behavior and driving decisions deserves exploration. "So you drink occasionally on weekends. Tell me more about how driving fits into those occasions." "What's your usual plan for getting home when you go out drinking?" "What was different about the night you got arrested?" These questions help identify whether the problem is overall drinking level, decision-making patterns around driving, or some combination.

10.3 Case Study: First Offense Minimization

Background

Leocadia, a 35-year-old accountant, was arrested for DUI after a work holiday party. Her blood alcohol content was .12, moderately above the legal limit. She had no prior criminal history and was devastated by the arrest. She maintained that this was completely out of character and that she didn't have a drinking problem.

Presentation

Leocadia appeared anxious and tearful during her pre-sentence investigation interview. She explained that she rarely drinks, had misjudged her consumption at the party, and felt confident this would never happen again. She was primarily concerned about the impact on her professional license and reputation.

Analysis

Leocadia's presentation suggested a genuinely situational offense rather than chronic alcohol misuse. Her distress indicated she took the arrest seriously. However, her focus on external consequences (license, reputation) rather than internal reflection (understanding what happened, preventing recurrence) suggested some minimization of the underlying issue. The goal was supporting her genuine motivation while also deepening her reflection.

Intervention

The officer validated Leocadia's distress: "This has been really upsetting for you. You see yourself as someone who makes good decisions, and this doesn't fit." Leocadia agreed. The officer explored: "Help me understand how it happened. You said you misjudged your consumption. What does that look like for you?"

Leocadia described drinking quickly on an empty stomach, not tracking how many glasses of wine she had, and feeling fine when she decided to drive. The officer reflected: "So there were several points where things went differently than you expected. You drank faster than usual, didn't keep count, and your judgment about your impairment was off."

The officer then asked: "If you found yourself in a similar situation, a work event with drinking, what would you do differently?" This question invited Leocadia to develop her own prevention plan rather than imposing one on her. She identified several concrete strategies.

Outcome

Leocadia was assessed as low risk for alcohol use disorder and did not require intensive treatment. She completed an alcohol education program and developed clear plans for avoiding impaired driving. The MI approach helped her move from external concern about consequences to internal understanding of what happened and how to prevent recurrence.

Teaching Points

- First-time DUI offenders often minimize because they see the arrest as inconsistent with their self-image
- Exploring the specific circumstances helps identify what actually went wrong
- Having the person develop their own prevention plan increases ownership and likelihood of follow-through

10.4 MI Across DUI Supervision

Different points in DUI supervision present different opportunities for MI application.

Pre-sentence investigation interviews provide early opportunities to engage with the person's perspective and begin planting seeds of reflection. Officers gathering information for sentencing recommendations can use open questions that serve both purposes: gathering data for assessment while prompting the person to examine their behavior.

Ignition interlock compliance discussions arise when devices are ordered. Rather than simply explaining requirements, officers can explore the person's reaction: "What's your sense of having an interlock device on your vehicle?" "How do you think that will affect your daily life?" "What concerns do you have about it?" These conversations reveal attitudes and potential compliance issues while also normalizing the experience.

Alcohol education program engagement parallels treatment engagement for other populations. "What are you learning in the program?" "What, if anything, has been useful?" "How does what they're teaching apply to your situation?" These questions support genuine engagement rather than mere attendance.

License reinstatement conversations occur at supervision's end and provide opportunities for consolidation. "You're about to get your license back. What have you learned through this process?" "What will you do differently now that you couldn't do before?" "What concerns you about having full driving privileges again?" These questions help ensure that lessons learned remain active as restrictions lift.

10.5 Assessing Treatment Needs

Not all DUI offenders require intensive substance abuse treatment. Over-treating low-risk individuals wastes resources and may actually increase recidivism by exposing them to higher-risk peers (Andrews & Bonta, 2010). Under-treating high-risk individuals misses opportunities for intervention. MI can help with appropriate assessment and triaging.

Assessing severity involves exploring the person's drinking patterns, consequences, and prior attempts to change. Open questions gather information while prompting self-reflection: "Tell me about your drinking over the past year." "How does alcohol fit into your typical week?" "Have you ever thought you should cut down?" "Has anyone expressed concern about your drinking?"

Standardized instruments like the AUDIT (Alcohol Use Disorders Identification Test) provide structured assessment (Babor et al., 2001). Officers can present these questionnaires in MI spirit: "I'd like you to complete this screening to help us understand what kind of support might be helpful. Answer honestly; the goal is to figure out what you actually need, not to make your situation worse."

Motivating treatment entry for those who need it involves the change talk evocation strategies discussed in Chapter 5.0. Importance and confidence rulers help identify barriers: "How important is it to you to change your relationship with alcohol?" "How confident are you that you could make those changes if you decided to?" Follow-up questions ("Why not lower?" "What would increase that number?") evoke the person's own arguments for change.

For **low-risk offenders**, brief intervention may be sufficient. A single session exploring what happened, developing a prevention plan, and checking in periodically can produce lasting change for individuals whose DUI represented a poor decision rather than a pattern. Research supports the effectiveness of brief interventions for this population (Gaume et al., 2008).

10.6 Essential Points

DUI offenders represent a population where brief MI interventions demonstrate strong effectiveness, with randomized trials showing reduced recidivism extending years beyond single-session interventions. Most DUI offenders do not have severe alcohol use disorders, making them responsive to interventions that prompt reflection rather than requiring extensive treatment.

Exploring ambivalence about drinking and driving involves distinguishing between overall alcohol use and specific decisions about driving while impaired. Minimization is common and should be explored rather than confronted directly. Questions that help the person examine their own behavior produce better results than arguments about their statements.

MI applies across DUI supervision, from pre-sentence investigation through license reinstatement. Each contact provides opportunities to reinforce reflection and support change. Assessment should match intervention intensity to risk level, with brief intervention for low-risk offenders and intensive treatment for those with significant alcohol problems.

Chapter 11.0 examines drug courts and specialty courts, settings where MI serves as the communication style for entire treatment teams rather than just individual practitioners.

Chapter 11.0: Drug and Specialty Courts

The judge looks down at a participant who has just tested positive for methamphetamine after three months of sobriety. In traditional court, this would trigger a scripted sanction. In drug court, it becomes a conversation. "I see you've had a setback," the judge says. "Help me understand what happened." The participant describes a family crisis that triggered the relapse. The judge asks what the participant learned and what support might help prevent recurrence. This exchange, taking place in a formal courtroom but using motivational principles, exemplifies how specialty courts integrate MI throughout the system.

This chapter examines motivational interviewing in drug courts and specialty court settings, where MI serves as the communication approach for entire treatment teams. You will learn:

- How MI principles match treatment court philosophy
- Specific MI applications for different team members
- Approaches to phase advancement and setback conversations
- Unique considerations for mental health court populations

11.1 MI and Treatment Court Philosophy

Drug courts and other specialty courts emerged from recognition that traditional criminal justice processing fails to address underlying issues driving criminal behavior. The **treatment court model** combines judicial supervision with therapeutic intervention, creating an approach that neither purely punitive nor purely therapeutic systems provide (National Association of Drug Court Professionals, 2015).

MI fits treatment court philosophy because both share core assumptions about change. Treatment courts assume that participants can change, that motivation matters, and that relationship quality affects outcomes. These assumptions contrast with traditional court models that focus on punishment rather than rehabilitation. MI provides the communication approach that puts treatment court philosophy into practice.

The **team-based structure** of treatment courts creates opportunities for MI integration across all participant contacts. Judges, case managers, treatment providers, probation officers, prosecutors, and defense attorneys all interact with participants. When team members share a common MI approach, participants receive consistent messages regardless of which team member they encounter. This consistency reinforces change-oriented communication and reduces the mixed messages that undermine progress.

Research on drug court effectiveness shows better outcomes compared to traditional court processing. A meta-analysis by Mitchell, Wilson, Eggers, and MacKenzie (2012) found that drug court participants had significantly lower recidivism rates than comparison groups. While studies specifically isolating MI's contribution within drug courts are limited, the communication quality between team members and participants appears to influence outcomes (Carey, Mackin, & Finigan, 2012).

11.2 Team Member Applications

Each team member role involves different interactions with participants, and MI adapts to each context while maintaining consistent spirit.

Judges hold unique positions for motivational communication. The courtroom setting carries weight that other contexts do not. When a judge demonstrates MI spirit, showing genuine interest in a participant's welfare, reflecting their statements, and expressing belief in their capacity to change, the impact can exceed that of identical communication from other team members. Bench conversations can include open questions ("What's been your biggest challenge this month?"), affirmations ("You've worked hard to get to this point"), and reflections ("It sounds like you're proud of the progress you've made").

Case managers coordinate services and often have the most frequent contact with participants. MI helps case managers build relationships that support genuine engagement rather than mere compliance. When participants experience case managers as allies invested in their success, they disclose problems earlier and accept help more readily. Case management conversations benefit from the OARS skills detailed in Chapter 4.0.

Treatment providers working in drug court settings should use MI as their primary clinical approach. This creates alignment between what happens in treatment sessions and what happens in other court contacts. When treatment providers use MI and court team members use MI, participants experience consistent engagement regardless of setting.

Defense attorneys and prosecutors in treatment courts often struggle most with MI adoption because their traditional roles emphasize advocacy or punishment rather than therapeutic engagement. Defense attorneys can use MI when discussing participant progress and options with their clients. Prosecutors can adopt MI spirit in staffing discussions and courtroom interactions, focusing on supporting participant success rather than purely pursuing sanctions.

11.3 Case Study: Team Consistency

Background

Marius, a 32-year-old drug court participant, had completed six months of the program with good compliance. Then he tested positive for alcohol (not his primary substance of concern) and appeared evasive when discussing it with his case manager. The team needed to respond, but team members initially disagreed about the appropriate approach.

Presentation

In staffing, the prosecutor favored immediate sanctions for the positive test. The treatment provider worried that harsh response would damage therapeutic alliance. The defense attorney advocated for minimal consequences. The case manager noted that Marius's evasiveness was unusual and suggested there might be underlying issues to explore.

Analysis

The team's disagreement reflected different professional orientations and priorities. Without MI as a shared framework, each member applied their traditional role perspective. With MI as a common language, the team could focus on how to respond in ways that maintained engagement while addressing the violation.

Intervention

The judge facilitated a discussion framed around MI principles: "Our goal is helping Marius succeed. The violation needs to be addressed, and so does whatever is going on that led to it. How can we do both?" The team agreed that the judge would address the violation directly in court while using MI to explore what happened.

In court, the judge said: "Marius, you tested positive for alcohol. That's concerning. Before we talk about what happens next, I want to understand what's going on. Help me understand what led to this." Marius eventually disclosed that his mother had been diagnosed with cancer, triggering the relapse.

The team adjusted its response based on this information, providing additional support while also implementing a modest sanction for the violation. The judge concluded: "You're dealing with something really difficult. That doesn't excuse the alcohol use, and there are consequences. It also means we need to figure out how to support you through this crisis."

Outcome

The MI-informed approach allowed the team to address the violation while maintaining engagement. Marius received increased counseling support and remained in the program. He later cited the court's response to this incident as a turning point in his perception of the program, noting that he felt supported rather than just punished.

Teaching Points

- Team disagreements can be resolved by returning to shared MI principles and goals
- Exploring circumstances before imposing sanctions often reveals information that affects appropriate response
- Combining accountability with support maintains engagement through difficult moments

11.4 Phase Advancement Conversations

Drug courts typically operate in phases, with participants advancing as they meet benchmarks. **Phase advancement conversations** provide opportunities for MI application that celebrates progress while maintaining momentum.

Celebrating progress using MI principles means affirming effort and recognizing change without becoming patronizing. Judges and case managers can reflect specific changes: "When you started this program, you were homeless and using daily. Today you have an apartment, a job, and six months clean. How does that feel?" This reflection invites the participant to articulate their own progress.

Questions about the advancement process invite reflection on change: "What's been different about the last few months?" "What do you think has made the difference?" "What have you learned about yourself through this process?" These questions help participants consolidate their understanding of their own change process, strengthening maintenance.

Addressing setbacks without derailing engagement requires balancing acknowledgment of problems with continued support. When participants experience relapses or violations, team responses should explore what happened (MI's curious, non-judgmental stance) while also addressing accountability (the court's enforcement function). As discussed in section 7.6, sanctions and support are not mutually exclusive.

Sustaining **motivation through phases** involves recognizing that enthusiasm often peaks early and may wane as the program extends. Later phases should continue evoking change talk and affirming progress rather than assuming sustained motivation. Questions like "What keeps you going at this point?" and "What would make you consider giving up, and what would keep you from doing that?" address maintenance challenges directly.

11.5 Mental Health Court Considerations

Mental health courts serve individuals with serious mental illness (SMI) whose criminal behavior connects to their psychiatric conditions. MI applies in these settings with adaptations for the population's unique characteristics.

Individuals with SMI may present communication challenges including disorganized thinking, paranoia, cognitive limitations, or medication effects. Officers should adjust their MI approach accordingly: using simpler language, checking understanding frequently, allowing more time for responses, and being patient with tangential or disorganized communication (Stinson & Clark, 2017).

Medication adherence represents a common focus in mental health court supervision. Traditional approaches often frame this as compliance: take your medications or face consequences. MI approaches medication as a choice with consequences, exploring the person's relationship with medication, concerns about side effects, and connection between medication and their goals. "What's your experience been with your medication?" "What do you notice when you take it versus when you don't?" "How does medication fit with what you want for your life?"

Coordinating with mental health treatment requires understanding how psychiatric symptoms affect motivation. Someone experiencing a depressive episode may have low energy and hopelessness that looks like resistance but reflects their illness. Someone with paranoia may be suspicious of the court team's intentions in ways that require patience and trust-building. Officers should communicate with treatment providers about how symptoms may be affecting presentation.

Understanding that **symptoms affect motivation** prevents misattribution of psychiatric symptoms to character or willfulness. An officer who understands that their participant's irritability reflects a manic episode responds differently than one who interprets it as defiance. Regular consultation with mental health professionals helps officers calibrate their expectations and responses appropriately.

11.6 Chapter Overview

Drug courts and specialty courts provide settings where MI can serve as the communication approach for entire treatment teams rather than individual practitioners. The philosophical alignment between MI and treatment court models creates natural fit. When team members share MI as a common language, participants receive consistent messages that reinforce engagement and change.

Different team members apply MI in different ways depending on their roles, but all can incorporate MI spirit and skills. Judges using MI in bench conversations create powerful motivational moments. Case managers and treatment providers using MI build relationships that support genuine change. Even prosecutors and defense attorneys can adopt MI principles in their treatment court interactions.

Phase advancement conversations provide opportunities to celebrate progress while maintaining momentum. Mental health court participants require adaptations for communication challenges and symptom effects while maintaining MI's core principles.

Chapter 12.0 addresses sex offender supervision, exploring whether and how MI applies to this challenging population.

Chapter 12.0: Sex Offender Supervision

The probation officer reviews her new case assignment: a 45-year-old man convicted of possession of child pornography, now on supervised release following federal prison. The offense triggered automatic registration, residence restrictions, and computer monitoring. The man has completed prison-based treatment and presents as cooperative but emotionally distant. The officer wonders how to establish genuine engagement with someone whose offense provokes such visceral reactions. Can motivational interviewing work with sex offenders? If so, how must it be adapted? These questions challenge officers to apply MI principles to perhaps the most difficult population in community corrections.

This chapter examines MI application to sex offender supervision, exploring evidence, adaptations, and boundaries. You will learn:

- What research indicates about MI effectiveness with sex offenders
- Strategies for engaging resistant clients around difficult material
- MI applications to specific sex offender supervision requirements
- How to balance risk management with therapeutic engagement

12.1 Evidence and Possibilities

Research specifically examining MI with sex offenders remains limited, but available evidence suggests potential value, particularly for treatment engagement and working alliance development. The **Good Lives Model (GLM)** of sex offender rehabilitation explicitly incorporates MI principles as the approach for engaging clients and supporting change (Ward & Stewart, 2003).

Marshall and colleagues (2005) examined therapist variables in sex offender treatment and found that therapist empathy, warmth, and directiveness (without aggressiveness) predicted better treatment outcomes. These therapist characteristics align with MI spirit. Confrontational treatment approaches, once common in sex offender treatment, have been associated with poorer outcomes in multiple studies (Serran, Fernandez, Marshall, & Mann, 2003).

The challenge with sex offenders involves the prevalence of **denial and minimization**. Many sex offenders deny their offenses entirely, admit to some but not all behavior, or acknowledge behavior while minimizing harm. Traditional approaches viewed denial as a risk factor requiring aggressive confrontation. More recent research suggests that denial's relationship to recidivism is more complex, and that confrontational approaches to denial may be counterproductive (Hanson & Morton-Bourgon, 2005).

MI offers an alternative to confrontation that may be more effective. Rather than attacking denial directly (which typically produces more denial), MI explores the person's perspective, identifies any acknowledgments that exist, and builds from there. This approach aligns with the GLM's emphasis on approach goals (building a good life) rather than avoidance goals (not reoffending), though both treatment frameworks maintain clear focus on community safety.

12.2 Engaging Resistant Clients

Sex offenders often present as highly resistant, and their resistance may have multiple sources. Some resist because they maintain innocence despite conviction. Others resist because shame makes acknowledging their behavior unbearable. Still others resist because they distrust a system that has labeled and restricted them. Understanding the source of resistance helps officers respond appropriately (Stinson & Clark, 2017).

Building working alliance with sex offenders requires demonstrating genuine interest in the person beyond their offense. This does not mean ignoring the offense or minimizing its seriousness. It means recognizing that the person existed before the offense and will exist after supervision ends, and that engaging with their full humanity creates better conditions for change than treating them only as their criminal behavior.

Questions that explore **values beyond the offense** help establish connection: "What was important to you before all this happened?" "What do you want your life to look like ten years from now?" "What kind of person do you want to be?" These questions identify motivations that can be connected to supervision goals.

Finding **motivation for positive change** often involves identifying what the person values and how current behavior threatens those values. Someone who values his relationship with his adult children can explore how continued violation of conditions might affect that relationship. Someone who values his professional identity can consider how his current path serves or threatens that identity.

12.3 Case Study: Engaging Through Values

Background

Simeon, a 52-year-old former high school teacher, was convicted of sexual contact with a 16-year-old student. He maintained that the relationship was consensual (though legally it could not be) and that the student had initiated contact. He completed prison-based treatment but was assessed as still minimizing responsibility.

Presentation

On supervision, Simeon was technically compliant but emotionally disengaged. He answered questions minimally, completed requirements mechanically, and seemed to be waiting out his supervision term. His officer noted that he never discussed his offense voluntarily and deflected any questions about it.

Analysis

Simeon's presentation suggested shame-based avoidance rather than genuine denial. His identity as an educator had been destroyed by his offense, and engaging with what he had done meant confronting this loss. Direct approaches to discussing the offense were unlikely to succeed. Connection to other values might provide a pathway to engagement.

Intervention

The officer explored Simeon's history and interests. Simeon had been married for 25 years and had two adult children who had largely cut off contact since his arrest. He spoke with obvious pain about missing his grandchildren. The officer reflected: "You've lost a lot. Your career, your reputation, and now much of your family."

Simeon agreed, adding that he didn't know how to repair things. The officer asked: "If you could have a different relationship with your children, what would that look like?" Simeon described wanting to apologize, to explain without excusing, and to rebuild trust slowly. The officer explored: "What do you think it would take for your children to trust you again?"

This question led Simeon to acknowledge that trust required demonstrating he understood what he had done wrong and was committed to being different. For the first time, he began discussing his offense in terms of its impact on the student rather than defending himself.

Outcome

Engagement with Simeon improved substantially after the values-based conversation opened a pathway to discussing his offense. He remained in supervision successfully and eventually had supervised contact with his grandchildren. The approach did not excuse or minimize his behavior but found motivation for genuine reflection that direct confrontation had not achieved.

Teaching Points

- Shame-based avoidance may look like resistance but requires different response than defiant denial
- Exploring values beyond the offense can create pathways to discussing the offense itself
- Identifying what the person wants to rebuild provides motivation for the work of change

12.4 Specific MI Applications

Sex offender supervision involves specific requirements that benefit from MI approaches.

Polygraph appointments generate anxiety and resistance. Officers can explore concerns about polygraphs using MI: "What are your thoughts about the polygraph requirement?" "What worries you about it?" Understanding concerns helps address them while also identifying potential issues the person may be avoiding.

Treatment group engagement involves similar principles to substance abuse treatment engagement. Exploring concerns about group treatment, connecting participation to personal goals, and supporting genuine engagement rather than mere attendance all apply. "What's been useful in group?" "What's been challenging?" "How does what you're learning apply to your situation?"

Registration and restriction compliance creates ongoing challenges. Rather than simply monitoring compliance, officers can explore the person's experience: "What's it like living with these restrictions?" "What's been hardest about the registration requirements?" "How do you manage the limitations on where you can live and go?" These conversations identify stressors that might lead to violation while also demonstrating understanding.

Social support and relationship building present particular challenges for sex offenders, who often face isolation and relationship restrictions. MI can help explore what healthy social connection looks like within the boundaries of supervision: "Who are the people in your life now?" "What kind of relationships would you like to have?" "How do you build connections while meeting your supervision requirements?"

12.5 Risk Management Balance

Throughout sex offender supervision, **community safety** remains the overriding priority. MI is a tool for engagement that may improve outcomes, but it cannot supersede protection of potential victims. Officers must maintain clarity about this priority even while using collaborative engagement approaches.

Using MI to **improve risk disclosure** means that better relationships may lead to more honest communication about risk factors. When supervisees trust their officers and experience supervision as supportive rather than purely punitive, they may disclose concerning thoughts or behaviors earlier. This disclosure allows for intervention before harm occurs. Conversely, purely punitive relationships may drive concerning behavior underground where it cannot be addressed.

When confrontation is necessary, officers should not hesitate to use it. If evidence suggests a supervisee is violating conditions, planning new offenses, or creating risk to potential victims, direct intervention takes precedence over maintaining collaborative rapport. The difference between MI and permissiveness is important: MI maintains clear boundaries while engaging collaboratively within them.

After confrontational interventions, officers can return to MI approaches: "I had to respond to that situation the way I did because safety comes first. That's not going to change. Now I want to understand what was going on for you."

12.6 Summary and Implications

MI application to sex offender supervision requires careful adaptation that maintains focus on community safety while engaging clients more effectively than purely confrontational approaches. Research suggests that therapist characteristics associated with MI predict better treatment outcomes, and that confrontational approaches may be counterproductive.

Engaging resistant sex offenders involves exploring values beyond the offense, building working alliance through genuine interest, and finding motivation for change that connects to what the person values. Specific supervision requirements including polygraph, treatment, registration, and relationship building all benefit from MI approaches.

Risk management remains paramount, and MI does not mean compromising safety. Better engagement may actually improve safety by increasing honest disclosure of concerning thoughts and behaviors. When direct intervention is necessary, officers should use it, then return to collaborative approaches afterward.

Chapter 13.0 examines high-risk offenders more broadly, exploring why MI matters more, not less, as risk level increases.

Chapter 13.0: Working with High Risk

The intensive supervision unit handles caseloads with individuals assessed as high risk for reoffending. These supervisees have extensive criminal histories, multiple criminogenic needs, and often resist intervention. An officer reviewing her caseload notes that most are on electronic monitoring, several have gang affiliations, and nearly all have failed on standard supervision before. She meets with one supervisee three times weekly, and these contacts feel more like surveillance than relationship. How does she engage meaningfully with someone who sees her as just another part of the system trying to control him?

This chapter examines MI application with high-risk offenders, exploring why relationship quality matters more, not less, as risk increases. You will learn:

- Why research shows high-risk individuals benefit most from quality intervention
- MI techniques adapted for intensive supervision contexts
- Approaches to gang-involved individuals
- How MI integrates with cognitive-behavioral programming

13.1 Why MI Matters More

Research from the Risk-Need-Responsivity (RNR) model demonstrates that high-risk individuals benefit most from intensive services (Andrews & Bonta, 2010). This finding seems counterintuitive; shouldn't difficult cases be the hardest to change? The explanation lies in the relationship between risk level and intervention intensity. Low-risk individuals often change on their own and may actually be harmed by intensive intervention. High-risk individuals have more room to improve and more potential to benefit from quality services.

The **responsivity principle** within RNR specifically addresses how services should be delivered. General responsivity indicates that cognitive-behavioral and social learning approaches work best. Specific responsivity calls for matching intervention style to individual characteristics. MI addresses responsivity by providing a communication approach that increases receptivity to intervention regardless of specific content.

Research specifically examining the officer-supervisee relationship with high-risk populations shows that relationship quality predicts outcomes. Kennealy, Skeem, Manchak, and Eno Louden (2012) found that "firm, fair, and caring" relationships protected against supervision failure even among high-risk offenders. Officers who maintained clear boundaries while demonstrating genuine care produced better outcomes than those who were either purely punitive or excessively lenient.

The **trap of pure surveillance** emerges when intensive supervision focuses only on monitoring without engagement. Increasing contact frequency without improving contact quality simply produces more opportunities for violation detection without corresponding increases in behavior change. MI provides the quality dimension that makes intensive supervision genuinely intensive rather than merely frequent.

13.2 Intensive Supervision Techniques

More frequent contacts in intensive supervision create more opportunities for MI application. Each contact represents a potential moment for relationship building and motivation enhancement, or alternatively, another reminder of external control. How officers use these contacts determines their impact.

Building rapport in high-stakes relationships requires demonstrating trustworthiness over time. High-risk supervisees often distrust the system based on extensive prior experience. They have encountered officers who made promises and broke them, who claimed to want to help but seemed focused only on catching violations. Building trust requires consistent demonstration that this relationship is different.

Electronic monitoring conversations can be conducted in MI spirit. Rather than simply verifying compliance, officers can explore experience: "What's it been like wearing the monitor?" "What's been hardest about the restrictions?" "How do you manage when you get frustrated with it?" These questions acknowledge the burden while also gathering information about potential compliance challenges.

Home visit dialogue benefits from MI techniques. Officers entering someone's home are in their space, which changes the dynamic from office visits. Beginning home visits with open questions about how things are going, noticing and commenting on positive elements in the environment, and conducting conversations rather than interrogations all maintain MI spirit in the home setting.

13.3 Case Study: Intensive Supervision

Background

Aurelian, a 28-year-old man with seven felony convictions, was assigned to intensive supervision following prison release. His officer was required to see him three times weekly plus conduct random home visits. Aurelian had failed standard supervision twice before and was assessed as high risk on all validated instruments.

Presentation

Aurelian presented as hostile and uncooperative initially. He made clear that he saw supervision as just another way the system kept him down. He completed required contacts but offered nothing more than necessary, treating each meeting as an adversarial encounter to survive.

Analysis

Aurelian's presentation reflected years of experience with the criminal justice system. His resistance protected against involvement with yet another authority figure likely to disappoint or betray him. The intensity of his supervision (three contacts weekly) meant that relationship quality would determine whether these became opportunities for change or just repeated confrontations.

Intervention

The officer recognized that building trust would take time and began by being consistent, honest, and respectful in every contact. She asked about his life beyond supervision requirements: his interests, his family, his hopes. She noticed when he was having good days and commented on it. She was clear about requirements and honest about consequences, but she also expressed genuine interest in his success.

Over weeks of consistent contact, Aurelian's hostility decreased. The officer asked: "You've been through supervision before, and it didn't work out. What would make this time different?" Aurelian began articulating what he needed to change and what barriers he faced. The officer reflected: "You're seeing that some things have to be different this time."

Outcome

Aurelian successfully completed intensive supervision and stepped down to standard supervision. He later credited the relationship with his officer as the factor that made the difference: "She actually gave a damn. First PO I ever had who seemed like she wanted me to make it."

Teaching Points

- High-risk supervisees often have extensive negative experience with the system that must be overcome
- Consistency over time builds trust that cannot be established quickly
- The quantity of contacts in intensive supervision creates opportunities that the quality of contacts determines

13.4 Gang Involved Individuals

Gang-involved supervisees present specific challenges that require adapted MI approaches. **Understanding loyalty and identity** is essential. Gang membership often provides belonging, purpose, protection, and identity that pro-social alternatives do not readily replace. Simply demanding that someone leave their gang without offering alternatives ignores the real functions gang membership serves.

Exploring ambivalence about gang life recognizes that many gang members have mixed feelings about their involvement. They may value the brotherhood while recognizing the costs. They may want out but not know how, or fear consequences of leaving. MI questions can explore this ambivalence: "What do you get from being in the gang?" "What has it cost you?" "How do you see your future with the gang?" (Stinson & Clark, 2017).

Finding **alternative sources of belonging** involves exploring what needs the gang met and identifying how those needs might be met differently. Employment programs, community organizations, mentoring relationships, and family connections can provide some of what gang membership provided. Officers can help supervisees identify and pursue these alternatives.

Addressing safety concerns openly acknowledges that leaving gang life carries real risks. Officers should not pretend these risks do not exist. Instead, they can explore what the person fears and what might mitigate those fears. This honest conversation builds trust and allows for realistic planning.

13.5 Criminal Thinking Patterns

Many high-risk offenders display **criminal thinking patterns**, cognitive distortions that support antisocial behavior. Programs like "Thinking for a Change" address these patterns through cognitive-behavioral intervention (National Institute of Corrections, 2019). MI can serve as a gateway to this work and complement it during participation.

MI as a **gateway to cognitive-behavioral work** helps prepare supervisees for programs they might otherwise resist. Exploring what cognitive-behavioral programs offer, addressing concerns about participation, and connecting program content to personal goals all increase engagement. "The thinking skills program focuses on how we think about situations and make decisions. How do you see your thinking affecting your choices?"

Exploring thinking errors without lecturing uses MI's reflective approach. When supervisees describe decisions that reflect distorted thinking, officers can reflect without judging: "So you saw it as okay to take the money because the company wouldn't miss it." This reflection invites the supervisee to examine their thinking without triggering defensiveness.

Integrating MI with programs like Thinking for a Change involves supporting the program's content during supervision contacts. When supervisees learn concepts in the program, officers can reinforce them: "You've been learning about thinking traps. How does that apply to what you're describing?"

13.6 Bringing It Together

High-risk offenders benefit most from quality intervention, making MI more important with this population, not less. The responsivity principle indicates that how services are delivered affects outcomes, and MI provides a delivery approach that increases receptivity. Pure surveillance without engagement wastes the opportunity intensive supervision provides.

MI techniques adapt to intensive supervision contexts including frequent contacts, electronic monitoring, and home visits. Each contact represents an opportunity for relationship building and motivation enhancement. Gang-involved individuals require understanding of the functions gang membership serves and exploration of alternatives that meet similar needs. Criminal thinking patterns can be addressed through MI-informed engagement that prepares for and complements cognitive-behavioral programming.

Chapter 14.0 examines reentry and parole, exploring MI application during the critical transition from incarceration to community.

Chapter 14.0: Reentry and Parole

After twelve years in federal prison, a man walks through the gate with $50 and a list of parole conditions. Within 72 hours, he must report to his parole officer, find housing that meets approval, and begin looking for employment. He has no driver's license, no recent work history, and a felony record that will follow him on every application. His parole officer meets him at the first appointment and asks what his plans are. This moment, and the hundreds of decisions and interactions that follow over the next months, will determine whether reentry succeeds or whether he returns to the system that just released him.

This chapter examines MI application during reentry and parole, the transition from incarceration back to community. You will learn:

- What research indicates about successful reentry
- How to build relationship and conduct MI before release
- Approaches to common reentry challenges
- Coordination strategies with reentry services and providers

14.1 The Reentry Challenge

Research consistently shows that the period immediately following release from incarceration presents the highest risk for reoffending. Studies indicate that approximately two-thirds of released prisoners are rearrested within three years, and many reoffenses occur within the first months after release (Durose, Cooper, & Snyder, 2014). The **first 90 days** represent a particularly critical window where the foundations for successful reentry are established or where patterns of failure take hold.

Returning citizens face substantial barriers including housing restrictions, employment discrimination, identification challenges, transportation limitations, family relationship strain, and the requirement to meet supervision conditions while simultaneously addressing survival needs (Travis, Western, & Redburn, 2014). These barriers can overwhelm even motivated individuals, leading to violations or new offenses driven by desperation rather than criminal intent.

The parole officer's role during reentry involves both monitoring compliance and supporting successful transition. Officers who focus only on monitoring may document failures without preventing them. Officers who actively support transition using MI principles may prevent failures from occurring in the first place. The evidence reviewed throughout this text suggests that relationship quality between officer and supervisee affects outcomes, and this relationship matters particularly during the vulnerable reentry period.

14.2 Pre Release Conversations

Building relationship before release, when possible, improves reentry outcomes. **Pre-release MI conversations** establish connection, begin realistic planning, and allow the parole officer and soon-to-be-released individual to develop working rapport before the stresses of release complicate the relationship.

Realistic **planning using MI** involves exploring expectations and developing achievable goals. Many incarcerated individuals have unrealistic expectations about reentry, imagining that securing housing and employment will be straightforward or that family relationships will immediately resume pre-incarceration patterns. MI questions can explore these expectations: "What are you expecting when you get out?" "What do you think will be hardest?" "What concerns you most?"

Addressing **expectations and fears** openly prepares for challenges that lie ahead. Fear of failure, fear of the unknown, fear of rejection by family, and fear of returning to circumstances that led to incarceration all warrant exploration. Officers can reflect these fears without minimizing them while also evoking the person's own resources and motivations: "You're worried about going back to the same neighborhood. What would help you stay on track despite that?"

Pre-release conversations also allow officers to begin gathering information that will inform supervision planning. Understanding the person's history, relationships, skills, and goals helps officers make appropriate referrals and develop supervision strategies tailored to individual circumstances.

14.3 Case Study: Pre Release Planning

Background

Nephele, a 34-year-old woman, was scheduled for release after serving five years for drug trafficking. Her parole officer was able to meet with her twice before release as part of a pilot pre-release program. Nephele expressed both excitement and anxiety about release.

Presentation

In pre-release meetings, Nephele described plans to return to her mother's home, reconnect with her teenage children who had been raised by her mother during her incarceration, and find a job in healthcare (her pre-incarceration field). She seemed optimistic but also acknowledged fears about how her children would receive her.

Analysis

Nephele's plans contained both realistic elements (staying with family initially) and potentially unrealistic expectations (quick return to healthcare employment with a felony record, immediate reconnection with children). The pre-release conversations provided opportunity to explore these plans while she still had time and space to prepare.

Intervention

The officer explored Nephele's expectations using MI questions: "Tell me more about how you see things going with your children." Nephele described imagining that they would be happy to have her back and that things would return to how they were before her incarceration. The officer reflected: "You're hoping to pick up where you left off. What do you think it's been like for them while you've been gone?"

This question prompted Nephele to consider her children's perspective more fully. She acknowledged that they might have complicated feelings and that rebuilding trust would take time. The officer helped her develop realistic expectations and identify concrete steps for gradual reconnection.

Regarding employment, the officer explored: "What do you know about working in healthcare with a felony conviction?" Nephele was unsure. The officer provided information about restrictions while also exploring alternative paths: "Given these limitations, what other work options would interest you?"

Outcome

When Nephele released, she had more realistic expectations and a more developed plan than she would have without pre-release conversations. Family reconnection proceeded gradually, employment took longer than hoped but eventually stabilized, and the relationship with her parole officer began with trust already established.

Teaching Points

- Pre-release conversations allow for planning and relationship building before release stresses begin
- Exploring expectations helps identify unrealistic hopes that can be gently recalibrated

- Providing information within MI framework maintains engagement while ensuring realistic planning

14.4 Reentry Challenges

Common reentry challenges benefit from MI approaches that support problem-solving while maintaining collaborative relationship.

Housing conversations address one of the most immediate reentry needs. "What are your options for housing?" "What concerns do you have about where you'll stay?" "What would you need to feel stable in your living situation?" When housing options are limited, officers can help prioritize while respecting autonomy: "Given the restrictions, what matters most to you in where you end up?"

Employment and job search discussions recognize both the importance of employment and the barriers returning citizens face. "What kind of work are you looking for?" "What's been your experience with job applications so far?" "How do you handle questions about your record?" Officers can provide information about reentry-friendly employers while also supporting the person's own efforts and maintaining realistic expectations.

Family reconnection involves complex emotions and relationships that supervision can support but not control. "How have things been with your family since you got out?" "What do you hope for in those relationships?" "What's been challenging?" These questions acknowledge that family matters deeply while respecting that the person makes their own choices about relationships.

Navigating conditions and restrictions requires balancing compliance requirements with reentry demands. When multiple conditions compete for limited time and resources, officers can help prioritize: "You have a lot of requirements. What's been hardest to manage?" "How can we make this work better?" Problem-solving collaboratively maintains MI spirit while also addressing compliance needs.

14.5 Service Coordination

Successful reentry typically involves multiple service providers: case managers, treatment providers, employment specialists, housing services, and others. Effective supervision coordinates these services rather than operating in isolation.

Working with service providers using MI principles means communicating about shared clients in ways that support engagement. When officers and treatment providers share MI as a common approach, the returning citizen experiences consistent messages regardless of setting. Differences in approach between providers can confuse clients and undermine progress.

Advocating for clients while maintaining accountability involves helping returning citizens access services and overcome barriers while also holding them accountable for their responsibilities. These functions are not contradictory. Officers who advocate for their clients demonstrate care that builds trust, making accountability conversations easier.

Communication between officers and service providers should focus on supporting success rather than merely documenting problems. "What's working well with this client?" and "What does he need that he's not getting?" are more productive questions than "Is he complying?"

14.6 Concluding Thoughts

Reentry represents perhaps the most challenging period in the criminal justice continuum, with the highest rates of failure occurring in the months immediately following release. MI provides a communication approach that can improve outcomes by building relationships that support transition, helping returning citizens develop realistic plans, and coordinating services effectively.

Pre-release conversations establish relationship and begin planning before the stresses of release complicate engagement. Post-release conversations address the concrete challenges of housing, employment, family, and conditions while maintaining collaborative spirit. Coordination with service providers ensures that multiple supports work together rather than at cross-purposes.

This chapter concludes Part III of the text, which has examined MI application across special populations and specific offense types. Part IV will address implementation, including how individual officers develop MI skills and how agencies support MI adoption system-wide.

PART IV: IMPLEMENTATION & SUSTAINABILITY

Chapter 15.0: Integrating MI Into Practice

A probation officer attends a two-day motivational interviewing workshop. She learns about OARS, change talk, and the spirit of MI. She practices with colleagues, receives positive feedback, and leaves feeling equipped to transform her practice. Six weeks later, she realizes she has barely used any of what she learned. Her conversations with supervisees look much like they did before the training. The workshop materials sit in a drawer, and the enthusiasm has faded into the demands of daily caseload management. This scenario repeats across agencies nationwide, representing millions of dollars in training investment that fails to produce lasting practice change.

This chapter addresses the gap between learning MI in a workshop and actually using it in daily practice. Building on the skills and applications covered in Parts I through III, you will learn:

- The stages of MI learning and why single trainings fail
- How to target specific situations for deliberate practice
- Methods for self-assessment and ongoing skill development
- Common pitfalls that derail MI implementation and how to avoid them

15.1 Stages of Learning MI

Miller and Moyers (2006) proposed an eight-stage model for learning motivational interviewing that explains why brief training exposures rarely produce competent practitioners. Understanding these stages helps officers set realistic expectations and plan their learning path.

Stage 1 involves openness to collaboration with clients. Before any techniques matter, the practitioner must be willing to work with rather than on people. Officers who believe their job is to tell supervisees what to do and enforce compliance when they do not will struggle with MI regardless of technical training. This openness represents a philosophical shift that some officers resist.

Stage 2 involves proficiency in client-centered counseling skills, particularly reflective listening. The ability to hear what someone says, understand it accurately, and reflect it back forms the foundation on which all other MI skills build. Officers who cannot reflect skillfully cannot practice MI, regardless of how many other techniques they know (Miller & Rollnick, 2013).

Stage 3 requires recognizing and reinforcing client change talk. As discussed in Chapter 5.0, change talk signals movement toward change and predicts outcomes.

Officers must develop ears for change talk, hearing it when it appears and recognizing its absence.

Stage 4 involves eliciting and strengthening change talk. Beyond recognizing it, practitioners must be able to evoke change talk through strategic questioning and respond to it in ways that strengthen and extend it.

Stage 5 requires rolling with resistance, now more commonly termed responding to sustain talk and discord. As Chapter 6.0 detailed, arguing against resistance produces more resistance. Officers must learn to acknowledge, reflect, and redirect rather than confront.

Stage 6 involves developing a change plan. MI is not merely a relationship-building exercise; it moves toward specific behavioral change. Officers must be able to help supervisees develop concrete, achievable plans when readiness emerges.

Stage 7 requires consolidating commitment. Once a plan exists, helping the supervisee strengthen their commitment increases the likelihood of follow-through.

Stage 8 involves switching between MI and other intervention styles as appropriate. MI does not replace all other approaches; it provides one tool among many. Knowing when to use MI and when other approaches fit better represents advanced practice (Miller & Moyers, 2006).

Research on MI training consistently shows that brief workshops alone do not produce sustained behavior change in practitioners. A meta-analysis by Schwalbe, Oh, and Zweben (2014) found that workshop training alone showed minimal effects on practitioner behavior, while training combined with ongoing coaching and feedback produced substantial improvements. The difference was not the initial workshop quality but the presence of follow-up support.

15.2 Starting With Practice

Given the complexity of full MI competence, officers benefit from starting small rather than trying to change everything at once. Targeting specific skills in specific situations allows deliberate practice that builds genuine competence.

One skill at a time prevents overwhelm. An officer might spend two weeks focusing solely on asking open questions, tracking how many open versus closed questions she asks in each contact. Once open questions feel natural, she adds reflections. Then affirmations. Then summaries. This sequential approach builds skills systematically rather than attempting everything simultaneously and doing nothing well.

Targeting specific situations focuses practice where it matters most. An officer might decide that intake interviews represent his best opportunity for MI practice because they are longer and less rushed than routine check-ins. He practices MI during intakes while maintaining his usual approach in other contacts. As competence builds, he expands to routine visits, then to violation conversations.

Tracking progress provides feedback that sustains motivation. Simple tracking might involve noting after each contact how many reflections were offered, or rating on a one-to-ten scale how well MI spirit was maintained. More sophisticated tracking might involve recording sessions (with appropriate permissions) and counting specific behaviors. Whatever the method, measurement creates accountability and makes progress visible (Moyers et al., 2016).

Sample tracking questions officers might ask themselves after each contact include: Did I ask at least one open question that I would not have asked before learning MI? Did I reflect at least twice? Did I hear any change talk, and if so, how did I respond? Did I notice and resist any urges to argue or lecture?

15.3 Self Assessment Methods

Ongoing self-assessment distinguishes officers who maintain and improve their MI skills from those who drift back to old habits. Several methods support this self-assessment.

Recording and reviewing conversations provides the most direct feedback on actual practice. Audio recording, where legally and ethically permitted, allows officers to listen to themselves and evaluate their skill use. The distance of recording often reveals patterns invisible in the moment. An officer might discover she interrupts more than she realized, or that her reflections are actually questions in disguise.

Peer feedback and buddy systems create accountability and support. Two officers learning MI together can observe each other's work, offer constructive feedback, and troubleshoot challenges. Regular meetings to discuss cases and practice skills maintain momentum that isolated individual effort often cannot sustain (Madson et al., 2009).

The **Motivational Interviewing Treatment Integrity (MITI)** code provides a standardized measure of MI quality. The MITI assesses both global dimensions (cultivating change talk, softening sustain talk, partnership, and empathy) and specific behavior counts (questions, reflections, affirmations, seeking collaboration, emphasizing autonomy, and confronting). While full MITI coding typically requires trained raters, officers can use simplified versions for self-assessment (Moyers et al., 2016).

A simplified self-reflection worksheet might include questions such as: What open questions did I ask? What did I reflect, and were my reflections simple or complex? Did I offer any affirmations, and if so, what specifically did I affirm? When I heard sustain talk, how did I respond? Did I notice any moments where I fell into old patterns? What will I try to do differently next time?

15.4 Case Study: Skill Development

Background

Dorothea, a probation officer with 12 years of experience, attended a three-day MI training and found it conceptually interesting but struggled to implement the skills with her caseload. She returned to work intending to use MI but found herself defaulting to her usual directive style within days.

Presentation

Dorothea described feeling overwhelmed by trying to remember everything from training while managing high caseload demands. When contacts went well, she was not sure if it was MI or just luck. When contacts went poorly, she blamed her supervisees' resistance rather than examining her own approach. After three months, she concluded MI "didn't work for her population."

Analysis

Dorothea's experience illustrates the workshop-to-practice gap that research consistently documents. She attempted global implementation without systematic skill building or feedback mechanisms. Her attribution of contact outcomes to external factors (supervisee resistance) rather than examining her own behavior prevented learning from experience.

Intervention

A colleague who had successfully integrated MI suggested a structured approach. Dorothea identified one skill (reflections) and one context (intake interviews) for focused practice. She used a simple tracking form after each intake, noting how many reflections she offered and rating her satisfaction with each. She scheduled weekly check-ins with her colleague to discuss what she was learning.

Outcome

After four weeks of focused practice, Dorothea noticed her reflections becoming more natural. She began hearing change talk she had previously missed. Her intakes were taking slightly longer but producing substantially more engagement. She expanded her practice to routine visits while continuing to track her progress. Six months later, she described MI as "just how I work now."

Teaching Points

- Global implementation attempts often fail; focused skill-building succeeds
- Self-tracking creates accountability and makes progress visible
- Peer support sustains motivation through the difficult learning period

15.5 Common Pitfalls

Several pitfalls commonly derail MI implementation. Recognizing them helps officers avoid or recover from them.

MI as manipulation occurs when officers use MI techniques to get supervisees to do what the officer wants rather than to help supervisees explore their own motivation. This fundamentally violates MI spirit. The difference between MI and manipulation lies in whose agenda drives the conversation. If the officer has a predetermined outcome and uses MI techniques to engineer compliance, that is manipulation regardless of how skillfully the techniques are applied (Miller & Rollnick, 2013).

"MI lite" involves going through motions without genuine engagement. An officer might ask open questions but not listen to the answers. She might reflect but without genuine curiosity about the supervisee's experience. She might affirm mechanically rather than noticing and acknowledging genuine strengths. This surface-level implementation produces neither the relationship benefits nor the behavioral outcomes that genuine MI achieves.

Abandoning MI when stressed happens because MI requires cognitive resources that stress depletes. Under pressure, officers revert to overlearned patterns, which for many means directive, confrontational approaches. Recognizing this tendency helps officers prepare for it. Some plan specific stress management strategies. Others identify particular stressors (certain supervisees, certain situations) where they know they are likely to abandon MI and prepare accordingly.

The **gradual drift back to old habits** occurs without active maintenance. Even officers who successfully implement MI may find their skills eroding over months without practice feedback and renewal. Research on MI skill retention suggests that without ongoing support, practitioners' skills decline toward pre-training levels within months (Schwalbe et al., 2014). Continuous practice, tracking, and peer support prevent this drift.

15.6 Avoiding the Pitfalls

Strategies exist for avoiding or recovering from each pitfall.

For manipulation concerns, officers should regularly examine their motivations. Before a conversation, ask: Am I genuinely curious about this person's perspective, or do I already know what they should do? During conversation, notice if frustration arises when the supervisee does not move toward predetermined outcomes. After conversation, reflect on whose agenda drove the interaction.

For MI lite, officers should periodically return to fundamentals. Reread Chapter 2.0 on MI spirit. Listen to recordings and assess not just technique but genuine engagement. Ask whether conversations feel different to supervisees or just to the officer. Peer observation can help identify when technical proficiency masks spiritual emptiness.

For stress-induced abandonment, officers should identify their triggers and prepare responses. An officer who knows he reverts to confrontation with hostile supervisees might develop specific phrases to use when hostility emerges. Another who abandons MI when running behind schedule might build buffer time into her calendar on demanding days.

For gradual drift, ongoing practice structures provide protection. Continued tracking, periodic peer observation, refresher training, and professional reading all maintain skills. Officers who treat MI learning as a one-time event will likely lose it; those who treat it as ongoing professional development will likely sustain and improve.

15.7 Putting Knowledge Into Practice

MI competence develops through stages that single workshops cannot traverse. Understanding these stages helps officers set realistic expectations and plan systematic skill development rather than hoping that training exposure alone will produce lasting change.

Starting small with focused practice on specific skills in specific situations builds competence incrementally. Tracking progress provides feedback that sustains motivation and identifies areas needing attention. Peer support creates accountability and helps troubleshoot challenges.

Common pitfalls including manipulation, superficial implementation, stress-induced abandonment, and gradual drift all threaten sustained MI practice. Recognizing these pitfalls and implementing preventive strategies protects the investment in learning.

Chapter 16.0 shifts focus from individual skill development to agency-level implementation, examining how supervisors and administrators can support MI adoption across their organizations.

Chapter 16.0: Agency MI Implementation

A probation department director reviews her agency's training budget and wonders if the motivational interviewing training they have been providing for three years has made any difference. Officers attend workshops, express enthusiasm, and then return to caseloads where little seems to change. Outcome data show no improvement in supervision completion rates or recidivism. The director suspects the training is not working but cannot explain why, and she faces pressure to continue because MI has become the expected approach in community corrections. She needs a different strategy but is not sure what it should be.

This chapter addresses agency-level MI implementation for supervisors and administrators seeking to move beyond ineffective training models. You will learn:

- How to make the evidence-based case for MI investment
- What training models work versus what fails
- How to create organizational conditions that support MI practice
- Methods for measuring implementation success

16.1 Making the Evidence Case

Presenting the case for MI to agency leadership requires translating research findings into language that resonates with administrative priorities. Different arguments appeal to different decision-makers.

The **evidence base** for MI in criminal justice, reviewed throughout this text, shows improved treatment engagement, better supervision outcomes, and in some studies, reduced recidivism. Meta-analyses demonstrate effect sizes that, while modest individually, aggregate to meaningful population-level impact when applied across large caseloads (Lundahl et al., 2010). These findings should be presented specifically, with citations, rather than vaguely claiming that "research shows MI works."

Cost-benefit arguments quantify MI's value. Training costs represent upfront investment that produces returns through improved outcomes. If MI reduces revocations by even a small percentage, the avoided incarceration costs (averaging $35,000 or more per person annually) quickly exceed training expenses (Vera Institute of Justice, 2019). Reduced officer turnover, which may accompany more satisfying work relationships, represents additional savings.

Alignment with existing priorities connects MI to what the agency already values. Most agencies espouse goals around rehabilitation, successful supervision completion, and reduced recidivism. MI directly serves these goals. Agencies using Risk-Need-Responsivity frameworks (discussed in Chapter 2.0) can frame MI as addressing the responsivity principle. Agencies emphasizing evidence-based practice can position MI as one of the best-supported interventions available for community corrections populations.

Leadership buy-in requires addressing concerns as well as presenting benefits. Common concerns include: "We don't have time for lengthy conversations" (address with research showing brief MI effectiveness), "Our population is too difficult" (address with research specifically in criminal justice settings), and "We've tried training before and it didn't stick" (address with research on effective versus ineffective training models).

16.2 Effective Training Models

Research clearly distinguishes training approaches that work from those that fail. Understanding this distinction prevents wasted investment and failed implementation.

What does not work includes single-day exposure trainings, self-study without practice opportunities, and any training without follow-up support. Studies consistently show that one-time training events produce temporary skill increases that decay to baseline within weeks to months (Schwalbe et al., 2014). The common agency practice of sending officers to a workshop and expecting sustained behavior change has no empirical support.

What works includes intensive initial training combined with ongoing coaching, feedback, and support. The initial training should span at least two days, preferably longer, with substantial practice opportunities rather than just didactic presentation. After initial training, ongoing support is essential. This support might include individual coaching sessions, group supervision focused on MI cases, regular skill assessments with feedback, and booster trainings (Madson et al., 2009).

The **MINT (Motivational Interviewing Network of Trainers)** maintains a directory of trainers who have completed standardized training in MI training. Using MINT-registered trainers provides some quality assurance, though trainer quality still varies. Agencies should ask about trainers' backgrounds, approach to ongoing support, and experience with criminal justice populations specifically.

Effective implementation budgets for ongoing support, not just initial training. A rough guideline suggests that ongoing support costs should equal or exceed initial training costs over the first year post-training. Agencies that invest heavily in initial training but nothing in follow-up typically see their investment wasted through skill decay.

16.3 Case Study: Failed Implementation

Background

A state probation department invested $200,000 in MI training over three years. Each year, a group of officers attended a two-day workshop provided by qualified trainers. Officers reported enjoying the training and intending to use the skills. However, supervision outcome data showed no changes over the three-year period.

Presentation

When administrators examined what happened after officers returned from training, they found a consistent pattern. Officers returned to full caseloads with no protected time for practice or reflection. Supervisors did not ask about MI use and did not observe or provide feedback on officer contacts. No systems existed to track MI implementation. The organizational culture valued efficiency and compliance monitoring over relationship-building conversations.

Analysis

This implementation failed not because of poor training but because of absent follow-up support. Officers faced no accountability for using MI, no feedback on their skill level, and no organizational support for practice. The training content was sound, but the implementation model (train and hope) had no research support.

Intervention

Based on this analysis, administrators restructured the approach. They designated agency MI champions who received advanced training. They built MI observation and feedback into supervisory practice. They created tracking systems to monitor officer skill use. They adjusted productivity expectations to allow time for meaningful conversations. They scheduled regular booster sessions rather than treating training as a one-time event.

Outcome

Two years after restructuring, the agency observed measurable improvements in both officer MI skill levels (assessed through recorded sessions) and supervision outcomes (completion rates, revocations). The total cost was higher than the original training-only model, but the investment produced actual returns rather than being wasted.

Teaching Points

- Training alone, no matter how high quality, does not produce sustained behavior change
- Organizational conditions either support or undermine what training teaches
- Effective implementation requires ongoing support, feedback, and accountability structures

16.4 Supporting Officer Practice

Creating organizational conditions that support MI practice requires attention to supervision structures, workload, culture, and recognition systems.

Supervision and feedback structures provide ongoing support for skill development. Supervisors should observe officer contacts (in person or through recording review), provide specific feedback on MI skill use, and discuss challenging cases using MI principles. This requires that supervisors themselves understand MI, which may mean prioritizing supervisor training before or alongside frontline staff training.

Reducing barriers addresses practical obstacles to MI implementation. Time is the most commonly cited barrier; officers with crushing caseloads feel unable to have the extended conversations MI seems to require. However, as Chapter 7.0 discussed, brief MI techniques work within time-limited contacts, and MI-informed conversations often prove more efficient than resistance-generating confrontational ones. Workload management, protected time for skill practice, and realistic productivity expectations all help.

Cultural change addresses the values and norms that shape officer behavior. If agency culture implicitly rewards tough, directive approaches and views relationship-building as soft or naïve, officers face pressure to conform regardless of what training taught. Changing culture requires consistent messaging from leadership, modeling by supervisors, and systems that make MI the path of least resistance rather than a countercultural deviation.

Recognizing and rewarding MI practice reinforces desired behavior. This might include incorporating MI skill assessment into performance evaluations, highlighting successful MI-informed outcomes in staff meetings, and creating advancement opportunities for officers who demonstrate MI competence. What gets measured and rewarded is what gets done.

16.5 Measuring Success

Implementation without measurement cannot be evaluated or improved. Multiple measurement levels provide information about whether MI implementation is succeeding.

Officer-level competence measures assess whether officers are actually using MI skills. The MITI (Moyers et al., 2016) provides standardized assessment based on recorded sessions. Simplified versions can be used for routine quality assurance. Without skill measurement, agencies cannot know whether training translated into practice.

Client-level process measures assess whether supervisees experience supervision differently. Surveys of supervisee perceptions about their officer's approach can detect changes in relationship quality. Working alliance measures adapted for criminal justice settings capture whether supervisees experience their officers as collaborative and supportive.

Client-level outcome measures assess whether MI implementation affects the ultimate goals of supervision. Relevant outcomes include treatment engagement, supervision completion, technical violations, new arrests, and revocations. These measures require comparison to baseline or to control groups to determine whether changes reflect MI implementation or other factors.

Building data systems for continuous improvement means collecting relevant data routinely rather than as special projects. Embedding skill assessment into supervisory practice, surveying supervisees systematically, and tracking outcomes by officer or unit all provide ongoing feedback for improvement. Data should flow to decision-makers in timely, usable formats.

16.6 Case Study: Successful Implementation

Background

A county probation department committed to evidence-based practice decided to implement MI agency-wide. Leadership received consultation on effective implementation models and designed a multi-year strategy rather than expecting immediate transformation.

Presentation

The implementation plan included: training supervisors before line staff; intensive initial training followed by monthly coaching sessions; integration of MI observation into routine supervision; workload adjustments to allow time for practice; creation of MI champions in each unit; tracking systems for skill levels and outcomes; and commitment to continuing support for at least three years.

Analysis

This implementation design addressed the common failure points that research identifies. Training was not treated as sufficient on its own. Organizational conditions were adjusted to support what training taught. Measurement systems provided feedback for continuous improvement.

Intervention

Implementation proceeded as planned over three years. Initial skill assessments showed wide variation among officers. Monthly coaching addressed individual development needs. Quarterly reviews examined outcome data and made adjustments. Officers who struggled received additional support. Officers who excelled became resources for their colleagues.

Outcome

After three years, skill assessments showed consistent MI use across officers. Treatment engagement rates increased significantly. Supervision completion rates improved. Officer satisfaction surveys showed improved morale. The investment paid for itself through reduced revocation costs within the first year of measurable outcome improvement.

Teaching Points

- Successful implementation requires multi-year commitment with sustained support
- Supervisor training and involvement are essential for sustainable change
- Measurement systems enable continuous improvement and demonstrate value

16.7 Chapter Synthesis

Agency-level MI implementation requires more than training. Research clearly shows that single training events, no matter how well delivered, do not produce sustained behavior change without ongoing support. Effective implementation combines intensive initial training with coaching, feedback, and accountability structures that continue indefinitely.

Making the case for MI investment involves presenting evidence specifically relevant to agency goals, quantifying cost-benefit relationships, and addressing leadership concerns. Training model selection should favor approaches with research support (intensive training plus ongoing support) and avoid those without support (single exposures without follow-up).

Supporting officers to use MI requires attention to supervision structures, workload management, organizational culture, and recognition systems. Measurement at officer, process, and outcome levels provides feedback for continuous improvement and demonstrates value to leadership.

Chapter 17.0 addresses sustainability from a different angle: the self-care and personal sustainability needs of officers implementing MI in demanding work environments.

Chapter 17.0: Self Care and Sustainability

A veteran probation officer sits in his car after a particularly difficult day. One supervisee disclosed suicidal thoughts, requiring emergency intervention. Another became hostile when confronted about a violation. A third, whom he had invested months of effort into helping, was arrested on new charges. He thinks about the 89 other people on his caseload, each with their own problems, needs, and demands. He wonders how long he can keep doing this work and finds himself caring less than he used to about whether his supervisees succeed or fail. Something has shifted, and he is not sure how to address it.

This chapter examines the personal sustainability needs of officers practicing MI in demanding corrections environments. Building on the implementation content from Chapters 15.0 and 16.0, you will learn:

- How compassion fatigue affects corrections workers and how MI might protect against it
- Strategies for maintaining MI spirit when conditions challenge your patience
- Ways to find ongoing meaning in difficult work
- Pathways for continued professional growth as an MI practitioner

17.1 Compassion Fatigue in Corrections

Compassion fatigue, sometimes called secondary traumatic stress or vicarious trauma, occurs when helping professionals experience emotional exhaustion from ongoing exposure to others' suffering and need (Figley, 1995). Corrections workers face particular risk factors including high caseloads, chronic exposure to client distress and trauma histories, limited resources, and work with populations who may not seem to appreciate or respond to help.

Research indicates that probation and parole officers experience burnout at rates comparable to or exceeding other human service professions. Lewis and colleagues (2013) found that correctional staff reported higher levels of emotional exhaustion and depersonalization than comparable samples of social workers and mental health professionals. Factors contributing to this included role ambiguity, limited control over outcomes, and organizational stressors.

Burnout manifests in three dimensions: emotional exhaustion (feeling drained and depleted), depersonalization (treating clients as objects rather than people), and reduced personal accomplishment (feeling ineffective regardless of actual outcomes). Officers experiencing burnout may stop caring about supervisee success, go through motions without genuine engagement, and struggle to maintain the empathic presence that MI requires (Maslach & Leiter, 2016).

Paradoxically, **MI may protect against burnout** rather than depleting already exhausted officers. Research on therapist experience with MI suggests that practitioners find it more satisfying than confrontational approaches (Miller & Moyers, 2006). The collaborative nature of MI reduces the adversarial dynamic that can make corrections work particularly draining. When supervisees engage and change, officers experience the professional satisfaction that sustains motivation.

However, this protective effect requires genuine MI practice, not superficial technique application. Officers going through MI motions without authentic engagement may experience neither the relationship benefits nor the protective effects. The spirit of MI, including the genuine belief in client capacity for change, provides the foundation for sustainable practice.

17.2 MI Under Pressure

Maintaining MI spirit becomes difficult when conditions conspire against it. High caseloads, difficult clients, and systemic obstacles all challenge the officer's ability to remain collaborative, empathic, and evocative.

High caseloads and limited time force officers to prioritize. When seeing 20 or more people in a day, the temptation to cut corners, ask only compliance questions, and move to the next person becomes powerful. Brief MI techniques (discussed in Chapter 7.0) help, but officers must also accept that not every contact can be deeply MI-informed. Identifying which contacts offer the best opportunities for meaningful MI work and focusing effort there may be more sustainable than attempting perfect MI with everyone and achieving it with no one.

Difficult clients test patience and challenge assumptions. Supervisees who are hostile, manipulative, or seemingly committed to failure trigger reactions that MI training may not overcome. When an officer genuinely dislikes a supervisee, maintaining MI spirit becomes performance rather than authentic engagement. Strategies include: recognizing one's own reactions without judgment, consulting with colleagues about challenging cases, and finding something genuinely true to affirm about even the most difficult person (even if it is just that showing up took effort).

Systemic obstacles include agency cultures that do not support MI, supervisors who do not value relationship-building, and outcome metrics that reward compliance monitoring over genuine engagement. Officers practicing MI in unsupportive environments face additional strain from swimming against organizational current. Building alliances with like-minded colleagues, seeking supervision from MI-supportive sources, and focusing on what can be controlled rather than what cannot all help manage this strain.

17.3 Case Study: Preventing Burnout

Background

Jessamine, a parole officer with eight years of experience, had been a skilled and dedicated practitioner. She learned MI early in her career and found it genuinely changed how she approached supervision. Over time, however, increasing caseloads, agency pressures, and a series of difficult outcomes eroded her enthusiasm and skill.

Presentation

Jessamine noticed herself caring less about her supervisees, completing contacts as quickly as possible, and reverting to purely compliance-focused interactions. She stopped asking open questions because she did not want to hear long answers. She stopped reflecting because the effort seemed pointless when supervisees would do what they wanted regardless. Her supervisor noted declining quality in her case notes.

Analysis

Jessamine displayed classic burnout symptoms: emotional exhaustion (depletion), depersonalization (treating supervisees as cases rather than people), and reduced personal accomplishment (believing her efforts were futile). Her MI skills had eroded not through lack of knowledge but through the accumulation of emotional burdens without adequate recovery or support.

Intervention

Jessamine's supervisor recognized the signs and responded not with criticism but with support. She reduced Jessamine's caseload temporarily. She connected Jessamine with an employee assistance counselor. She arranged for Jessamine to attend an MI refresher training, not as remediation but as renewal. She paired Jessamine with a newer officer for peer support, recognizing that teaching can restore sense of competence.

Outcome

Over several months, Jessamine's engagement improved. The temporary caseload reduction allowed recovery time. The refresher training reminded her why she had valued MI initially. The peer relationship provided accountability and support. She did not return to naive enthusiasm but developed a more sustainable practice that acknowledged both the possibilities and limits of her work.

Teaching Points

- Burnout is a predictable occupational hazard requiring systemic response, not individual blame
- Supervisory support that addresses underlying causes proves more effective than criticism
- MI skill erosion often reflects emotional depletion rather than knowledge deficits

17.4 Finding Meaning

Sustaining motivation for difficult work requires connection to meaning and purpose. Officers who understand why their work matters and who can perceive its effects maintain engagement better than those who work only for paycheck and pension.

Celebrating small wins counteracts the discouragement of large-scale failure rates. Recidivism statistics suggest that many people under supervision will fail, but this statistical reality obscures the individual successes that occur daily. An officer who notices when a supervisee attends treatment consistently, maintains employment, or shows increased engagement has something to celebrate, even if the ultimate outcome remains uncertain. Focusing solely on failures makes the work seem hopeless; noticing successes provides balance.

Connecting to personal values grounds work in authentic motivation. Why did the officer enter this field? What does she believe about human capacity for change? What kind of professional does she want to be? Reconnecting with these foundational values, particularly when daily pressures obscure them, sustains commitment that external rewards alone cannot maintain.

Building supportive colleague relationships provides both practical and emotional resources. Colleagues who share MI commitments can discuss cases, troubleshoot challenges, and remind each other why this approach matters. Isolation, whether physical or professional, erodes sustainability. Seeking connection with like-minded colleagues, within or beyond the immediate agency, builds resilience.

17.5 Continued Professional Growth

MI mastery is not a destination but an ongoing process. Officers who continue developing maintain interest and skill that stagnant practitioners lose.

Advanced training opportunities extend beyond the basic MI that initial trainings cover. Specialized trainings address MI with particular populations, integration with other approaches, and trainer development. MINT (Motivational Interviewing Network of Trainers) regional events provide advanced learning and connection with the broader MI community.

MINT membership offers access to resources, forums, and community that support continued growth. The MINT network includes practitioners and trainers across disciplines and settings who can provide consultation, collaboration, and support. While membership requirements include trainer certification, attending MINT-sponsored events and utilizing MINT resources benefits all practitioners.

Staying current with research ensures that practice remains evidence-based. New studies on MI effectiveness, mechanism, training, and application appear regularly. Officers who read selectively from this literature maintain connection to the broader field and learn about developments that might improve their practice.

Professional growth also involves contributing to others' development. Experienced MI practitioners can mentor newer colleagues, present at professional conferences, participate in training, and contribute to the growing body of practice wisdom. Teaching often deepens one's own understanding while supporting the broader field.

17.6 Case Study: Sustained Growth

Background

Erasmus, a probation officer who learned MI early in his career, deliberately cultivated continued development over 15 years. Rather than treating initial training as sufficient, he approached MI as an ongoing professional commitment requiring continued investment.

Presentation

Erasmus sought advanced training opportunities, attending specialized workshops on MI with particular populations. He joined a regional MI interest group that met monthly to discuss cases and practice skills. He began recording selected sessions (with supervisee permission) for self-review. Eventually, he became certified to train others, which deepened his own understanding through teaching.

Analysis

Erasmus treated MI competence as a professional identity rather than a technique to be learned and forgotten. His continued investment prevented the skill decay that affects most practitioners and produced genuine expertise rather than initial exposure. His teaching role created accountability for maintaining skill and staying current with developments.

Intervention

Erasmus's approach involved proactive self-development rather than response to problems. He budgeted time and resources for professional growth just as he would for any important commitment. He sought community with other committed practitioners to maintain motivation and learning.

Outcome

After 15 years, Erasmus demonstrated advanced MI competence on formal assessments and was regarded as a resource within his agency and region. He reported continued satisfaction with his work, experiencing MI as a renewable source of professional meaning rather than a depleting burden.

Teaching Points

- MI mastery requires ongoing investment, not just initial training
- Teaching others deepens one's own understanding and creates accountability
- Building community with other committed practitioners sustains motivation

17.7 Core Principles Recap

Corrections work exposes officers to suffering, frustration, and failure in ways that produce compassion fatigue and burnout. MI practice may protect against burnout by making work more satisfying and relationships less adversarial, but this protection requires genuine engagement rather than mechanical technique application.

Maintaining MI spirit under pressure involves realistic expectations, strategic focus on high-opportunity contacts, self-management when difficult clients trigger reactance, and building resilience against systemic obstacles. Finding meaning through celebrating small wins, connecting to personal values, and building supportive colleague relationships sustains motivation that external rewards alone cannot maintain.

Continued professional growth through advanced training, community involvement, and staying current with research ensures that MI skills improve rather than decay over a career. MI mastery is an ongoing process, and officers who approach it as such maintain interest, skill, and satisfaction that stagnant practitioners lose.

This chapter concludes the main text. The appendices that follow provide practical tools for implementing and sustaining MI practice in criminal justice settings.

PART V: CASE STUDIES

Chapter 18: Foundation Cases

Case Study 1: Initial Intake Interview with Resistant Client

Case Background

Supervisee: Marcus Ellsworth, 34-year-old African American male

Offense: Felony possession with intent to distribute (cocaine), second offense

Sentence: 3 years probation following 18 months incarceration

Risk Level: High (LSI-R score: 32)

History: Previous probation revocation at age 26 for technical violations including missed appointments and positive drug screens. Marcus served 14 months before release. He has expressed distrust of the criminal justice system and stated during his presentence investigation that probation is "designed to fail people like me."

Criminogenic Needs: Substance abuse (cocaine, alcohol), antisocial peers, unemployment, antisocial attitudes toward supervision

Context: This is Marcus's first meeting with his new probation officer, Officer Denise Whitfield, following his release from incarceration. Marcus arrives 10 minutes late, arms crossed, minimal eye contact.

Session Script

[Marcus enters the office, does not extend hand for handshake, sits down heavily in the chair across from Officer Whitfield]

OFFICER WHITFIELD: Marcus, thank you for coming in today. I know you've had a long journey to get here after your release last week. How are you settling in?

[MI Skill: Open question to establish rapport; acknowledges transition difficulty]

MARCUS: [Shrugs] It is what it is. Look, I've done this before. I know how it works. You're gonna tell me all the things I can't do, I'm gonna nod my head, and then we'll see each other every month until one of us gets tired of the game.

OFFICER WHITFIELD: You've been through this process before, and it sounds like that experience left you feeling like probation is more of a game than something that actually helps.

[MI Skill: Complex reflection capturing both content and underlying emotion]

MARCUS: [Makes eye contact for first time] Help? Nobody's trying to help me. Last time, my PO was just waiting for me to mess up. Three dirty UAs and I was back inside. Didn't matter that I was working, didn't matter that I was trying. One slip and it's over.

OFFICER WHITFIELD: That must have been incredibly frustrating. You were making real effort in some areas of your life, and it felt like none of that counted when you struggled with the drug testing.

[MI Skill: Reflection with emotional labeling; validates experience without endorsing substance use]

MARCUS: Exactly. So why should this time be any different? You're gonna have the same rules, same tests, same everything.

OFFICER WHITFIELD: You're wondering if anything has actually changed, or if we're just going to repeat the same pattern that didn't work before.

[MI Skill: Reflection reframing skepticism as a reasonable question]

MARCUS: [Slight nod] Yeah.

OFFICER WHITFIELD: That's a fair question, Marcus. I don't have a magic answer that's going to convince you right now that this will be different. What I can tell you is that I'm genuinely curious about what you think would actually be helpful for you during this supervision period. Not what the court thinks, not what I think. What would make a difference for you?

[MI Skill: Open question evoking client's perspective; emphasizes autonomy; acknowledges limitations honestly]

MARCUS: [Pauses, uncrosses arms slightly] What would make a difference? Nobody's ever asked me that before.

OFFICER WHITFIELD: I'm asking now. You know your life better than anyone else. You know what worked before and what didn't. If you could design your own supervision, what would it look like?

[MI Skill: Continued open questioning; affirms client expertise on own life]

MARCUS: [Long pause] I mean... last time, everything was about the drugs. Every meeting, every conversation. "Are you using? Did you go to NA? When's your next UA?" Like that's all I am. A drug addict.

OFFICER WHITFIELD: The focus on substance use made you feel like that was all anyone saw when they looked at you.

[MI Skill: Simple reflection]

MARCUS: I'm more than that, you know? I had a job. I was paying child support. My daughter was starting to trust me again. But none of that mattered when I had one bad week.

OFFICER WHITFIELD: Let me make sure I'm understanding this correctly. You were working, you were being a father and supporting your daughter financially, and you were rebuilding trust with her. Those are significant accomplishments that got overlooked. And it sounds like those things actually matter a lot to you.

[MI Skill: Summary with affirmation embedded; identifies values]

MARCUS: My daughter matters. Keisha. She's twelve now. She barely knew me before I went in this time. Her mother... we're not together, but she's been good about letting me call from inside.

OFFICER WHITFIELD: Keisha is important to you. You want to be present in her life in a way you haven't been able to be.

[MI Skill: Reflection highlighting value/motivation]

MARCUS: [Voice softens] She deserves a real father. Not some dude who shows up when it's convenient and then disappears. I've been that guy too many times.

OFFICER WHITFIELD: You've been thinking about what kind of father you want to be for Keisha, and it's different from the pattern you've had in the past.

[MI Skill: Complex reflection introducing change talk]

MARCUS: I have to be different. She's getting older. These are the years that matter. If I'm not there now, she's gonna write me off just like I wrote off my old man.

OFFICER WHITFIELD: [Leans forward slightly] I'm hearing something really important here, Marcus. You're saying you have to be different for Keisha, that these years are critical, and that you don't want to repeat the pattern you experienced with your own father. Can you tell me more about what being different would look like for you?

[MI Skill: Summary followed by open question to elaborate change talk]

MARCUS: Being there. Not just sending money, but actually being there. Going to her school stuff. Teaching her to drive in a few years. Being someone she can call when things get hard.

OFFICER WHITFIELD: Being a present, available father who Keisha can count on.

[MI Skill: Simple reflection]

MARCUS: Yeah. But I can't do that if I'm locked up. I can't do that if I'm high. I know that. It's just... the drugs, man. When things get hard, that's what I know.

OFFICER WHITFIELD: So on one hand, you know that using cocaine has taken you away from Keisha and the father you want to be. And on the other hand, it's been your way of coping when life gets overwhelming. Both of those things are true at the same time.

[MI Skill: Double-sided reflection acknowledging ambivalence]

MARCUS: [Nods slowly] That's it exactly. I'm not stupid. I know the drugs are the problem. But knowing it and doing something about it are two different things.

OFFICER WHITFIELD: You've got the awareness. The gap is between knowing what you need to do and actually being able to do it consistently.

[MI Skill: Reflection affirming insight while acknowledging challenge]

MARCUS: Last time, I went to NA like they told me. Sat in the meetings. Said the words. But it never really clicked, you know? It felt like going through the motions for the PO.

OFFICER WHITFIELD: The NA attendance was compliance with supervision rather than something that genuinely connected with you.

[MI Skill: Reflection distinguishing compliance from engagement]

MARCUS: Right. So what's the point of doing the same thing again?

OFFICER WHITFIELD: What would be different from going through the motions? If there was something that actually helped you manage the hard times without using, what would that look like?

[MI Skill: Open question exploring alternatives]

MARCUS: I don't know. Something real. Something that gets it. Not a bunch of people telling me I'm powerless. I'm not powerless. I made choices that got me here.

OFFICER WHITFIELD: You want something that acknowledges your agency, that you make choices and can make different ones. You don't connect with the powerlessness message.

[MI Skill: Reflection capturing client's perspective on recovery approach]

MARCUS: I need to learn how to make better choices when everything in me is screaming to get high. That's the part I don't know how to do.

OFFICER WHITFIELD: That's a really important insight, Marcus. You're clear that the challenge isn't about willpower or wanting it enough. It's about having actual skills for those moments when the craving is intense and everything feels overwhelming.

[MI Skill: Affirmation with reflection; reframes problem as skills gap]

MARCUS: Yeah. So what, you got a magic class for that?

OFFICER WHITFIELD: [Slight smile] No magic. But there are some options that focus specifically on what you're describing, building skills for managing cravings and making different choices in high-risk moments. One is called cognitive behavioral therapy, and there's a specific version for substance use that some people find more practical than traditional 12-step approaches. Would you be interested in hearing more about it?

[MI Skill: Providing information with permission; offering options rather than prescribing]

MARCUS: [Shrugs, but maintains eye contact] I mean, I'll listen. Can't promise anything.

OFFICER WHITFIELD: That's completely fair. All I'm asking is that you stay open to exploring options. You're the one who gets to decide what makes sense for your life.

[MI Skill: Affirming autonomy]

MARCUS: [Nods] Okay. So what are these conditions I gotta follow? Let's get that part over with.

OFFICER WHITFIELD: We'll go through all of that. But before we do, I want to circle back to something you said earlier that stuck with me. You talked about Keisha and being a different kind of father. And you talked about needing real skills, not just going through the motions. As we go through these conditions, I want us to keep connecting them back to your goals, not just what the court requires. Does that work for you?

[MI Skill: Summary linking conditions to client values; collaborative framing]

MARCUS: [First genuine half-smile] Yeah. That works.

MI Skills Demonstrated

Skill	Frequency	Examples
Open Questions	7	"What would make a difference for you?"
Affirmations	4	"Those are significant accomplishments"
Reflections (Simple)	6	"Keisha is important to you"
Reflections (Complex)	8	Double-sided reflection on ambivalence
Summaries	3	Collecting, linking, and transitional
Autonomy Support	4	"You're the one who gets to decide"
Asking Permission	1	"Would you be interested in hearing more?"

Reflection

This initial intake session illustrates several critical MI principles for working with resistant clients. Marcus arrived with a defensive posture shaped by negative previous experiences with supervision. His expectation was that Officer Whitfield would follow the same pattern as his previous officer: focus exclusively on compliance, ignore his efforts in other life domains, and wait for him to fail.

Officer Whitfield's approach began with genuine curiosity rather than rule recitation. By asking what would actually help Marcus, she communicated that his perspective mattered, something he explicitly noted no one had asked before. This single question began shifting the dynamic from adversarial to collaborative.

The session demonstrates the importance of following the client's lead. When Marcus mentioned his daughter Keisha, Officer Whitfield recognized this as a potential source of change motivation and explored it thoroughly. She did not introduce Keisha; Marcus did. Her role was to notice the emotional shift when he spoke about his daughter and create space for him to elaborate.

The double-sided reflection regarding ambivalence about substance use was a pivotal moment. Rather than arguing that drugs were problematic (which Marcus already knew), Officer Whitfield acknowledged both sides simultaneously. This response communicated understanding without judgment and allowed Marcus to voice his own recognition that cocaine was interfering with his goals.

Officer Whitfield also demonstrated appropriate information sharing by waiting for Marcus to express interest in alternatives before describing cognitive behavioral approaches. She asked permission, offered options rather than mandates, and emphasized that Marcus retained decision-making authority.

The session did not resolve Marcus's ambivalence or create immediate buy-in to all supervision conditions. What it accomplished was establishing the foundation for a working relationship built on respect, curiosity, and connection to Marcus's own values.

Outcome Analysis

Immediate Outcomes:

- Marcus's body language shifted from closed (arms crossed, no eye contact) to more open (uncrossed arms, direct eye contact, half-smile)
- He identified his daughter Keisha as a core motivation for change

- He articulated his own understanding that substance use interferes with his parenting goals
- He expressed interest in skills-based treatment approaches
- He engaged collaboratively in framing how conditions would be discussed

Intermediate Outcomes (3-month follow-up):

- Marcus attended all scheduled appointments on time
- He enrolled in cognitive behavioral therapy for substance use at a community provider
- He had one positive drug screen at week 6, which was addressed using MI principles (see Case Study 16)
- He reported increased contact with Keisha, including attending her school play

Long-term Outcomes (12-month follow-up):

- Marcus completed the CBT program and continued with monthly aftercare
- He had no positive drug screens after month 3
- He obtained stable employment as a warehouse supervisor
- He established a consistent visitation schedule with Keisha
- He was transferred to low-intensity supervision at month 10

Key Success Factors:

- Initial session established relational foundation that survived later setback
- Connection to intrinsic motivation (daughter) provided anchor during difficult periods
- Treatment matching (CBT vs. 12-step) aligned with client's stated preferences
- Officer maintained MI approach even when addressing violation

Case Study 2: Using Open Questions to Build Engagement

Case Background

Supervisee: Priya Chandrasekaran, 28-year-old South Asian female

Offense: Felony theft (embezzlement from employer), first offense

Sentence: 5 years probation, restitution of $47,000

Risk Level: Low (LSI-R score: 12)

History: No prior criminal history. Priya was a trusted accountant at a small manufacturing company for four years. Over 18 months, she diverted funds totaling $47,000 through falsified vendor payments. She was caught during a routine audit and immediately confessed. She has expressed profound shame and has been minimally communicative in previous contacts.

Criminogenic Needs: Financial pressure (gambling debt), limited prosocial supports (estranged from family following disclosure of offense)

Context: Fourth monthly meeting. Previous sessions have been brief, with Priya providing one-word answers and avoiding detailed discussion. Officer Raymond Chen has decided to shift his approach from closed compliance questions to open exploration.

Session Script

[Priya enters office, sits in chair, looks at floor, hands clasped tightly in lap]

OFFICER CHEN: Good afternoon, Priya. Thanks for coming in. [Pauses] Before we go through the usual check-in items, I wanted to do something different today if that's okay with you.

[MI Skill: Asking permission; signaling change in approach]

PRIYA: [Barely audible] Okay.

OFFICER CHEN: I've noticed that our meetings tend to be pretty quick. I ask questions, you give me answers, and then you're on your way. And I've been wondering if there's more going on for you that we haven't really talked about.

[MI Skill: Naming the pattern; expressing genuine curiosity]

PRIYA: [Slight shrug] I don't know what else there is to say.

OFFICER CHEN: What's it been like for you these past few months, adjusting to everything that's happened?

[MI Skill: Open question inviting reflection on experience]

PRIYA: [Long pause] Hard.

OFFICER CHEN: Hard. Can you help me understand what's been the hardest part?

[MI Skill: Simple reflection followed by open elaboration question]

PRIYA: [Voice strained] Everything. I lost everything. My job, obviously. My family won't speak to me. My parents... [trails off]

OFFICER CHEN: [Waits in silence for 10 seconds]

[MI Skill: Strategic silence to create space]

PRIYA: My parents are traditional. Very traditional. They came here with nothing and built a life. They sacrificed everything for me and my brother. Education, reputation, honor. These things matter more than money. And I... I destroyed all of that. I brought shame on them.

OFFICER CHEN: The disappointment from your parents feels even heavier than the legal consequences.

[MI Skill: Complex reflection identifying core emotional weight]

PRIYA: [Eyes fill with tears, nods] They told me I'm dead to them. My mother said that. Her own daughter. Dead.

OFFICER CHEN: [Softly] That must be incredibly painful to hear from your mother.

[MI Skill: Reflection with emotional attunement]

PRIYA: [Wipes eyes] I don't blame them. I don't. What I did was unforgivable.

OFFICER CHEN: You understand their reaction, even though it causes you tremendous pain. It sounds like you hold yourself to the same standards they do.

[MI Skill: Complex reflection connecting family values to self-judgment]

PRIYA: Higher. I hold myself to higher standards. That's what makes this so... I can't even look at myself in the mirror. I was supposed to be the success story. The first one in my family to get a professional job. A CPA. And I threw it all away.

OFFICER CHEN: What happened, Priya? Not the mechanics of what you did. But what led you to a place where this seemed like an option?

[MI Skill: Open question seeking understanding rather than details of offense]

PRIYA: [Long pause] I've never told anyone the whole thing.

OFFICER CHEN: You don't have to tell me anything you're not ready to share. I'm asking because I want to understand you, not just your case file.

[MI Skill: Affirming autonomy; expressing genuine interest in person]

PRIYA: [Takes deep breath] It started with online poker. Just for fun, at first. A way to unwind after work. But I was good at it. Or I thought I was. I started winning. Then I started playing for real money. Small amounts. Then bigger amounts.

OFFICER CHEN: The gambling started as recreation and gradually became something more serious.

[MI Skill: Simple reflection to keep story flowing]

PRIYA: I won $10,000 one night. And I thought... I thought I had figured something out. I was smarter than the other players. I had a system. So I kept playing. And then I started losing. But I knew I could win it back. I just needed to play through the bad streak.

OFFICER CHEN: The losses felt temporary, like you could recover if you just kept playing.

[MI Skill: Reflection capturing gambling cognitive distortion]

PRIYA: I lost $30,000 of my savings. Then I maxed out my credit cards. Then I took a payday loan. And I was so deep in debt that I couldn't see any way out. I couldn't ask my family. They would have helped me, but I couldn't face telling them. So I started taking from the company. Just to pay off the loans. I told myself I would pay it back.

OFFICER CHEN: You were trying to solve a problem without anyone knowing you had a problem in the first place.

[MI Skill: Reflection capturing core pattern of secrecy]

PRIYA: [Crying openly now] I was so ashamed. The gambling, the debt, the stealing. Each thing I did to fix it just made it worse. And I couldn't tell anyone because then they would know who I really was.

OFFICER CHEN: [Offers tissue box, waits]

PRIYA: [Takes tissue, wipes eyes] Now everyone knows anyway. And they know the worst version. The thief. The criminal.

OFFICER CHEN: The secret you were so desperate to protect came out in the worst possible way.

[MI Skill: Reflection capturing tragic irony]

PRIYA: [Nods] And I lost everything I was trying to protect.

OFFICER CHEN: Priya, I want to reflect something back to you that I've been hearing throughout this conversation. You've described carrying an enormous amount of shame, both before the offense and now. You've described being unable to ask for help because of what people might think. And you've described a pattern where trying to fix things alone just made everything worse. What do you make of that pattern?

[MI Skill: Summary followed by open question inviting self-reflection]

PRIYA: [Long pause] I don't know how to ask for help. I never have. In my family, you handle your problems. You don't burden others. You succeed quietly and struggle silently.

OFFICER CHEN: Asking for help feels like failure, like admitting you can't handle things yourself.

[MI Skill: Reflection on family-of-origin pattern]

PRIYA: Yes. Exactly.

OFFICER CHEN: And yet, here you are. You're on probation now. You have to meet with me, attend these appointments, complete these requirements. In a way, you're being forced to accept help even though you didn't choose it. What's that like for you?

[MI Skill: Open question exploring current experience of mandated support]

PRIYA: [Considers] Humiliating. But also... maybe... a little relieving? I don't know. That sounds strange.

OFFICER CHEN: It doesn't sound strange at all. Say more about the relief.

[MI Skill: Normalizing response; inviting elaboration]

PRIYA: I don't have to pretend anymore. Everyone already knows. The worst has already happened. I don't have to keep the secret because there is no secret anymore.

OFFICER CHEN: The exposure you dreaded has actually lifted some of the weight of hiding.

[MI Skill: Reflection reframing disclosure]

PRIYA: [Nods slowly] I never thought of it that way. But yes. I'm still ashamed. But I'm not lying anymore. I'm not hiding. This is just... who I am now.

OFFICER CHEN: And who do you want to be going forward, Priya? Not who your parents want you to be, or who you think you should be. Who do you want to become?

[MI Skill: Open question evoking future self; emphasizing autonomy]

PRIYA: [Long pause] I want to be someone who can ask for help before things get catastrophic. Someone who doesn't have to be perfect to be acceptable. Someone who made a terrible mistake and found a way to... I don't know... live with it. Maybe even grow from it.

OFFICER CHEN: Someone who learns from this instead of being defined forever by it.

[MI Skill: Reflection capturing growth orientation]

PRIYA: Yes. I don't want to be "the embezzler" for the rest of my life. I want this to be part of my story, not the whole story.

OFFICER CHEN: Priya, what you just said is really significant. You're not just talking about getting through probation. You're talking about genuinely changing the patterns that got you here. Not being able to ask for help. Needing to be perfect. Hiding when you're struggling. Those are the things you want to work on.

[MI Skill: Summary highlighting deeper change goals beyond compliance]

PRIYA: [Nods] Yes. That's what I want.

OFFICER CHEN: And what would be one small step toward becoming that person who can ask for help?

[MI Skill: Open question moving toward commitment/action]

PRIYA: [Thinks] Maybe... telling you when things are hard? Instead of just saying "fine" when you ask how I'm doing?

OFFICER CHEN: That would be different from what you've done before. Are you willing to try that?

[MI Skill: Eliciting commitment language]

PRIYA: Yes. I'll try.

MI Skills Demonstrated

Skill	Frequency	Examples
Open Questions	11	"What's been the hardest part?"
Affirmations	2	"What you just said is really significant"
Reflections (Simple)	5	"The gambling started as recreation"
Reflections (Complex)	9	"The exposure you dreaded has lifted some weight"

Skill	Frequency	Examples
Summaries	2	Collecting themes, linking to change goals
Strategic Silence	2	Allowing space after emotional statements
Asking Permission	2	"If that's okay with you"

Reflection

This session illustrates how open questions can transform a superficial compliance-focused interaction into a meaningful therapeutic conversation. Priya had been providing minimal responses in previous sessions, creating a pattern where Officer Chen asked closed questions and received brief answers. By explicitly naming this pattern and expressing genuine curiosity about her experience, he invited a different kind of engagement.

The key turning point came when Officer Chen asked about Priya's experience rather than her compliance. "What's it been like for you these past few months?" created an opening for her to share the emotional reality behind the offense. This question communicated that her internal experience mattered, not just her adherence to conditions.

Officer Chen's use of strategic silence was particularly important with Priya. Her cultural background emphasized restraint and not burdening others, which manifested as brief responses. The silence created space without pressure, allowing her to decide how much to share. When she chose to share more, the depth of her disclosure surprised even her.

The session also demonstrates the importance of exploring the function of the offense rather than just its mechanics. By asking what led Priya to a place where embezzlement seemed like an option, Officer Chen opened a conversation about the underlying gambling problem and the pattern of shameful secrecy that preceded and drove the criminal behavior.

Officer Chen's reflections consistently went beyond surface content to capture emotional meaning. When Priya described being "dead" to her parents, he reflected not just the words but the devastating pain of that rejection. This level of empathic attunement built trust and encouraged continued disclosure.

The session concluded by eliciting Priya's own vision of who she wanted to become, then connecting that vision to a concrete first step. By having Priya identify her own change goals and first action, Officer Chen ensured the commitment was intrinsically motivated rather than externally imposed.

Outcome Analysis

Immediate Outcomes:

- First substantive conversation in four months of supervision
- Priya disclosed underlying gambling problem not previously known to officer
- She articulated her own analysis of the patterns that led to her offense
- She identified specific changes she wanted to make beyond compliance
- She made a commitment to be more honest about her struggles in supervision

Intermediate Outcomes (6-month follow-up):

- Priya enrolled in Gamblers Anonymous and cognitive behavioral therapy for gambling
- She was honest in subsequent sessions about moments of temptation
- She began rebuilding relationship with brother (parents remained estranged)
- She obtained employment as bookkeeper for small nonprofit (with disclosure of offense)
- Restitution payments began on schedule

Long-term Outcomes (24-month follow-up):

- Priya completed full restitution ahead of schedule
- No gambling relapses reported
- She reconnected with mother (father remained estranged)
- She became a peer support volunteer for others with gambling problems
- Early termination granted at month 30 (of 60-month sentence)

Key Success Factors:

- Open questions uncovered underlying problem (gambling) requiring treatment
- Emotional attunement built trust that enabled honesty
- Connection to deeper values (integrity, not being defined by mistake) provided motivation
- Identification of core pattern (inability to ask for help) created treatment target
- Client-identified first step ensured genuine commitment

Case Study 3: Strategic Affirmations with a Defensive Supervisee

Case Background

Supervisee: Terrence "Terry" McCullough, 45-year-old white male

Offense: Felony DUI (fourth offense), causing bodily injury

Sentence: 5 years probation following 2 years incarceration, ignition interlock device required

Risk Level: Moderate-High (LSI-R score: 26)

History: Three prior DUI convictions (ages 24, 31, and 38). Previous probation periods completed with multiple technical violations but no new offenses. Incarcerated this time because fourth DUI caused injury to another driver (broken arm, lacerations). Terry completed prison-based alcohol treatment program but has expressed skepticism about whether he has "a real problem" versus "bad luck with cops."

Criminogenic Needs: Alcohol abuse, minimization of problem severity, antisocial attitudes toward authority

Context: Second month of supervision. Terry completed intake with another officer and was transferred to Officer Juanita Reyes. He arrives for the appointment defensive and argumentative, apparently expecting confrontation about his alcohol use.

Session Script

[Terry enters, sits down with arms crossed, jaw set]

TERRY: Look, before you start, I already know what you're going to say. I've heard it all before. "Terry, you have a drinking problem. Terry, you need to go to AA. Terry, you're going to end up dead or in prison." Save it.

OFFICER REYES: [Calmly] You've heard a lot of people tell you what's wrong with you.

[MI Skill: Simple reflection without defensiveness]

TERRY: Damn right I have. Every probation officer, every judge, every counselor, my ex-wife, my kids. Everyone's got an opinion about Terry's drinking.

OFFICER REYES: That must get exhausting, having everyone line up to point out your flaws.

[MI Skill: Reflection with empathy for his experience]

TERRY: [Slightly taken aback] Yeah. It does. [Pause] So what, you're going to be different? Let me guess, you're going to "meet me where I'm at" or some crap like that.

OFFICER REYES: [Slight smile] I can tell you've been through some treatment programs.

[MI Skill: Gentle humor acknowledging his familiarity with therapeutic language]

TERRY: [Snorts] Four of them. Prison made number four. I can recite the twelve steps in my sleep. Doesn't mean I believe any of it.

OFFICER REYES: You've put in the time, sat through the programs, learned the material. And you're still not convinced it applies to you.

[MI Skill: Reflection acknowledging both compliance and skepticism]

TERRY: It doesn't. Look, I'm not saying I've never had too much to drink. I'm not stupid. Four DUIs, I'm obviously doing something wrong. But this disease stuff, this "powerless over alcohol" business. That's not me. I'm not some homeless guy under a bridge.

OFFICER REYES: When you think about what an "alcoholic" looks like, it doesn't match the image you see in the mirror.

[MI Skill: Reflection capturing his self-concept]

TERRY: Exactly. I held down a job for twenty-two years. Same company. Supervisor position. I paid my bills, raised two kids, kept a roof over my head. Does that sound like someone whose life is unmanageable?

OFFICER REYES: Terry, those are real accomplishments. Twenty-two years at one company, working your way up to supervisor, raising two children. That takes responsibility, showing up day after day, even when it's hard. A lot of people can't sustain that kind of commitment.

[MI Skill: Affirmation recognizing genuine strengths]

TERRY: [Uncrosses arms slightly] Thank you. That's the first time a PO has ever said anything like that to me.

OFFICER REYES: It seems like most people focus on the DUIs and forget about everything else you've managed to do.

[MI Skill: Reflection acknowledging pattern of deficit-focused feedback]

TERRY: That's all anyone sees. Four DUIs. Never mind the thousands of times I drove perfectly fine. Never mind the years between incidents. Just the four times I got caught.

OFFICER REYES: Help me understand something, Terry. You mentioned the thousands of times you drove fine. Can you tell me about your thinking on the times when things didn't go fine?

[MI Skill: Open question inviting reflection without arguing]

TERRY: [Sighs] Bad luck, mostly. Wrong place, wrong time. Cops fishing for arrests at bar closing time.

OFFICER REYES: And the last one? The one where the other driver got hurt?

[MI Skill: Specific open question about most serious incident]

TERRY: [Long pause, jaw tightens] That was different.

OFFICER REYES: [Waits in silence]

TERRY: I shouldn't have been driving that night. I knew it. I could barely see straight. But I was pissed off at my ex, and I just wanted to get home, and I didn't think about anyone else.

OFFICER REYES: That night was different. You knew before you got in the car that you shouldn't drive.

[MI Skill: Simple reflection of his admission]

TERRY: [Quietly] Yeah. I knew.

OFFICER REYES: Terry, I want to acknowledge something. It takes a certain kind of honesty to admit that, especially to a probation officer. You could have given me the same "bad luck" story, and I couldn't have proven otherwise. The fact that you're willing to say you knew you shouldn't drive tells me something about your character.

[MI Skill: Affirmation recognizing honesty and courage]

TERRY: [Looks uncomfortable] I'm not a liar. Whatever else I am, I'm not a liar.

OFFICER REYES: Honesty is important to you. It's part of how you see yourself.

[MI Skill: Reflection identifying value]

TERRY: My old man was a liar. Lied about everything. Lied about where he was, lied about money, lied about other women. I swore I'd never be like him.

OFFICER REYES: You've deliberately chosen to be different from your father in that way.

[MI Skill: Reflection connecting to intentional value choice]

TERRY: Damn right.

OFFICER REYES: So let me ask you something, and I'm asking because you value honesty. When you think about your drinking over the years, not compared to some homeless guy under a bridge, but compared to your own standards, how do you feel about it?

[MI Skill: Open question using client's own value as frame]

TERRY: [Long pause] I don't know. [Another pause] Not great, I guess.

OFFICER REYES: Not great?

[MI Skill: Simple reflection inviting elaboration]

TERRY: There are things I've done drunk that I wouldn't do sober. Things I've said to my kids. Times I missed stuff because I was hungover. The divorce... I can't blame that all on drinking, but it didn't help.

OFFICER REYES: When you're honest with yourself, you can see ways that alcohol has affected more than just the driving.

[MI Skill: Reflection connecting honesty value to self-assessment]

TERRY: [Nods slowly] Yeah. Maybe.

OFFICER REYES: Terry, I'm not going to tell you that you're an alcoholic or that you need AA or that you have a disease. Those labels will mean something to you or they won't. What I'm hearing from you is that you're someone who values honesty, who has accomplished real things in your life, and who can admit that drinking has created problems beyond the legal consequences. What do you want to do with that?

[MI Skill: Summary affirming strengths and honesty, followed by open question about next steps]

TERRY: What do you mean, what do I want to do?

OFFICER REYES: I mean, you've got five years of probation ahead of you. You've got an ignition interlock device, so you physically can't drive drunk. The question is whether you want to just get through the next five years, or whether you want something to actually be different when it's over.

[MI Skill: Presenting choice without prescribing answer]

TERRY: [Thinks] I don't want to lose my license permanently. I don't want to go back to prison. And I don't want to hurt anyone else like I hurt that woman.

OFFICER REYES: You want to make sure what happened with that other driver never happens again.

[MI Skill: Reflection emphasizing commitment to not harming others]

TERRY: She's got a scar on her face now. Because of me. Her arm still bothers her. I found that out at the sentencing. [Pause] I did that to her. She was just driving home from work, and I did that to her.

OFFICER REYES: That's a heavy thing to carry, knowing you caused that harm to someone who was just going about her life.

[MI Skill: Reflection acknowledging emotional weight]

TERRY: [Voice rough] I've done a lot of things I'm not proud of. But I never hurt anyone before. Not physically.

OFFICER REYES: This one is different because someone else paid the price.

[MI Skill: Reflection distinguishing this incident]

TERRY: Yeah. [Wipes eye] Look, I'm not going to sit here and cry. But yeah. I think about her sometimes.

OFFICER REYES: It would be easier if you didn't care. The fact that you think about her, that it bothers you, that's actually a sign that your conscience is working.

[MI Skill: Affirmation reframing remorse as moral capacity]

TERRY: Never thought of it that way.

OFFICER REYES: So what's one thing you could do, not for probation, not because I'm telling you to, but for yourself and because you don't want to risk hurting anyone else?

[MI Skill: Open question emphasizing autonomy and intrinsic motivation]

TERRY: [Long pause] I guess I could actually try to pay attention in the outpatient program instead of just counting down the hours.

OFFICER REYES: Engage with it instead of just getting through it.

[MI Skill: Simple reflection]

TERRY: Yeah. Maybe there's something in there for me. I don't know. But I've never really tried.

OFFICER REYES: That's an honest assessment. And it takes strength to consider trying something you've been resistant to.

[MI Skill: Affirmation recognizing openness]

TERRY: We'll see. I'm not making any promises.

OFFICER REYES: I'm not asking for promises. I'm just glad we could have this conversation.

[MI Skill: Closing affirmation without pushing for commitment]

MI Skills Demonstrated

Skill	Frequency	Examples
Open Questions	6	"What do you want to do with that?"
Affirmations	7	"Twenty-two years takes responsibility"
Reflections (Simple)	8	"That night was different"
Reflections (Complex)	7	"When you're honest with yourself..."
Summaries	2	Collecting strengths and honest admissions
Strategic Silence	2	Allowing space after difficult admissions
Autonomy Support	4	"Not because I'm telling you to"

Reflection

This session demonstrates the strategic use of affirmations with a defensive client who expected criticism and arrived prepared to argue. By refusing to engage in the anticipated confrontation, Officer Reyes disarmed Terry's defensiveness and created space for genuine reflection.

The affirmations in this session were carefully chosen and specific. Rather than generic praise, Officer Reyes recognized concrete accomplishments: twenty-two years at one company, raising two children, maintaining responsibilities. These affirmations communicated that she saw Terry as a whole person, not just as "the fourth-time DUI offender." This recognition was so unexpected that Terry explicitly commented on it.

Importantly, the affirmations did not ignore or excuse Terry's harmful behavior. Officer Reyes used affirmations to create safety, then gently invited Terry to examine his drinking using his own value of honesty as the frame. By asking how he felt about his drinking "compared to your own standards," she made it impossible for him to deflect to comparisons with "worse" alcoholics.

The session also illustrates rolling with resistance. When Terry offered the "bad luck" explanation for his DUIs, Officer Reyes did not argue. Instead, she asked about the most serious incident specifically. This invitation allowed Terry to arrive at his own differentiated assessment without being told he was wrong.

The disclosure about the injured woman represented a significant shift. Terry moved from defensive justification to genuine remorse. Officer Reyes recognized this as meaningful change talk and affirmed it appropriately, noting that his conscience was functioning, which was a sign of moral capacity rather than weakness.

By the end of the session, Terry had not committed to dramatic change. He made a modest commitment to "actually try to pay attention" in treatment rather than just getting through it. This incremental movement was appropriate for someone at his stage of change. Officer Reyes wisely accepted this step without pushing for more.

Outcome Analysis

Immediate Outcomes:

- Terry's defensive posture softened throughout session
- He made honest admissions he had previously avoided
- He connected his drinking to broader life problems beyond legal consequences
- He expressed genuine remorse about the injured victim
- He committed to engaging authentically with treatment program

Intermediate Outcomes (6-month follow-up):

- Terry completed outpatient treatment with positive feedback from counselor
- He requested referral to individual therapy to address "anger stuff"
- He reconnected with adult children who had been estranged
- No positive alcohol screens; ignition interlock device recorded no violations
- He wrote letter of apology to victim (not sent, therapeutic exercise)

Long-term Outcomes (24-month follow-up):

- Terry maintained sobriety with one brief relapse addressed through additional treatment
- He became active in SMART Recovery (chose this over AA based on fit)
- He retired from company and began volunteering with DUI victim impact panels
- He testified at legislature hearing supporting ignition interlock requirements
- Supervision transferred to low intensity at month 18

Key Success Factors:

- Affirmations recognized whole person, reducing defensiveness
- Using client's own value (honesty) as frame for self-examination
- Not arguing against "bad luck" narrative; inviting specific reflection instead
- Recognizing remorse as moral capacity rather than weakness
- Accepting incremental commitment without pushing for dramatic change

Case Study 4: Reflective Listening with an Ambivalent Client

Case Background

Supervisee: Gabriela Fuentes, 31-year-old Latina female

Offense: Felony fraud (identity theft scheme), first offense

Sentence: 4 years probation, restitution of $23,000

Risk Level: Low-Moderate (LSI-R score: 18)

History: No prior criminal history. Gabriela was involved in an identity theft scheme orchestrated primarily by her then-boyfriend. She obtained victim information through her job at a medical billing company and provided it to her boyfriend, who created fraudulent credit accounts. She received approximately $23,000 in merchandise and cash over 18 months. She maintains she did not fully understand the scope of the scheme initially but admits she continued participating after she understood. She ended the relationship six months before her arrest and has been cooperative with investigation.

Criminogenic Needs: Financial stress, relationship dependency, limited assertiveness, employment uncertainty (terminated from medical billing position)

Context: Fifth month of supervision. Gabriela has been compliant but seems stuck, uncertain about what direction to take her life. She has expressed interest in returning to healthcare administration but fears her conviction will be a permanent barrier.

Session Script

OFFICER PATTERSON: Good to see you, Gabriela. How have things been since we last met?

GABRIELA: Okay, I guess. Same as always. Looking for work. Waiting for something to change.

OFFICER PATTERSON: Waiting for something to change. What would you like to see change?

[MI Skill: Simple reflection followed by open question]

GABRIELA: I don't know. Everything? My whole life is just... stuck. I can't move forward. I can't go back. I'm just here.

OFFICER PATTERSON: You feel frozen in place, unable to move in any direction.

[MI Skill: Reflection using client's metaphor]

GABRIELA: Exactly. I had a plan, you know? I was going to work my way up in healthcare administration, maybe get my bachelor's degree, eventually become a practice manager. That was the plan. And now I can't even get a job filing papers because of my record.

OFFICER PATTERSON: The future you were working toward feels out of reach now.

[MI Skill: Reflection capturing sense of lost future]

GABRIELA: It is out of reach. Who's going to hire someone convicted of identity theft to handle patient records? I might as well have "don't trust me" tattooed on my forehead.

OFFICER PATTERSON: You're worried that your conviction will define you forever in employers' eyes.

[MI Skill: Reflection naming core fear]

GABRIELA: Won't it? I mean, I looked it up. This stays on my record forever in this state. Every background check, for the rest of my life, there it is.

OFFICER PATTERSON: You've researched it and found that this will follow you permanently. That must feel overwhelming.

[MI Skill: Reflection acknowledging both action and emotional response]

GABRIELA: [Sighs] Yeah. Some days I wonder why I even bother trying. Maybe I should just take whatever job doesn't do background checks and accept that this is my life now.

OFFICER PATTERSON: One part of you wants to give up on your goals and just settle for whatever you can get.

[MI Skill: Reflection emphasizing "part of you" to leave room for other parts]

GABRIELA: That's the realistic part. The part that sees things as they are.

OFFICER PATTERSON: And is there another part?

[MI Skill: Open question exploring ambivalence]

GABRIELA: [Pause] There's a stupid part that still thinks maybe I can figure this out. That maybe it's not completely over.

OFFICER PATTERSON: There's a part of you that isn't ready to give up on your original goals.

[MI Skill: Reflection without labeling hope as "stupid"]

GABRIELA: It's not realistic. I'm thirty-one. I have a felony conviction. I don't have a degree. The healthcare field does extensive background checks. The math doesn't work.

OFFICER PATTERSON: The logical analysis says it's impossible.

[MI Skill: Simple reflection]

GABRIELA: Right.

OFFICER PATTERSON: And yet that part of you that still hopes keeps hanging on anyway.

[MI Skill: Reflection returning to ambivalence]

GABRIELA: I don't know why. Hope is dangerous. It just sets you up for disappointment.

OFFICER PATTERSON: Hope feels risky because it means you might try and fail.

[MI Skill: Complex reflection identifying function of hopelessness]

GABRIELA: If I don't try, I can't fail.

OFFICER PATTERSON: Giving up protects you from the pain of trying and not succeeding.

[MI Skill: Reflection on protective function of resignation]

GABRIELA: [Long pause] That sounds really sad when you say it out loud.

OFFICER PATTERSON: What sounds sad about it to you?

[MI Skill: Open question inviting self-reflection]

GABRIELA: That I'm so afraid of failing that I won't even try. That I'm going to spend the rest of my life working some minimum wage job because I was too scared to find out if something better was possible.

OFFICER PATTERSON: The idea of living a limited life because of fear, not because of actual barriers, that's what feels sad.

[MI Skill: Complex reflection distinguishing internal and external barriers]

GABRIELA: But there are actual barriers. The conviction is real.

OFFICER PATTERSON: Absolutely. The conviction is real and it creates real obstacles. And at the same time, you just said something about fear holding you back, not just the barriers themselves.

[MI Skill: Double-sided reflection acknowledging both external and internal factors]

GABRIELA: [Thinks] I guess... I don't know which obstacles are real and which ones I'm creating because I'm scared.

OFFICER PATTERSON: You're not sure where the actual barriers end and where your own fear begins.

[MI Skill: Reflection capturing uncertainty]

GABRIELA: Yeah. Like, I've applied for exactly three jobs since I've been on probation. Three. In five months. And every time I see the background check question, I just stop.

OFFICER PATTERSON: The background check question stops you before you even finish the application.

[MI Skill: Simple reflection]

GABRIELA: Because what's the point? They're going to find out and reject me anyway.

OFFICER PATTERSON: You've decided the outcome before you've even applied.

[MI Skill: Reflection naming premature conclusion]

GABRIELA: [Pause] When you put it that way...

OFFICER PATTERSON: What are you noticing?

[MI Skill: Open question inviting awareness]

GABRIELA: I'm the one stopping me. I mean, maybe they would reject me. Probably they would reject me. But I don't actually know because I never find out.

OFFICER PATTERSON: You've been protecting yourself from rejection by never giving anyone the chance to accept you.

[MI Skill: Complex reflection capturing paradox]

GABRIELA: [Tears forming] That's exactly what I do. That's what I did with Marco, too. The guy who got me into this. I knew he was bad news, but I stayed because I was afraid no one else would want me.

OFFICER PATTERSON: The same pattern shows up in different areas of your life, staying with what feels safe even when it's harmful, rather than risking rejection.

[MI Skill: Reflection linking patterns across life domains]

GABRIELA: I'm so tired of being scared all the time.

OFFICER PATTERSON: What would it be like to not let the fear make your decisions?

[MI Skill: Open question evoking alternative]

GABRIELA: Terrifying. [Laughs slightly] But maybe also... freeing?

OFFICER PATTERSON: Terrifying and freeing at the same time.

[MI Skill: Reflection honoring both emotions]

GABRIELA: If I actually tried, even if I failed, at least I would know. At least I wouldn't be standing still forever.

OFFICER PATTERSON: Movement feels better than being frozen, even if you don't know where it leads.

[MI Skill: Reflection using client's earlier metaphor]

GABRIELA: Yeah. I don't want to be stuck anymore. I'd rather fail trying than never try at all.

OFFICER PATTERSON: That's a significant shift, Gabriela. You came in today talking about being stuck and giving up, and now you're talking about preferring to try even if you might fail. What changed?

[MI Skill: Affirmation and open question exploring change]

GABRIELA: I think... I think I realized that I'm more scared of looking back at sixty and knowing I never tried than I am of getting rejected right now.

OFFICER PATTERSON: The long-term regret of inaction scares you more than the short-term pain of possible rejection.

[MI Skill: Reflection amplifying insight]

GABRIELA: When you put it like that, it's obvious. Of course it does.

OFFICER PATTERSON: So what's one step you could take to start moving again?

[MI Skill: Open question moving toward action]

GABRIELA: I could actually finish applying for jobs. Like, actually submit applications instead of closing the browser when I hit the background check question.

OFFICER PATTERSON: Complete the applications you start.

[MI Skill: Simple reflection of commitment]

GABRIELA: Yes. And I've been thinking... there's a certificate program for health information technician at the community college. It's all online. It wouldn't erase my conviction, but it would show employers I'm serious about the field.

OFFICER PATTERSON: You've already been thinking about concrete steps to strengthen your credentials.

[MI Skill: Affirmation noting proactive thinking]

GABRIELA: I have. I just kept talking myself out of it. "What's the point, they won't hire you anyway." But that's the fear talking.

OFFICER PATTERSON: And you're starting to recognize the fear voice for what it is.

[MI Skill: Reflection affirming growing self-awareness]

GABRIELA: I am. [Takes breath] Okay. I'm going to look at that program today. And I'm going to finish at least one job application this week. A real one, with the background check question answered honestly.

OFFICER PATTERSON: You've identified two specific steps: exploring the certificate program and submitting at least one complete application. Those are concrete, doable actions.

[MI Skill: Summary of commitments]

GABRIELA: They are. [Small smile] I feel different than when I walked in here.

OFFICER PATTERSON: You came in feeling stuck and you're leaving with a plan. That's significant work you did today.

[MI Skill: Affirmation attributing change to client's own effort]

MI Skills Demonstrated

Skill	Frequency	Examples
Open Questions	8	"What would it be like to not let fear decide?"
Affirmations	4	"That's significant work you did today"

Skill	Frequency	Examples
Reflections (Simple)	9	"Complete the applications you start"
Reflections (Complex)	12	"Protecting yourself from rejection by never giving anyone the chance to accept you"
Summaries	2	Summarizing commitments at end
Strategic Silence	2	After emotional moments
Autonomy Support	3	Attributing change to client effort

Reflection

This session exemplifies MI's approach to ambivalence through sophisticated reflective listening. Gabriela arrived expressing hopelessness and resignation, but Officer Patterson's reflections revealed that both despair and hope existed simultaneously. Rather than challenging the hopelessness directly, Officer Patterson used reflections to make room for the hopeful part that Gabriela herself identified.

The critical technique in this session was the use of "part of you" language. When Gabriela said she wondered why she bothered trying, Officer Patterson reflected "one part of you wants to give up," which implicitly invited exploration of other parts. This framing acknowledges ambivalence as normal rather than pathological.

The session demonstrates how reflection can illuminate patterns the client has not consciously recognized. When Officer Patterson reflected that Gabriela was "protecting yourself from rejection by never giving anyone the chance to accept you," this reframing created a moment of insight. Gabriela immediately connected this pattern to her relationship history, seeing for the first time how the same dynamic operated across different life domains.

Officer Patterson also used Gabriela's own metaphor of being "stuck" and "frozen" throughout the session. Returning to this language at the end, reflecting that "movement feels better than being frozen," showed that the officer was tracking her internal experience closely.

The shift in the session came not from Officer Patterson providing solutions or reassurance but from creating space for Gabriela to examine her own relationship with fear. By asking "What would it be like to not let fear make your decisions?" the officer invited imagination of an alternative self without prescribing what that should look like.

Significantly, the concrete steps Gabriela committed to at the end were ones she generated herself. She had already been thinking about the certificate program; she had simply been talking herself out of it. The session gave her permission to honor her own aspirations rather than automatically deferring to her fears.

Outcome Analysis

Immediate Outcomes:

- Gabriela shifted from hopeless resignation to active planning within single session
- She identified long-standing pattern of fear-based avoidance
- She connected this pattern across multiple life domains
- She articulated specific, concrete commitments
- She reported feeling different and more hopeful

Intermediate Outcomes (6-month follow-up):

- Gabriela enrolled in health information technician certificate program
- She submitted 14 job applications over 3 months
- She received 3 interviews; one resulted in job offer (declined due to low salary)
- She accepted position as medical records clerk at physical therapy clinic
- Employer was aware of conviction; supervisor valued her honesty

Long-term Outcomes (18-month follow-up):

- Gabriela completed certificate program with 3.8 GPA
- She was promoted to medical records supervisor at same clinic
- Restitution payments on schedule; 40% completed
- She began dating relationship with someone she described as "healthy"
- She reported ongoing pattern recognition around fear-based decision making

Key Success Factors:

- Reflections illuminated ambivalence without judging either side
- "Part of you" language created space for hope
- Connecting patterns across life domains increased insight
- Client generated own solutions rather than receiving officer's advice
- Concrete commitments were specific and achievable

Case Study 5: Summarizing to Consolidate Change Talk

Case Background

Supervisee: Darnell Washington, 26-year-old African American male

Offense: Robbery (second degree), accomplice role

Sentence: 6 years probation following 3 years incarceration

Risk Level: High (LSI-R score: 34)

History: Juvenile record including theft and assault. Adult record includes two prior convictions for burglary. This offense involved robbery of a convenience store; Darnell served as driver while two co-defendants entered the store. No weapon was used by Darnell, but co-defendants displayed firearms. Darnell received lesser sentence due to cooperation with investigation and lack of direct victim contact.

Criminogenic Needs: Criminal peers, unemployment, limited education (dropped out at 11th grade), antisocial cognitions, unstable housing

Context: Ninth month of supervision. Darnell has been compliant but ambivalent about making major life changes. He still associates with some criminal peers, saying they are "all he has." Today he arrived appearing agitated after an argument with his mother about his living situation.

Session Script

[Darnell enters looking stressed, sits down heavily]

OFFICER BRYANT: Darnell, you look like you're carrying something heavy today. What's going on?

[MI Skill: Open question acknowledging visible distress]

DARNELL: Man, my mom is trippin'. Told me I have thirty days to find somewhere else to live. Thirty days! Where am I supposed to go?

OFFICER BRYANT: Your mom gave you an ultimatum, and you're not sure how to handle it.

[MI Skill: Simple reflection]

DARNELL: She says she's tired of my "associates" coming around. That's what she calls them. My associates. These are my boys. They've had my back since I was twelve years old.

OFFICER BRYANT: The people your mom is concerned about are the same people who've been there for you most of your life.

[MI Skill: Reflection acknowledging positive aspect of friendships]

DARNELL: Exactly. But she doesn't see that. She just sees guys with records. Guys who might get me in trouble again.

OFFICER BRYANT: What do you think about her concern?

[MI Skill: Open question inviting reflection rather than arguing either side]

DARNELL: I mean... [sighs] I get it, I guess. Marcus just caught another charge last week. Tyrell's been locked up more than he's been out. And Jamal... I don't know where Jamal's head is at right now, to be honest.

OFFICER BRYANT: When you think about where your friends are at, you can see why your mom is worried.

[MI Skill: Reflection connecting his own assessment to mom's concern]

DARNELL: But that's them. That doesn't have to be me.

OFFICER BRYANT: You see yourself as different from them in some ways.

[MI Skill: Reflection highlighting differentiation]

DARNELL: I'm trying to be. I've been doing everything probation asks. Haven't missed an appointment. Pissing clean. Got that job at the warehouse, even though it doesn't pay nothing. I'm doing what I'm supposed to do.

OFFICER BRYANT: You're putting in real effort to make this probation period different from the past.

[MI Skill: Affirmation recognizing compliance efforts]

DARNELL: But it doesn't matter to her. She just sees who I hang out with and assumes the worst.

OFFICER BRYANT: Her judgment feels unfair when you're working so hard.

[MI Skill: Reflection capturing emotional response]

DARNELL: It is unfair. I'm not out there doing dirt anymore. I'm just... I'm just trying to figure out my life, and these are the only people who understand what I'm going through.

OFFICER BRYANT: Your friends understand your situation in a way that other people don't.

[MI Skill: Simple reflection]

DARNELL: They get it. When I say prison was hard, they get it. When I talk about how POs look at me, they get it. When I say I feel like I'm never going to catch a break, they get it. Who else is going to understand that?

OFFICER BRYANT: The shared experiences create a bond that's hard to replace.

[MI Skill: Complex reflection on function of friendships]

DARNELL: Right. So how am I supposed to just cut them off like everyone keeps telling me to?

OFFICER BRYANT: It feels like an impossible ask, like people want you to give up your support system without offering anything in return.

[MI Skill: Reflection acknowledging unfairness of demand]

DARNELL: That's exactly it. Everyone tells me what I should stop doing, but nobody tells me what I'm supposed to do instead.

OFFICER BRYANT: Darnell, I've heard a lot in what you've just shared. Can I try to pull it together and see if I'm understanding correctly?

[MI Skill: Asking permission to summarize]

DARNELL: Go ahead.

OFFICER BRYANT: Your mom gave you thirty days to move out, and the immediate trigger is her concern about your friends. These friends are people who've been in your life since childhood, who understand your experiences in ways that others don't. They're your support system, especially after prison. At the same time, when you honestly look at where they are in their own lives, you can see why people are worried. Marcus, Tyrell, Jamal, they're struggling, getting locked up, catching charges. And you said something important: "That's them, that doesn't have to be me." You're trying to be different. You're compliant with probation, working a job, testing clean. You want to break the pattern, but you don't know how to do that without losing the only people who understand you. Does that capture it?

[MI Skill: Comprehensive summary collecting key themes and ending with change talk]

DARNELL: [Pause] Yeah. That's it. That's exactly it.

OFFICER BRYANT: What stands out to you in hearing all that together?

[MI Skill: Open question inviting reflection on summary]

DARNELL: The part about them struggling. I don't usually think about it that way. They're my boys, so I just... I accept where they're at. But hearing it all together like that... it sounds pretty bad.

OFFICER BRYANT: Looking at the pattern from the outside gives you a different view than you have from the inside.

[MI Skill: Reflection on perspective shift]

DARNELL: And I said I don't want that to be me. I said that, right?

OFFICER BRYANT: You did. You said, "That's them, that doesn't have to be me."

[MI Skill: Affirming by repeating his own words]

DARNELL: But how do I make that true? How do I stay different when I'm around the same people doing the same things?

OFFICER BRYANT: That's a critical question you're asking yourself. How can you maintain a different path while staying connected to people on a different path?

[MI Skill: Reflection emphasizing importance of question]

DARNELL: I don't know if I can. That's what scares me. Every time I'm around Marcus and them, I feel the pull. Like, "What's one beer gonna hurt?" or "This opportunity sounds easy." And so far I've said no, but how long can I keep doing that?

OFFICER BRYANT: You're noticing that being around them creates temptation, and you're not sure how long your resistance will hold.

[MI Skill: Reflection acknowledging vulnerability]

DARNELL: Right. And if I lose this housing situation... if I end up having to crash with one of them... I don't think I could stay clean. Not in that environment.

OFFICER BRYANT: The housing situation is connected to your ability to stay on track. If you end up living with one of these guys, you don't think you could maintain the changes you've been making.

[MI Skill: Reflection connecting housing to broader goals]

DARNELL: I know I couldn't. I've tried before.

OFFICER BRYANT: So let me pull together what I'm hearing now. You're worried that losing housing means ending up with friends whose lifestyle makes staying clean impossible. You've tried to maintain your commitments in that environment before and you couldn't. And you're at a point where you're questioning whether staying close to these friends is compatible with becoming the different person you want to be. Where does that leave you?

[MI Skill: Transitional summary ending with open question]

DARNELL: I don't know. [Long pause] I guess I have to figure out the housing thing first. Because if I don't have somewhere to go, I'm going back to what I know. And if I go back to what I know, I'm going back to prison.

OFFICER BRYANT: You're connecting the dots clearly. Housing leads to environment, environment leads to behavior, behavior leads to consequences.

[MI Skill: Reflection highlighting causal chain he identified]

DARNELL: Yeah. I've been trying not to think about it like that, but that's what's real.

OFFICER BRYANT: What would it take to find housing that supports the person you're trying to become?

[MI Skill: Open question toward problem-solving]

DARNELL: Money. Which I don't have enough of because the warehouse job barely covers anything. Maybe a roommate? But I don't know anybody I'd want to live with who isn't caught up in the same stuff.

OFFICER BRYANT: You need either more income or a roommate who's on a similar path to you.

[MI Skill: Simple reflection]

DARNELL: There's this guy Jerome I work with at the warehouse. He's been out a couple years, trying to stay straight. He's got a room he's been trying to rent. I kind of blew it off when he mentioned it because I wasn't trying to think about leaving my mom's place.

OFFICER BRYANT: Jerome sounds like he might be the kind of person who'd understand your situation but is also trying to build a different life.

[MI Skill: Reflection noting potential positive peer connection]

DARNELL: Yeah, actually. He's been straight for like three years. Got a kid now. He's different from how he used to be.

OFFICER BRYANT: Someone who's further along on the path you're trying to walk.

[MI Skill: Complex reflection framing Jerome as model]

DARNELL: I never thought about it like that. Maybe I should hit him up about that room.

OFFICER BRYANT: That sounds like it might address a few things at once: the housing, the environment, and even having someone who gets what you're going through but is making different choices.

[MI Skill: Summary linking housing option to multiple needs]

DARNELL: Yeah. [Nods] I'm gonna talk to him tomorrow. See if that room is still available.

OFFICER BRYANT: You've made a real shift today, Darnell. You came in frustrated about your mom's ultimatum, and you're leaving with a plan that might actually put you in a better situation than you were in before.

[MI Skill: Affirmation recognizing progress]

DARNELL: Weird how that works.

OFFICER BRYANT: Sometimes a crisis pushes us toward changes we needed to make anyway.

[MI Skill: Normalizing and reframing crisis as opportunity]

MI Skills Demonstrated

Skill	Frequency	Examples
Open Questions	7	"Where does that leave you?"
Affirmations	3	"You've made a real shift today"
Reflections (Simple)	10	"Money, which you don't have enough of"
Reflections (Complex)	8	"Someone further along on the path you're trying to walk"
Summaries	3	Collecting, transitional, and linking
Permission Seeking	1	"Can I try to pull it together?"
Autonomy Support	2	Solution emerged from client

Reflection

This session demonstrates the strategic use of summaries to consolidate scattered thoughts into a coherent narrative that amplifies change talk. Darnell arrived in crisis mode, focused on the immediate problem of his mother's ultimatum. Through careful listening and strategic summarizing, Officer Bryant helped him see connections between housing, social environment, and his ability to maintain behavioral changes.

The first major summary in the session was comprehensive, collecting multiple themes that had emerged across several minutes of conversation. Importantly, it ended with Darnell's own change talk: "That doesn't have to be me." This placement was strategic because ending a summary with change talk allows it to resonate as the final note.

When Officer Bryant asked "What stands out to you?" after the summary, Darnell identified the pattern of his friends struggling, something he had mentioned but not really examined. The summary created distance that allowed him to see the pattern objectively rather than defensively.

The session also illustrates how summaries can function as transitions. The second major summary ended with "Where does that leave you?" This moved the conversation from exploration into action planning. Rather than telling Darnell what to do, the summary invited him to draw his own conclusions.

Officer Bryant did not tell Darnell to distance himself from his friends. Instead, through reflections and summaries, Darnell arrived at his own recognition that his environment was threatening his goals. When he stated "if I go back to what I know, I'm going back to prison," this was his conclusion, carrying far more weight than if the officer had said it.

The emergence of Jerome as a positive peer connection came from Darnell, not the officer. By the time this option surfaced, the groundwork had been laid for Darnell to see Jerome not just as a potential roommate but as someone "further along on the path" he was trying to walk. The officer's reflection framed Jerome in terms of Darnell's own goals.

Outcome Analysis

Immediate Outcomes:

- Darnell reframed crisis as potential opportunity
- He recognized connection between environment and ability to change
- He identified specific plan (contact Jerome about housing)
- He articulated causal chain from housing to incarceration
- He left with different emotional state than when he arrived

Intermediate Outcomes (4-month follow-up):

- Darnell moved into shared apartment with Jerome
- He reduced contact with previous friend group (not eliminated)
- He obtained second part-time job to afford housing

- He reported Jerome as "accountability partner" who noticed when he seemed stressed
- His mother reported improved relationship

Long-term Outcomes (18-month follow-up):

- Darnell enrolled in GED program, completed at month 14
- He was promoted to shift supervisor at warehouse
- He had one significant setback when Marcus was shot; Darnell's response was addressed through additional support
- He began volunteering with youth mentorship program
- He reported dramatically reduced contact with previous friend group; said he "outgrew" them

Key Success Factors:

- Summaries made implicit connections explicit
- Crisis reframed as catalyst for positive change
- Ending summaries with change talk amplified client's own motivation
- Positive peer connection emerged from client's own knowledge
- Officer did not tell client to leave friends; client concluded this independently

Chapter 19: Change Talk and Sustain Talk Cases

Case Study 6: Recognizing and Evoking DARN-CAT Change Talk

Case Background

Supervisee: Vanessa Okonkwo, 38-year-old Nigerian American female

Offense: Felony drug possession (cocaine, personal use amount)

Sentence: 2 years probation, mandatory substance abuse treatment

Risk Level: Low-Moderate (LSI-R score: 16)

History: No prior criminal history. Vanessa is a registered nurse who was arrested when pulled over for erratic driving and found to possess cocaine. She disclosed during assessment that she has been using cocaine periodically for approximately two years, primarily to manage fatigue during demanding hospital shifts. Her nursing license is currently under review by the Board of Nursing. She has been compliant with probation but has resisted engaging authentically with treatment, describing it as "hoops to jump through."

Criminogenic Needs: Substance abuse, occupational stress, limited healthy coping mechanisms

Context: Third month of supervision. Vanessa continues to minimize the significance of her cocaine use, attributing it entirely to work stress. Officer Simone Dupree has decided to use this session to systematically evoke and strengthen change talk using the DARN-CAT framework.

Session Script

OFFICER DUPREE: Vanessa, thanks for coming in. Last time we talked about your treatment program, and you mentioned feeling like it's just hoops to jump through. I'm curious what would make it feel more meaningful to you.

[MI Skill: Open question about treatment engagement]

VANESSA: Honestly? I don't know if anything could. I'm not like those other people in the group. I don't wake up needing a fix. I don't steal from my family. I had a demanding job and found a way to keep up. That's different from being an addict.

OFFICER DUPREE: You see your situation as fundamentally different from the others in your treatment group.

[MI Skill: Simple reflection without arguing]

VANESSA: It is different. I was a functional professional. Twelve years as an RN with excellent reviews. No one ever suspected anything because I kept it completely separate from my work. I never used before a shift. Only on my off days to recover.

OFFICER DUPREE: You maintained clear boundaries around your use and protected your professional performance.

[MI Skill: Reflection acknowledging her perspective]

VANESSA: Exactly. Until I made one stupid mistake and got caught.

OFFICER DUPREE: Tell me about the mistake.

[MI Skill: Open question inviting exploration]

VANESSA: I used on a day I wasn't planning to drive. Then my sister called. Emergency with my nephew. I thought I was fine. Obviously I wasn't.

OFFICER DUPREE: The situation changed and you made a decision that you wouldn't normally make.

[MI Skill: Reflection]

VANESSA: I would never put a patient at risk. Never. But my nephew... I wasn't thinking about risk assessments. I was just trying to get to my sister.

OFFICER DUPREE: Family emergency overrode the careful boundaries you usually maintain.

[MI Skill: Complex reflection connecting exception to values]

VANESSA: Yes. And now I'm paying for it. The arrest, the probation, the nursing board investigation. All because of one bad call.

OFFICER DUPREE: Let me ask you something, Vanessa. If we set aside the legal consequences for a moment, just between us, are there other times when the cocaine use has affected your life in ways you didn't intend?

[MI Skill: Open question exploring broader impact]

VANESSA: [Pause] What do you mean?

OFFICER DUPREE: You've described yourself as someone who keeps careful boundaries. I'm wondering if there have been other times when those boundaries got blurred, even if no one else knew.

[MI Skill: Continued exploration with specificity]

VANESSA: [Long pause] Maybe a few times. Sometimes I'd plan to use only on my day off, and then I'd use again the next day because I was coming down and felt terrible. And then I'd be going into work tired and irritable.

OFFICER DUPREE: The use sometimes extended beyond what you planned.

[MI Skill: Simple reflection of admission]

VANESSA: A few times I called in sick because I'd used more than I intended and couldn't face a twelve-hour shift.

OFFICER DUPREE: So even though you never used before a shift, the effects of using were sometimes still there when you got to work.

[MI Skill: Reflection connecting to previously stated boundary]

VANESSA: [Quietly] Yes. I never thought of it that way, but yes.

OFFICER DUPREE: What concerns you most about that pattern?

[MI Skill: Open question evoking Desire/Reason change talk]

VANESSA: [Sighs] I went into nursing because I wanted to help people. When I'm not at my best, I'm not giving my patients what they deserve.

OFFICER DUPREE: Being fully present for your patients matters deeply to you, and you're recognizing that the cocaine was interfering with that even when you didn't realize it.

[MI Skill: Complex reflection connecting concern to core value]

VANESSA: I always told myself it didn't affect my work. But if I was calling in sick, if I was tired and irritable... that's affecting my work.

OFFICER DUPREE: The story you told yourself is different from what was actually happening.

[MI Skill: Reflection highlighting cognitive shift]

VANESSA: [Nods] I've been lying to myself.

OFFICER DUPREE: That's a significant thing to recognize. A lot of people never get there.

[MI Skill: Affirmation of insight]

VANESSA: So what do I do with that?

OFFICER DUPREE: I'd like to explore that with you. On a scale of zero to ten, where zero is not at all important and ten is the most important thing in your life, how important is it to you to make sure cocaine never affects your nursing career again?

[MI Skill: Importance ruler to evoke Desire/Need change talk]

VANESSA: Nine. Maybe ten. Nursing is everything to me.

OFFICER DUPREE: A nine or ten. That's as high as it gets. Why a nine and not a five?

[MI Skill: Following up ruler by asking why not lower]

VANESSA: Because nursing isn't just a job to me. It's who I am. I fought so hard to get through school, to pass boards, to get to where I was. If I lose my license... I don't know who I am without it.

OFFICER DUPREE: Nursing is central to your identity. Protecting that license means protecting who you are.

[MI Skill: Reflection of identity-based motivation]

VANESSA: Yes. I have to protect it. I have to do whatever it takes.

OFFICER DUPREE: You said "I have to do whatever it takes." What does whatever it takes mean to you?

[MI Skill: Elaboration question on Commitment change talk]

VANESSA: I need to get serious about this treatment instead of just showing up. I need to figure out why I started using in the first place and find other ways to deal with the stress.

OFFICER DUPREE: You're talking about genuinely engaging with treatment rather than going through the motions, and addressing the underlying reasons for your use.

[MI Skill: Reflection consolidating Taking Steps change talk]

VANESSA: The hospital environment is brutal. The hours, the administration, the constant pressure to do more with less. Cocaine made me feel like I could handle it all. But obviously that was an illusion.

OFFICER DUPREE: The cocaine felt like a solution to a real problem, even though it was creating problems of its own.

[MI Skill: Double-sided reflection acknowledging function]

VANESSA: What am I supposed to do instead? The stress isn't going away.

OFFICER DUPREE: That's exactly the right question. You can't change the stressful environment, so you need sustainable ways to manage it. What's one thing that helped you manage stress before you started using cocaine?

[MI Skill: Open question evoking Ability change talk]

VANESSA: Before? I used to run. I ran a marathon in 2019. But then the pandemic hit, everything got crazy at the hospital, and I stopped making time for it.

OFFICER DUPREE: Running was something that worked for you, and it got lost when other demands took over.

[MI Skill: Reflection connecting to past success]

VANESSA: I was in the best shape of my life during training. Mentally and physically. I felt strong.

OFFICER DUPREE: Running gave you strength, not just physically but mentally too. Is that something you could bring back?

[MI Skill: Reflection followed by question about reinstatement]

VANESSA: I've been thinking about it. My sponsor in treatment is a runner. She's been inviting me to her running group.

OFFICER DUPREE: So you've already been thinking about this, and there's even someone offering to support you in getting back to it.

[MI Skill: Reflection noting preparation already underway]

VANESSA: I keep saying no because I'm out of shape and embarrassed.

OFFICER DUPREE: What would it take to say yes?

[MI Skill: Open question toward activation]

VANESSA: [Pause] Just doing it, I guess. Just showing up even though I'm slow and out of breath.

OFFICER DUPREE: Let me gather together what I've heard today, Vanessa. You came in seeing the treatment as hoops to jump through, something separate from your real life. But as we talked, you recognized that the cocaine was affecting your work in ways you hadn't admitted to yourself. You connected this to your deepest value, being fully present for your patients and protecting the nursing career that defines who you are. You said you need to do "whatever it takes," which includes genuinely engaging with treatment and finding healthy ways to manage stress. You've identified running as something that worked before, and you have a specific opportunity through your sponsor to reconnect with it. Where does this leave you?

[MI Skill: Comprehensive summary ending with collected change talk, then open question]

VANESSA: It leaves me with no more excuses. I know what I need to do. I just have to do it.

OFFICER DUPREE: What's your commitment?

[MI Skill: Eliciting Commitment change talk]

VANESSA: I'm going to tell my sponsor yes to the running group. And I'm going to actually talk in treatment instead of sitting in the back.

OFFICER DUPREE: Those are specific commitments. I'm glad you're ready to take these steps, Vanessa.

[MI Skill: Affirmation of commitment]

MI Skills Demonstrated

DARN-CAT Type	Example from Session
Desire	"I need to get serious about treatment"
Ability	"I used to run. I ran a marathon"
Reasons	"Nursing is everything to me"
Need	"I have to protect it"
Commitment	"I'm going to tell my sponsor yes"
Activation	"I'm ready" (implied in final statements)
Taking Steps	"I've been thinking about it. My sponsor is a runner"

Skill	Frequency	Examples
Open Questions	9	"What concerns you most about that pattern?"
Affirmations	3	"That's a significant thing to recognize"
Reflections (Simple)	7	"The use sometimes extended beyond what you planned"
Reflections (Complex)	10	"Nursing is central to your identity"
Summaries	2	Comprehensive final summary
Importance Ruler	1	"On a scale of 0-10..."

Reflection

This session demonstrates systematic evocation of all seven types of change talk in the DARN-CAT framework. Officer Dupree began with a client who was minimizing her substance use and resisting treatment engagement. Through strategic questioning and reflection, she guided Vanessa toward increasingly strong change talk.

The session started with exploration of Vanessa's self-protective narrative that she was "different" from other people in treatment. Rather than challenging this directly, Officer Dupree asked about exceptions to her careful boundaries. This approach allowed Vanessa to discover contradictions in her own narrative without becoming defensive.

The importance ruler technique was deployed at a strategic moment, after Vanessa had already acknowledged that cocaine was affecting her work. By asking "Why a nine and not a five?" Officer Dupree evoked the underlying reasons for Vanessa's motivation: nursing as identity, the struggle to achieve her career, the fear of losing it all.

Each type of change talk was recognized and reflected to amplify its strength. When Vanessa said "I have to do whatever it takes," Officer Dupree asked what that meant specifically, transforming a general statement into concrete intentions. When Vanessa mentioned running and her sponsor, Officer Dupree reflected this as Taking Steps already underway.

The comprehensive summary at the end collected all the change talk in a single narrative arc: from minimization to recognition of impact, to values clarification, to specific commitment. Ending the summary with "Where does this leave you?" invited Vanessa to draw her own conclusion.

The final commitments were specific and actionable: saying yes to the running group and actively participating in treatment. These emerged from the conversation rather than being prescribed, ensuring they carried the weight of Vanessa's own motivation.

Outcome Analysis

Immediate Outcomes:

- Vanessa shifted from minimization to acknowledgment of cocaine's impact
- She connected substance use to core professional identity
- She identified specific behavioral commitments
- She rated importance of change at 9-10 level
- She articulated desire, ability, reasons, need, commitment, and taking steps

Intermediate Outcomes (6-month follow-up):

- Vanessa fully engaged with treatment; counselor noted "complete turnaround"
- She joined running group and completed a 10K race
- Board of Nursing placed license on probation (not revoked)
- She returned to nursing at different hospital with disclosure of situation
- She maintained negative drug screens throughout

Long-term Outcomes (24-month follow-up):

- Vanessa completed probation successfully
- Nursing license restriction removed; full license restored
- She became peer mentor in treatment program
- She reported running as primary stress management strategy
- She received promotion to charge nurse at current hospital

Key Success Factors:

- Not arguing against minimization; inviting exploration of exceptions
- Importance ruler elicited strong values-based motivation
- All DARN-CAT types evoked and reflected
- Commitments were specific and emerged from client
- Treatment reframed from "hoops" to meaningful support for goals

Case Study 7: Responding to Sustain Talk Without Amplification

Case Background

Supervisee: Raymond "Ray" Kowalski, 52-year-old white male

Offense: Felony assault (bar fight resulting in serious injury)

Sentence: 3 years probation, anger management program, no contact with victim

Risk Level: Moderate (LSI-R score: 22)

History: One prior assault conviction fifteen years ago (domestic violence with ex-wife, misdemeanor). Ray has been separated from his second wife for six months following the assault incident. He maintains the assault was self-defense and that the victim "started it." He completed a court-ordered anger management program but continues to express resentment about his legal situation.

Criminogenic Needs: Anger management, alcohol use (was intoxicated during offense), interpersonal conflict patterns, victim stance

Context: Sixth month of supervision. Ray has been compliant but continues to minimize his responsibility for the assault and express frustration about "the system." Today's session occurs after Ray learned his estranged wife has filed for divorce.

Session Script

[Ray enters looking agitated, sits down with arms crossed]

RAY: Just so you know, I'm not in a great mood today. My wife's lawyer sent me papers. She wants a divorce. Thirty years, and she's throwing it away because I defended myself in a bar.

OFFICER MARTINEZ: You're dealing with divorce papers on top of everything else. That's a lot to handle.

[MI Skill: Simple reflection acknowledging stress without addressing narrative]

RAY: It's ridiculous. I didn't do anything wrong. Some drunk gets in my face, I push him back, and suddenly I'm the criminal? Now I've lost my job, my marriage, everything.

OFFICER MARTINEZ: You see the consequences as wildly disproportionate to what actually happened.

[MI Skill: Reflection of perspective without agreeing or disagreeing]

RAY: They are disproportionate. That guy called me every name in the book. He shoved me first. Anyone would have done what I did.

OFFICER MARTINEZ: From your perspective, anyone in your situation would have responded the same way.

[MI Skill: Simple reflection with "from your perspective" qualifier]

RAY: Exactly. It's human nature. You get attacked, you fight back. That's not a crime, that's survival.

OFFICER MARTINEZ: Fighting back felt like survival in that moment.

[MI Skill: Reflection on emotional experience without validating legal argument]

RAY: It was survival. The guy was bigger than me. If I hadn't put him down, he would have put me down.

OFFICER MARTINEZ: You were concerned he would seriously hurt you.

[MI Skill: Reflection on fear underlying aggression]

RAY: Yes. So what was I supposed to do, let him beat the crap out of me? Turn the other cheek like some kind of pushover?

OFFICER MARTINEZ: The choice felt like either fight back or be seen as weak.

[MI Skill: Reflection on binary framing]

RAY: Right. And I'm not weak. I've never been weak. I worked construction for thirty years. You can't be weak in that business.

OFFICER MARTINEZ: Strength has been important to your identity throughout your career.

[MI Skill: Reflection connecting to values]

RAY: Damn right it has.

OFFICER MARTINEZ: Ray, can I ask you something? When you think about strength, is fighting the only way to demonstrate it?

[MI Skill: Open question introducing alternative framings of value]

RAY: What do you mean?

OFFICER MARTINEZ: You said you're not weak, that you've demonstrated strength throughout your construction career. I'm curious how you showed that strength on the job. Was it through fighting?

[MI Skill: Elaboration question exploring value in different context]

RAY: [Pause] No. On the job, strength is about getting things done. Showing up every day. Handling the hard stuff without complaining. Keeping your word.

OFFICER MARTINEZ: Strength at work is about reliability, endurance, integrity. Not about physical confrontation.

[MI Skill: Reflection expanding definition of strength]

RAY: I mean, sure. You don't advance in construction by getting in fights. That would get you fired.

OFFICER MARTINEZ: So in that context, fighting would actually undermine your goals.

[MI Skill: Reflection noting context where aggression is counterproductive]

RAY: Obviously. Work is different.

OFFICER MARTINEZ: What makes it different?

[MI Skill: Open question inviting reflection on distinction]

RAY: At work, there are rules. There are consequences. You can't just punch someone who pisses you off.

OFFICER MARTINEZ: The existence of rules and consequences changes how you express strength.

[MI Skill: Reflection highlighting external regulation]

RAY: Right. Everyone knows that at work.

OFFICER MARTINEZ: I'm wondering about the bar that night. Were there rules and consequences there too?

[MI Skill: Open question applying same logic to offense context]

RAY: [Long pause] I mean... technically, yeah. But it didn't feel like that. It felt like the wild west.

OFFICER MARTINEZ: In the moment, it felt like there were no rules, even though looking back you know there were.

[MI Skill: Reflection distinguishing felt experience from reality]

RAY: Yeah. Everything was fuzzy. The alcohol, the adrenaline. I wasn't thinking about courts and lawyers. I was thinking about this guy in my face.

OFFICER MARTINEZ: The alcohol and adrenaline narrowed your focus to the immediate threat.

[MI Skill: Reflection introducing alcohol's role without lecturing]

RAY: [Quieter] I'd had a lot to drink. More than usual.

OFFICER MARTINEZ: That night was different from your typical drinking.

[MI Skill: Simple reflection of acknowledgment]

RAY: Things were bad with Sharon. The wife. We'd had a huge fight that morning. I went to the bar to cool off, and I just kept drinking.

OFFICER MARTINEZ: You were drinking to cope with the conflict at home, and it escalated beyond what you intended.

[MI Skill: Reflection connecting drinking pattern to emotional state]

RAY: [Nods] I don't usually get that drunk. I can usually handle my liquor.

OFFICER MARTINEZ: So the quantity that night was unusual for you.

[MI Skill: Simple reflection]

RAY: Yeah. And then this jackass... [sighs] Maybe if I'd been sober, I would have handled it different.

OFFICER MARTINEZ: You're thinking that your decision-making that night might have been affected by how much you drank.

[MI Skill: Reflection of emerging insight]

RAY: I'm not saying I was wrong to defend myself. But... maybe I took it further than I needed to.

OFFICER MARTINEZ: You still see the initial response as defensive, but you're questioning whether the level of force was necessary.

[MI Skill: Nuanced reflection honoring both positions]

RAY: The guy ended up in the hospital. Broken jaw. I didn't need to hit him that hard. I know that. I knew it as soon as I saw him on the ground.

OFFICER MARTINEZ: In that moment after, when he was on the ground, you had a realization.

[MI Skill: Reflection focusing on moment of awareness]

RAY: [Quietly] Yeah. I knew I'd gone too far.

OFFICER MARTINEZ: Ray, I want to acknowledge something. We started this conversation with you saying you didn't do anything wrong, and you've just acknowledged that you went too far. That's not an easy thing to admit.

[MI Skill: Affirmation recognizing shift]

RAY: [Looks uncomfortable] I'm not saying everything is my fault.

OFFICER MARTINEZ: You're not taking all the blame. And you're also recognizing your part in how things escalated.

[MI Skill: Double-sided reflection avoiding all-or-nothing framing]

RAY: He did start it. But I didn't have to finish it the way I did.

OFFICER MARTINEZ: Both of those can be true at the same time. He started it, and you finished it in a way you regret.

[MI Skill: Reflection honoring complexity]

RAY: [Long pause] I do regret it. Not the divorce so much. That was probably going to happen anyway. But that guy's jaw. The look on his face. I see that sometimes when I close my eyes.

OFFICER MARTINEZ: The image stays with you.

[MI Skill: Simple reflection of intrusive memory]

RAY: I'm not a bad person. I don't want to hurt people.

OFFICER MARTINEZ: You're someone who ended up hurting someone, and that conflicts with how you see yourself.

[MI Skill: Reflection on identity dissonance]

RAY: Yeah. I don't know how to square that.

OFFICER MARTINEZ: What would help you make sure something like this doesn't happen again?

[MI Skill: Open question moving toward future prevention]

RAY: [Thinks] Staying sober, probably. When I'm sober, I can walk away from stuff. When I'm drunk... everything feels like a threat.

OFFICER MARTINEZ: Alcohol changes how you perceive situations and what options you see.

[MI Skill: Reflection on alcohol's cognitive effects]

RAY: It does. I've known that for a while, I guess. I just didn't want to admit it.

OFFICER MARTINEZ: Where does that leave you with your drinking going forward?

[MI Skill: Open question eliciting change intention]

RAY: I don't know. I'm not ready to say I'll never drink again. But maybe... maybe I need to be more careful. Especially when I'm stressed.

OFFICER MARTINEZ: Being more careful when emotions are running high, so alcohol doesn't make things worse.

[MI Skill: Reflection supporting moderate change statement]

RAY: Yeah. That's something I can work on.

MI Skills Demonstrated

Skill	Frequency	Examples
Open Questions	7	"Is fighting the only way to demonstrate strength?"
Affirmations	2	"That's not an easy thing to admit"
Reflections (Simple)	12	"That night was different from your typical drinking"
Reflections (Complex)	9	"You're someone who ended up hurting someone, and that conflicts with how you see yourself"
Summaries	0	Session flowed without formal summaries
Double-Sided Reflections	3	"Both can be true at the same time"

Reflection

This session illustrates the MI principle of rolling with resistance rather than confronting sustain talk directly. Ray arrived committed to a narrative of complete innocence, attributing all consequences to an unjust system. Officer Martinez did not argue against this narrative, which would have triggered defensiveness. Instead, she reflected Ray's perspective while introducing subtle openings for reflection.

The key technique was reflecting sustain talk without amplification or endorsement. When Ray said "I didn't do anything wrong," Officer Martinez reflected "You see the consequences as wildly disproportionate." This acknowledged his perspective without agreeing that he did nothing wrong. This distinction is crucial: validating the person's experience of their perspective differs from validating the perspective itself.

The turning point came through exploring Ray's own value of strength. By asking how strength manifested at work, Officer Martinez helped Ray recognize that he had a more nuanced understanding of strength than "fighting back." When he acknowledged that fighting at work would get him fired, the same logic could be applied to other contexts.

Introducing the role of alcohol was done through reflection rather than assertion. When Ray mentioned his thoughts were "fuzzy," Officer Martinez reflected "the alcohol and adrenaline narrowed your focus." This allowed Ray to connect his own dots rather than being told that alcohol was the problem.

The session ended with a moderate change statement rather than dramatic transformation. Ray acknowledged he needed to "be more careful" with drinking when stressed. This incremental movement was appropriate for his stage of change. Officer Martinez did not push for abstinence or grand commitments, accepting the step he was ready to make.

Throughout the session, Officer Martinez avoided the common mistake of arguing with sustain talk, which typically produces more sustain talk. Instead, she redirected toward values, expanded definitions, and invited self-reflection, allowing Ray to arrive at his own modified perspective.

Outcome Analysis

Immediate Outcomes:

- Ray shifted from complete denial ("I didn't do anything wrong") to partial acknowledgment ("I took it further than I needed to")
- He recognized alcohol's role in the incident
- He identified stress as a trigger for problematic drinking
- He made moderate commitment to being more careful with alcohol
- He expressed genuine regret about the victim's injury

Intermediate Outcomes (6-month follow-up):

- Ray voluntarily enrolled in additional anger management sessions beyond court requirement
- He reduced drinking significantly, particularly when experiencing stress
- He had one incident of drinking heavily after divorce finalized; discussed openly with officer
- He began attending therapy to address "the stuff with Sharon"

- No new incidents of violence or aggression

Long-term Outcomes (20-month follow-up):

- Ray completed probation without violations
- He achieved moderate drinking pattern with abstinence during high-stress periods
- He reconciled partially with adult children who had been estranged
- He reported intrusive images of assault had significantly decreased
- He remained single but reported "healthier" interactions with women

Key Success Factors:

- Rolling with resistance rather than confronting sustain talk
- Using client's own values (strength) to introduce alternative perspectives
- Introducing alcohol's role through reflection rather than lecture
- Accepting moderate change commitment rather than pushing for abstinence
- Honoring complexity rather than demanding all-or-nothing acknowledgment

Case Study 8: Rolling with Resistance in a High-Conflict Session

Case Background

Supervisee: Destiny Jackson, 24-year-old African American female

Offense: Felony retail theft (organized retail crime ring)

Sentence: 4 years probation, restitution of $12,000

Risk Level: Moderate (LSI-R score: 20)

History: Two prior theft convictions as a juvenile, one prior misdemeanor theft as an adult. Destiny was part of an organized group that stole merchandise from retail stores and sold it online. She was identified as a "booster" who physically took items while others served as lookouts and handlers. She has been hostile toward supervision from the beginning, viewing probation as "harassment" and officers as "people who get paid to mess up my life."

Criminogenic Needs: Criminal peers, antisocial attitudes, unemployment, limited legitimate income sources, antisocial cognitions

Context: Fourth month of supervision. Destiny missed her previous appointment and is now in the office after Officer Kevin Park sent a warning letter. She arrives angry and confrontational.

Session Script

[Destiny enters, stands in doorway with arms crossed]

DESTINY: You happy now? You got me here. What do you want?

OFFICER PARK: Come on in and have a seat, Destiny. I'm glad you came.

[MI Skill: Calm, non-defensive response]

DESTINY: [Sits down aggressively] Let's just get this over with. I got things to do.

OFFICER PARK: You've got somewhere you need to be after this.

[MI Skill: Simple reflection without confronting rudeness]

DESTINY: Always got somewhere to be. Unlike you, I don't get to sit in an office all day doing nothing.

OFFICER PARK: Your schedule is demanding.

[MI Skill: Simple reflection, still not engaging with provocation]

DESTINY: [Narrows eyes, seemingly surprised by lack of defensiveness] Whatever. So what, you gonna violate me for missing one appointment?

OFFICER PARK: That's one option available to me. I'm more interested in understanding what happened.

[MI Skill: Acknowledging authority without leading with it; expressing curiosity]

DESTINY: What happened is I had something more important to do. Something that might actually help my life instead of just checking a box for you people.

OFFICER PARK: You prioritized something that felt more meaningful than this appointment.

[MI Skill: Reflection without judgment]

DESTINY: Job interview. At a warehouse. Only time they could see me was when I was supposed to be here.

OFFICER PARK: You had a job interview, and it conflicted with our meeting.

[MI Skill: Simple reflection]

DESTINY: Yeah. So was I supposed to blow off the interview so I could come tell you nothing's changed in my life? That makes a lot of sense.

OFFICER PARK: You made a judgment call. The interview felt more important than the appointment.

[MI Skill: Reflection framing as decision rather than defiance]

DESTINY: It was more important. Getting a job is the whole point, right? Isn't that what you people are always telling me? "Get a job, stay out of trouble." Well, I'm trying to get a job and you're mad about it.

OFFICER PARK: From your perspective, you're doing exactly what you're supposed to do, and the system is punishing you for it.

[MI Skill: Reflection capturing her logic]

DESTINY: Exactly! This is what I mean. You can't win with probation. Do nothing, you're a problem. Try to do something, you're still a problem.

OFFICER PARK: It feels like a no-win situation where you get criticized no matter what you choose.

[MI Skill: Reflection of frustration]

DESTINY: [Slightly less aggressive] That's exactly how it feels.

OFFICER PARK: I hear that. And I want to ask you something. What would it have taken to let me know about the conflict ahead of time?

[MI Skill: Open question about alternative action]

DESTINY: What, like call you?

OFFICER PARK: Yeah, or leave a message, send an email. Just a heads up that you had a conflict.

DESTINY: I didn't think you'd care. I figured you'd just say "too bad, miss the interview."

OFFICER PARK: You assumed I wouldn't work with you on it.

[MI Skill: Reflection of assumption]

DESTINY: Why would you? No PO has ever worked with me on anything.

OFFICER PARK: Past experience has taught you that probation officers don't collaborate, they just demand.

[MI Skill: Reflection of history shaping expectation]

DESTINY: That's been my experience, yeah.

OFFICER PARK: So based on that experience, it made sense to just skip the appointment rather than ask for flexibility.

[MI Skill: Reflection validating her reasoning given her experience]

DESTINY: [Pause] I mean... when you put it like that, I guess I could have asked. I didn't think about it.

OFFICER PARK: It wasn't on your radar because you didn't expect it to be an option.

[MI Skill: Reflection]

DESTINY: No, it wasn't. [Pause] So what, you would have rescheduled?

OFFICER PARK: For a job interview? Absolutely. That's exactly the kind of thing I want to support.

DESTINY: [Looks surprised] Really?

OFFICER PARK: Really. Look, Destiny, I know you think I'm here to mess up your life. But I actually want you to succeed. A job interview is progress. That's what we're working toward.

DESTINY: [Guard dropping slightly] That's not what I expected you to say.

OFFICER PARK: What did you expect?

[MI Skill: Open question about expectation]

DESTINY: Threats. Lectures. "You missed your appointment, that's a violation, don't let it happen again."

OFFICER PARK: The typical script.

[MI Skill: Simple reflection]

DESTINY: Yeah.

OFFICER PARK: I'm not saying there are no consequences for missed appointments. That's real. But I'm also genuinely interested in what's happening in your life and how I can help.

DESTINY: [Skeptical but listening] Help how?

OFFICER PARK: For starters, tell me about this interview. How did it go?

[MI Skill: Shifting focus to positive topic]

DESTINY: [Slight smile despite herself] It actually went pretty good. The manager said I was "direct." Said she likes that.

OFFICER PARK: You made a positive impression.

[MI Skill: Simple reflection]

DESTINY: I think so. She said they'd call this week.

OFFICER PARK: That's encouraging. What would getting this job mean for you?

[MI Skill: Open question evoking change talk]

DESTINY: It would mean I could stop depending on... other stuff. I could have my own money that's actually mine. Not always looking over my shoulder.

OFFICER PARK: Legitimate income that you earned, without the risk.

[MI Skill: Reflection highlighting contrast with illegal income]

DESTINY: [Nods] Yeah. I'm tired of the looking over my shoulder part. The money was good, but the stress... it wears on you.

OFFICER PARK: The lifestyle that paid well also came with constant anxiety.

[MI Skill: Reflection on cost of criminal income]

DESTINY: You don't know who's going to flip on you. Who's talking to police. Every time someone gets popped, you're wondering if you're next. I've been doing this since I was seventeen. I'm tired.

OFFICER PARK: Seven years of that stress has worn you down.

[MI Skill: Reflection emphasizing cumulative toll]

DESTINY: It has. I don't want to do this forever. I never wanted to do it forever. It was just... what was available.

OFFICER PARK: It was the option you saw when you were seventeen, and it's been hard to find a path to something different.

[MI Skill: Reflection on limited options without excusing behavior]

DESTINY: No one was offering me warehouse jobs when I was seventeen. This crew, they saw me. They gave me a role. It felt like family.

OFFICER PARK: They provided belonging and purpose when you needed it most.

[MI Skill: Reflection on function of criminal association]

DESTINY: [Voice softens] Yeah. I know they're not good for me. I'm not stupid. But they're my people. It's complicated.

OFFICER PARK: The relationship meets real needs even though you know it's pulling you toward trouble. It's not as simple as just walking away.

[MI Skill: Complex reflection honoring ambivalence]

DESTINY: It's not. But I'm twenty-four now. If I keep doing this, I'm going to prison. Real prison, not county. And my little brother... he looks up to me. I don't want him thinking this is the way.

OFFICER PARK: You're thinking about what message your choices send to your brother.

[MI Skill: Reflection on family motivation]

DESTINY: DeShawn's smart. Like, really smart. He could do things I never had the chance to do. But if I'm locked up, who's going to push him? Who's going to show him there's another way?

OFFICER PARK: You want to be the example for DeShawn that nobody was for you.

[MI Skill: Complex reflection capturing role model aspiration]

DESTINY: [Eyes moist] Yeah. I have to be.

OFFICER PARK: Destiny, I've seen a completely different side of you in the last few minutes. We started with you telling me this is all harassment, and now you're talking about wanting to be an example for your brother and finding a way out of the life. What's happening for you right now?

[MI Skill: Process comment and open question]

DESTINY: I don't know. You're different from what I expected. You actually listen.

OFFICER PARK: It sounds like being heard matters to you.

[MI Skill: Reflection of what worked]

DESTINY: Nobody listens. They just see my record and decide who I am.

OFFICER PARK: You're more than your record.

[MI Skill: Affirmation]

DESTINY: I'm trying to be.

OFFICER PARK: Here's what I want to propose. Let's set up a communication plan so situations like this interview don't turn into missed appointments. If you let me know ahead of time when conflicts come up, we can work together. That way you don't have to choose between progress and compliance.

DESTINY: [Nods] Okay. I can do that.

OFFICER PARK: And let me know when you hear back about that job. I want to celebrate with you if you get it.

DESTINY: [Half-smile] Celebrate? That's a first.

OFFICER PARK: Get used to it. We're in this together.

MI Skills Demonstrated

Skill	Frequency	Examples
Open Questions	6	"What would getting this job mean for you?"
Affirmations	3	"You're more than your record"
Reflections (Simple)	14	"You had a job interview"
Reflections (Complex)	9	"You want to be the example for DeShawn that nobody was for you"

Skill	Frequency	Examples
Non-Defensive Responses	5	Not engaging with provocations
Rolling with Resistance	4	Reflecting perspective without arguing

Reflection

This session demonstrates rolling with resistance in its most challenging form: a client who arrives hostile and expecting confrontation. Destiny entered ready for a fight, using aggression as a defense mechanism developed through years of negative experiences with authority.

Officer Park's most important intervention was refusing to engage with the conflict Destiny was inviting. When she insulted him ("you don't get to sit in an office all day doing nothing"), he reflected her schedule being demanding rather than defending himself or confronting her rudeness. This consistent non-defensiveness disarmed her because her usual strategy of provoking authority figures into adversarial postures did not work.

The turning point came when Officer Park validated the logic of Destiny's decision given her assumptions. By saying "based on that experience, it made sense to just skip the appointment rather than ask for flexibility," he acknowledged her reasoning without endorsing the action. This validation paradoxically opened space for her to recognize she "could have asked."

When Destiny expressed surprise that he would have rescheduled for a job interview, genuine relationship building began. Her entire framework had been that probation officers exist to "mess up" people's lives. Discovering an exception to this pattern created cognitive dissonance that opened her to engagement.

Officer Park then capitalized on this opening by shifting focus to the interview itself, a positive topic where Destiny could share a success. This demonstrated his stated interest in supporting her goals. When she began talking about wanting legitimate income and being tired of "looking over my shoulder," she was expressing change talk that had never emerged in previous hostile sessions.

The most powerful change talk came organically when Destiny mentioned her brother DeShawn. This deep motivation had never been explored because previous interactions never got past the defensive barrier. Officer Park's reflection that she wanted to be "the example for DeShawn that nobody was for you" captured both her aspiration and her own history of lacking role models.

The session concluded with a collaborative plan for communication, transforming the missed appointment from a potential violation into an opportunity to establish a different pattern of interaction.

Outcome Analysis

Immediate Outcomes:

- Destiny shifted from hostile and defensive to engaged and vulnerable
- She identified intrinsic motivation (brother DeShawn) for changing lifestyle
- She acknowledged weariness with stress of criminal income
- She agreed to communication plan for future conflicts
- She accepted collaborative rather than adversarial relationship frame

Intermediate Outcomes (6-month follow-up):

- Destiny obtained warehouse job (different than interviewed for, but same field)
- She communicated with officer about schedule conflicts three times; all rescheduled
- She reduced contact with criminal associates (not eliminated)
- She reported police contact once (witness to incident, not involved)
- She began attending GED program "for DeShawn's sake"

Long-term Outcomes (24-month follow-up):

- Destiny maintained employment with one job change
- She completed GED program
- She testified against former criminal associates in unrelated case (voluntary)
- DeShawn graduated middle school with honors; she attended ceremony
- Early termination granted at month 30 (of 48-month sentence)

Key Success Factors:

- Refusing to engage with invited conflict
- Non-defensive responses to insults and provocations
- Validating logic of decisions while introducing alternatives
- Genuine interest in positive developments (job interview)

- Allowing deep motivation (brother) to emerge naturally from conversation

Case Study 9: The Decisional Balance Conversation

Case Background

Supervisee: Evelyn Chambers, 46-year-old white female

Offense: Felony prescription fraud (doctor shopping)

Sentence: 3 years probation, substance abuse treatment

Risk Level: Low-Moderate (LSI-R score: 15)

History: No prior criminal history. Evelyn is a former elementary school teacher who developed opioid dependency following back surgery. When her physician reduced prescriptions due to new guidelines, she began seeing multiple doctors to maintain her supply. She was caught when a pharmacy monitoring program flagged her prescriptions. She has been cooperative with probation but reluctant to fully commit to recovery, expressing concern about managing chronic pain without opioids.

Criminogenic Needs: Substance abuse (prescription opioids), chronic pain management, social isolation, loss of professional identity

Context: Eighth month of supervision. Evelyn has been attending treatment but reports she is "going through the motions." Her counselor has indicated she seems ambivalent about full recovery. Officer Denise Howard decides to conduct a formal decisional balance exercise.

Session Script

OFFICER HOWARD: Evelyn, thanks for coming in. Last week you mentioned feeling stuck, like you're in the middle of something you can't quite resolve. I'd like to try something different today if you're open to it.

[MI Skill: Referencing previous conversation; seeking permission]

EVELYN: Sure. I don't know what's left to try, but sure.

OFFICER HOWARD: I'd like to do an exercise that helps people think through decisions they're facing. It's called a decisional balance. We'll look at the upsides and downsides of both sides of your situation. Would that be okay?

[MI Skill: Explaining exercise and seeking buy-in]

EVELYN: What decision are we talking about?

OFFICER HOWARD: The decision about where opioids fit in your life going forward. Whether to aim for complete abstinence or whether to try to find a way to still use them for pain management.

EVELYN: That's the million dollar question, isn't it?

OFFICER HOWARD: It is. And I'm not here to answer it for you. I want to help you think it through completely.

[MI Skill: Emphasizing autonomy]

EVELYN: [Nods] Okay. Let's try it.

OFFICER HOWARD: Let's start with continuing to use opioids for pain management. What are the benefits you've experienced from opioids?

[MI Skill: Beginning with sustain talk side per MI protocol]

EVELYN: The obvious one is pain relief. When my back flares up, nothing else works like opioids. I've tried everything else. Anti-inflammatories upset my stomach. Physical therapy helps some, but not when it's really bad.

OFFICER HOWARD: Effective pain relief that other options haven't matched.

[MI Skill: Reflection]

EVELYN: Right. And when the pain is under control, I can function. I can go to the grocery store. I can visit my grandchildren. Without something for the pain, I'm stuck on the couch.

OFFICER HOWARD: The opioids allow you to participate in life in ways you can't when pain is uncontrolled.

[MI Skill: Reflection on function]

EVELYN: Exactly. I'm not trying to get high. I'm trying to have a life.

OFFICER HOWARD: The motivation has always been about functioning, not about euphoria.

[MI Skill: Reflection honoring intention]

EVELYN: Yes.

OFFICER HOWARD: What else? Any other benefits?

[MI Skill: Elaboration question]

EVELYN: [Thinks] Peace of mind, I guess. Knowing that if the pain gets bad, I have something that will help. When I didn't have access after my doctor cut me off, I was terrified. Every twinge made me panic.

OFFICER HOWARD: The security of knowing relief is available if you need it.

[MI Skill: Reflection on psychological function]

EVELYN: Yes. That's important to me.

OFFICER HOWARD: I'm hearing three main benefits: effective pain relief, ability to function and participate in life, and psychological security knowing relief is available. Anything else before we move to the other side?

[MI Skill: Summary of benefits]

EVELYN: I think that covers it.

OFFICER HOWARD: Okay. Now let's look at the downsides of continuing with opioid use for pain management. What are the costs you've experienced?

[MI Skill: Transition to costs of status quo]

EVELYN: [Sighs] Well, the obvious one is that I'm a convicted felon now. I broke the law trying to get them.

OFFICER HOWARD: Legal consequences that you're still living with.

[MI Skill: Reflection]

EVELYN: And I lost my job. They can't have a teacher with a felony record. Twenty-two years in the classroom, and it's over.

OFFICER HOWARD: Your career ended because of this.

[MI Skill: Simple reflection]

EVELYN: [Voice breaking slightly] I loved teaching. It was everything to me. And now... I don't know who I am anymore.

OFFICER HOWARD: Teaching was central to your identity, and losing it has left you unmoored.

[MI Skill: Complex reflection on identity loss]

EVELYN: Yes. And my husband... we're still together, but things are different. He looks at me differently now. Like he's waiting for me to mess up again.

OFFICER HOWARD: The trust in your marriage has been damaged.

[MI Skill: Reflection]

EVELYN: [Nods] And the financial stress. I'm not working, we're paying legal fees, and I still need medical care for my back.

OFFICER HOWARD: Financial pressure on top of everything else.

[MI Skill: Simple reflection]

EVELYN: And honestly... even when I had access to the pills, I wasn't happy. I needed more and more to get the same relief. I was constantly counting, planning, worrying about running out. It took over my whole life.

OFFICER HOWARD: The opioids that were supposed to let you live your life ended up consuming it.

[MI Skill: Complex reflection capturing irony]

EVELYN: [Pause] When you put it that way... yes.

OFFICER HOWARD: Any other costs?

[MI Skill: Elaboration question]

EVELYN: My grandchildren. I was so preoccupied with managing the pills that I wasn't really present with them. I was physically there but mentally somewhere else.

OFFICER HOWARD: The very function the opioids were supposed to support, being with your grandchildren, was undermined by the preoccupation.

[MI Skill: Reflection highlighting contradiction]

EVELYN: [Tears forming] I didn't see it at the time. But looking back... I missed so much.

OFFICER HOWARD: Let me summarize the costs: felony conviction, lost career and professional identity, damaged trust with your husband, financial stress, increasing tolerance requiring more medication, and missing out on genuine connection with your grandchildren due to preoccupation with the pills.

[MI Skill: Summary of costs]

EVELYN: [Nods, wiping eyes] That's a lot.

OFFICER HOWARD: It is. Now let's look at the other side. What would be the benefits of moving toward life without opioids?

[MI Skill: Transition to change option]

EVELYN: [Thinks] I wouldn't be breaking the law. I wouldn't be living in fear of getting caught.

OFFICER HOWARD: Freedom from legal risk and fear.

[MI Skill: Reflection]

EVELYN: And my husband might start trusting me again. He could stop watching my every move, checking my purse, monitoring my doctor appointments.

OFFICER HOWARD: Possibility of restoring trust in your marriage.

[MI Skill: Reflection]

EVELYN: I could be present with my grandchildren. Really present, not just going through the motions while thinking about my next dose.

OFFICER HOWARD: Being truly there with the people you love.

[MI Skill: Reflection on relational benefit]

EVELYN: And maybe... maybe I could find a new sense of purpose. I can't teach anymore, but maybe there's something else. I can't even think about that right now because all my energy goes to managing the pain and the pills and the legal stuff.

OFFICER HOWARD: Having mental space to imagine a new chapter.

[MI Skill: Reflection on future possibility]

EVELYN: Yes.

OFFICER HOWARD: Any other benefits?

EVELYN: I'd have my self-respect back. Right now I feel like a criminal. An addict. Even though I never thought of myself that way, that's how the world sees me now.

OFFICER HOWARD: Reclaiming how you see yourself, not just how others see you.

[MI Skill: Reflection on identity recovery]

EVELYN: Yes. I want to be someone my grandchildren can be proud of.

OFFICER HOWARD: So the benefits of life without opioids include: legal safety, potential for restoring marital trust, being fully present with grandchildren, mental space to find new purpose, and reclaiming your self-respect. What would be the downsides of moving away from opioids?

[MI Skill: Summary followed by final quadrant]

EVELYN: [Long pause] The pain. I keep coming back to the pain. It's real. It's not going to go away just because I stop taking opioids.

OFFICER HOWARD: The underlying condition persists regardless of what you decide about medication.

[MI Skill: Reflection acknowledging reality]

EVELYN: And I don't know what else will work. I've tried so many things.

OFFICER HOWARD: Uncertainty about how you'll manage pain without opioids.

[MI Skill: Reflection on fear]

EVELYN: It terrifies me, honestly. Living with uncontrolled pain. I don't know if I can do it.

OFFICER HOWARD: The fear is real. What if you can't manage?

[MI Skill: Reflection honoring fear]

EVELYN: [Nods] And I might fail. What if I try to quit and I can't? Then everyone will know I'm weak.

OFFICER HOWARD: Fear of failure and judgment.

[MI Skill: Simple reflection]

EVELYN: Yes.

OFFICER HOWARD: Let me put all of this together. On one side, continuing with opioids offers effective pain relief, functional ability, and psychological security. The costs include felony status, lost career, damaged marriage, financial stress, tolerance requiring more medication, and missing genuine connection with grandchildren. On the other side, life without opioids offers legal safety, potential for restored trust, full presence with loved ones, mental space for new purpose, and reclaimed self-respect. The downsides are persistent pain, uncertainty about alternatives, fear you can't manage, and fear of failure and judgment. Looking at all four quadrants, what do you notice?

[MI Skill: Complete four-quadrant summary]

EVELYN: [Long pause] The costs of continuing are all things that already happened. I've already lost them. And the costs of quitting are things I'm afraid might happen, but I don't actually know.

OFFICER HOWARD: The losses from opioid use are real and concrete. The fears about quitting are projected possibilities.

[MI Skill: Reflection highlighting distinction she identified]

EVELYN: And the benefits of continuing... even those haven't really been benefits. The pain relief requires more and more. The functioning was compromised by preoccupation. The security was false because I was always afraid of getting caught.

OFFICER HOWARD: You're questioning whether the supposed benefits were actually delivering what they promised.

[MI Skill: Reflection on her reevaluation]

EVELYN: [Quietly] They weren't. [Pause] I don't think I realized that until just now.

OFFICER HOWARD: This exercise helped you see something you hadn't seen before.

[MI Skill: Process comment]

EVELYN: I've been clinging to opioids because I'm afraid of the pain. But the opioids have caused more pain than my back ever did.

OFFICER HOWARD: That's a profound recognition, Evelyn.

[MI Skill: Affirmation]

EVELYN: So where does that leave me?

OFFICER HOWARD: Where would you like it to leave you?

[MI Skill: Returning decision to client]

EVELYN: [Takes deep breath] I think I need to actually try. Not just go through the motions in treatment, but really try to build a life without opioids. I'm still terrified about the pain. But I'm more terrified of losing everything else.

OFFICER HOWARD: The fear of loss outweighs the fear of pain.

[MI Skill: Reflection]

EVELYN: I want my grandchildren to be proud of me. I want my husband to trust me again. I want to find out who I am without the pills.

OFFICER HOWARD: Those are powerful reasons to try. What would genuine engagement with treatment look like, different from going through the motions?

[MI Skill: Affirmation and open question toward action]

EVELYN: Being honest. Actually talking about what's hard instead of pretending I'm fine. Maybe asking about non-opioid pain management options that I haven't tried yet.

OFFICER HOWARD: Honesty, genuine participation, and exploring alternatives for your pain. Those sound like meaningful steps.

[MI Skill: Summary of commitments]

EVELYN: I'm going to try. I can't promise I'll succeed, but I'm going to actually try.

MI Skills Demonstrated

Skill	Frequency	Examples
Open Questions	6	"What do you notice?"
Affirmations	3	"That's a profound recognition"
Reflections (Simple)	12	"Freedom from legal risk"
Reflections (Complex)	10	"The opioids that were supposed to let you live your life ended up consuming it"
Summaries	5	Quadrant summaries and full decisional balance
Permission Seeking	2	"Would that be okay?"
Autonomy Support	4	"Where would you like it to leave you?"

Reflection

This session demonstrates the formal decisional balance exercise, a structured MI technique for exploring ambivalence comprehensively. The four-quadrant model examines both sides of a decision (status quo vs. change) in terms of both benefits and costs, creating a complete picture that often reveals imbalances the client had not previously recognized.

Officer Howard followed MI protocol by beginning with the reasons to continue the current behavior (sustain talk side). This sequencing honors the client's ambivalence and reduces defensiveness. If the exercise began with reasons to change, the client might argue for the status quo. Starting with benefits of continuation demonstrates that the officer understands the behavior serves purposes.

Each benefit and cost was reflected without judgment. When Evelyn identified pain relief and functioning as opioid benefits, Officer Howard reflected these genuinely. When she identified lost career and damaged marriage as costs, these too were reflected with equal weight. The officer's role was to help Evelyn complete her own analysis, not to weight the scales.

The turning point came when Evelyn herself noticed a pattern: the costs of continuing were concrete losses already experienced, while the costs of quitting were projected fears. This insight emerged from reviewing all four quadrants together, not from the officer pointing it out. Self-generated insight carries far more weight than external observation.

Evelyn's recognition that the "benefits" of opioids had been illusory was particularly powerful. She realized that pain relief required ever-increasing doses, that functioning was compromised by preoccupation, and that security was undermined by fear of detection. This reevaluation happened because the exercise created space for comprehensive reflection.

The session concluded with Evelyn committing to genuine treatment engagement rather than going through the motions. This commitment emerged from her own analysis, grounded in motivations she articulated herself: her grandchildren's pride, her husband's trust, discovering who she is without the pills.

Outcome Analysis

Immediate Outcomes:

- Evelyn completed comprehensive decisional balance exercise
- She recognized that opioid "benefits" had been illusory
- She distinguished concrete past losses from projected future fears
- She committed to genuine treatment engagement
- She identified specific behavioral changes (honesty, participation, exploring alternatives)

Intermediate Outcomes (6-month follow-up):

- Evelyn's treatment counselor reported "dramatic shift" in engagement

- She explored and began comprehensive pain management program including physical therapy, NSAID schedule, mindfulness-based pain management
- She reported reduced pain levels despite opioid abstinence
- Her husband accompanied her to several appointments; trust rebuilding began
- She completed treatment program with positive completion

Long-term Outcomes (24-month follow-up):

- Evelyn maintained opioid abstinence for full supervision period
- She reported manageable pain levels most of the time
- She began volunteering as reading tutor for elementary students
- Her marriage significantly improved; husband confirmed trust restored
- She became advocate for non-opioid pain management options at local level

Key Success Factors:

- Structured decisional balance allowed comprehensive ambivalence exploration
- Starting with sustain talk side reduced defensiveness
- Self-generated insight about concrete losses vs. projected fears was powerful
- Recognition that "benefits" were illusory emerged from client's own analysis
- Commitment was intrinsically motivated by values she identified

Case Study 10: Using Importance and Confidence Rulers

Case Background

Supervisee: Anthony Reyes, 29-year-old Hispanic male

Offense: Felony burglary (commercial building)

Sentence: 4 years probation, restitution of $8,500

Risk Level: Moderate-High (LSI-R score: 28)

History: Two prior theft convictions, one prior burglary as juvenile. Anthony has struggled with employment stability and has relied on theft income during periods of unemployment. He was recently laid off from a construction job and is facing financial pressure. He has completed previous supervision periods but returned to criminal behavior each time employment ended.

Criminogenic Needs: Unemployment/unstable employment, criminal thinking patterns, limited legitimate financial resources, antisocial peers

Context: Twelfth month of supervision. Anthony was doing well while employed but was recently laid off when a construction project ended. Officer Maria Santos is concerned about the pattern and decides to use importance and confidence rulers to assess his commitment to staying straight during unemployment.

Session Script

OFFICER SANTOS: Anthony, I know getting laid off is tough. You were doing really well at that job. How are you holding up?

[MI Skill: Empathic opening acknowledging difficulty]

ANTHONY: Trying to keep it together. Sent out some applications. Checking the union hall every day. Something will come up.

OFFICER SANTOS: You're actively looking.

[MI Skill: Simple reflection]

ANTHONY: Yeah. What else am I supposed to do?

OFFICER SANTOS: Anthony, I want to have an honest conversation with you. I've been doing this job for a while, and I've seen your history. I'm not saying this to lecture you, but because I want to understand where you really are.

[MI Skill: Setting up honest dialogue]

ANTHONY: [Tenses slightly] What do you mean?

OFFICER SANTOS: Each time you've been unemployed in the past, you've eventually gone back to stealing. The construction job kept you straight, but the pattern shows that when work ends, problems follow.

ANTHONY: You saying you think I'm going to mess up?

OFFICER SANTOS: I'm not predicting anything. I'm naming a pattern and asking where you're at right now. Because I think if we talk about it openly, there's a better chance we can do something about it.

[MI Skill: Direct but non-judgmental approach; collaborative framing]

ANTHONY: [Relaxes slightly] Okay. What do you want to know?

OFFICER SANTOS: I want to ask you a scaling question. On a scale of zero to ten, where zero is not at all important and ten is the most important thing in your life, how important is it to you to stay on the right side of the law during this unemployment period?

[MI Skill: Importance ruler]

ANTHONY: [Thinks] Seven. Maybe seven and a half.

OFFICER SANTOS: So not a two or three, but not a ten either. Tell me about the seven.

[MI Skill: Following up by exploring the number]

ANTHONY: It's important. I don't want to go back to prison. I'm almost thirty. I can't be doing this forever. But it's also... the bills don't stop. You know? Rent is due whether I'm working or not.

OFFICER SANTOS: The importance is real, and so is the financial pressure.

[MI Skill: Reflection honoring both]

ANTHONY: Exactly.

OFFICER SANTOS: What would make it an eight or nine?

[MI Skill: Exploring what would increase importance]

ANTHONY: [Pause] I don't know. Maybe if I had more at stake? Like, before, I didn't have much to lose. This time... I've been talking to someone. A woman. Isabella. It's not serious yet, but it could be. She doesn't know about my record. If I went back in, that would be it.

OFFICER SANTOS: Isabella represents something that matters enough to raise the stakes.

[MI Skill: Reflection identifying motivation]

ANTHONY: Yeah. She's different from women I usually date. She's got her act together. Good job, nice apartment, doesn't deal with drama. I like who I am when I'm with her.

OFFICER SANTOS: She brings out a version of yourself you want to keep.

[MI Skill: Complex reflection on relationship motivation]

ANTHONY: She does.

OFFICER SANTOS: Let me ask you another scaling question. Same scale, zero to ten. How confident are you that you can stay on the right side of the law during unemployment? That you can make it through without going back to theft?

[MI Skill: Confidence ruler]

ANTHONY: [Long pause] Honestly? Five. Maybe a four.

OFFICER SANTOS: So your importance is higher than your confidence. You want to stay straight, but you're not sure you can pull it off.

[MI Skill: Reflection noting discrepancy between importance and confidence]

ANTHONY: That's about right.

OFFICER SANTOS: Tell me about the five. What gives you that much confidence?

[MI Skill: Asking why not lower to evoke ability statements]

ANTHONY: I made it through three months unemployed once without doing anything. Three months was my longest stretch before. I know I can do it for a little while. And I've got more skills now than before. I'm a better worker. Jobs come easier than they used to.

OFFICER SANTOS: You've done it before for a period of time, and your marketability has improved.

[MI Skill: Reflection on ability and resources]

ANTHONY: Yeah. And this time I know the warning signs. Like, when I start thinking "just one time" or "it's easy money," that's when I'm in trouble.

OFFICER SANTOS: You've developed self-awareness about your own risk signals.

[MI Skill: Affirmation recognizing growth]

ANTHONY: I guess I have. Doesn't mean I always listen to them, but I know them.

OFFICER SANTOS: What makes it a five and not an eight?

[MI Skill: Exploring what would increase confidence]

ANTHONY: The pressure. When the money runs out, when I can't pay rent, when people I owe start calling... that's when it gets hard. I don't have a cushion. If I can't find work in the next month, I'm in trouble.

OFFICER SANTOS: The financial timeline creates urgency that pushes you toward options you don't want to choose.

[MI Skill: Reflection on structural vulnerability]

ANTHONY: Yeah. And my boys... they know when I'm hurting for money. They come around with opportunities. They make it sound easy.

OFFICER SANTOS: Old connections resurface when you're vulnerable.

[MI Skill: Reflection on peer pressure]

ANTHONY: Every time.

OFFICER SANTOS: Let me put this together. Your importance is a seven to seven and a half, high but not maximum. Isabella is something that could push it higher. Your confidence is a four or five, meaning you have some ability statements going for you, past success, better marketability, self-awareness of warning signs, but you're worried about what happens when money runs out and old connections show up with "opportunities." Does that sound accurate?

[MI Skill: Summary integrating both rulers]

ANTHONY: Yeah, that's where I'm at.

OFFICER SANTOS: So the question is: what would increase your confidence? What would help you get through the next month or two of unemployment without the pattern repeating?

[MI Skill: Open question toward problem-solving]

ANTHONY: [Thinks] Staying busy, probably. When I have too much time, that's when I start thinking about easy money. If I'm doing something productive, I'm not sitting around being tempted.

OFFICER SANTOS: Structure and productive activity fill the space that could otherwise become risky.

[MI Skill: Reflection]

ANTHONY: And staying away from certain people. I know who's going to come to me with offers. If I don't answer their calls, if I stay out of the places where they hang out, I'm safer.

OFFICER SANTOS: Limiting exposure to the people and places connected to criminal opportunities.

[MI Skill: Reflection on avoidance strategy]

ANTHONY: Yeah. [Pause] And maybe... maybe telling Isabella the truth. About my record. Because right now I'm keeping this secret, and secrets are dangerous for me. If she knows, and she still wants to be with me, that's real. If she doesn't, at least I'll know before I'm in too deep.

OFFICER SANTOS: Honesty with Isabella both removes a secret you're carrying and tests whether the relationship can survive the truth.

[MI Skill: Complex reflection on multiple functions of disclosure]

ANTHONY: I've been afraid to tell her. But keeping this secret is the same pattern as before. Hiding. Pretending. It never works out.

OFFICER SANTOS: You're recognizing that the pattern of hiding connects to other patterns you're trying to break.

[MI Skill: Reflection on interconnection]

ANTHONY: Yeah.

OFFICER SANTOS: Anthony, if you did all three of those things, staying busy, limiting exposure to risky people and places, and being honest with Isabella, where would your confidence be?

[MI Skill: Revisiting ruler after identifying supports]

ANTHONY: Maybe a seven? Still not guaranteed, but a lot better than a five.

OFFICER SANTOS: That's a meaningful increase. You've identified strategies that make a real difference in your confidence.

[MI Skill: Affirmation of identified solutions]

ANTHONY: I have to actually do them, though. Knowing what to do and doing it aren't the same.

OFFICER SANTOS: What would help you actually do them, not just know them?

[MI Skill: Open question about implementation]

ANTHONY: Accountability, I guess. Someone checking in.

OFFICER SANTOS: What if we increased our contact frequency during this unemployment period? Weekly check-ins instead of monthly?

ANTHONY: That might help. Not because you're watching me, but because I'd have to tell you how I'm doing.

OFFICER SANTOS: The accountability of having to report keeps you honest with yourself.

[MI Skill: Reflection on function of supervision]

ANTHONY: Yeah.

OFFICER SANTOS: And one more thing. If you do tell Isabella, and it doesn't go well, I want you to call me. Not because you're in trouble, but because that's exactly the kind of moment when old patterns kick in. Rejection, disappointment, feeling like "what's the point." That's when you need support, not isolation.

ANTHONY: [Nods] Okay. I can do that.

OFFICER SANTOS: Let's set a specific day and time for our weekly check-ins. And let's set a deadline for when you're going to have the conversation with Isabella.

[MI Skill: Moving to concrete commitments]

ANTHONY: How about... I'll tell her this weekend. Get it over with.

OFFICER SANTOS: This weekend. And our first weekly check-in will be Tuesday?

ANTHONY: Tuesday works.

OFFICER SANTOS: I'm going to ask you one more time. After everything we've talked about, how confident are you now that you can make it through this unemployment without going back to theft?

[MI Skill: Final confidence check]

ANTHONY: Seven. Solid seven.

MI Skills Demonstrated

Skill	Frequency	Examples
Open Questions	7	"What would make it an eight?"
Affirmations	4	"You've developed self-awareness"

Skill	Frequency	Examples
Reflections (Simple)	10	"You're actively looking"
Reflections (Complex)	9	"She brings out a version of yourself you want to keep"
Summaries	2	Integration of ruler results
Importance Ruler	1	"Scale of 0-10, how important..."
Confidence Ruler	3	Initial, hypothetical after strategies, final

Reflection

This session demonstrates the use of importance and confidence rulers as assessment and intervention tools simultaneously. The rulers served multiple functions: assessing readiness, evoking change talk, identifying motivations, uncovering barriers, and generating solutions.

Officer Santos began with the importance ruler, and the follow-up question "tell me about the seven" evoked Anthony's articulation of why staying straight matters (avoiding prison, age considerations) and why it's not a ten (financial pressure). The question "what would make it an eight or nine?" introduced Isabella as a significant motivation that might not have surfaced otherwise.

The confidence ruler revealed a critical discrepancy: importance (7-7.5) exceeded confidence (4-5). This gap indicates someone who wants to change but doubts their ability, a pattern requiring support rather than motivation. The follow-up "why not lower?" evoked ability statements: past success, improved marketability, self-awareness of warning signs.

Critically, Officer Santos asked what would increase confidence before offering solutions. Anthony identified his own strategies: staying busy, avoiding risky people and places, and telling Isabella the truth. The solution to increase honesty emerged organically as Anthony recognized that secret-keeping connected to other problematic patterns.

The creative intervention of revisiting the confidence ruler after strategies were identified ("If you did all three, where would your confidence be?") allowed Anthony to experience the impact of his own ideas. Moving from 5 to 7 provided concrete evidence that his strategies were meaningful.

The practical steps established at the end, weekly check-ins and a deadline for talking to Isabella, created accountability structures that Anthony identified as helpful. The final confidence assessment at 7 represented substantial movement from the initial 4-5.

Outcome Analysis

Immediate Outcomes:

- Anthony articulated reasons for importance (prison avoidance, age, Isabella)
- He identified confidence-building strategies (structure, avoidance, honesty)
- He committed to telling Isabella about his record
- He agreed to increased supervision contact during unemployment
- Confidence increased from 5 to 7 within session

Intermediate Outcomes (4-month follow-up):

- Anthony told Isabella; she remained in relationship
- He obtained new construction job after 6 weeks of unemployment
- He maintained weekly check-ins even after employment resumed
- He reported two approaches from criminal associates; did not respond
- He disclosed to Isabella that he was on probation (additional honesty)

Long-term Outcomes (18-month follow-up):

- Anthony remained employed with one job transition (lateral, not layoff)
- He and Isabella moved in together
- He completed probation without violations
- He reported pattern of calling Officer Santos during stress periods
- No new criminal charges

Key Success Factors:

- Rulers identified gap between importance and confidence requiring support
- "Why not lower?" questions evoked ability statements and resources
- Client generated own strategies; officer did not prescribe
- Revisiting ruler after strategies showed meaningful change
- Practical accountability structures matched what client identified as helpful
- Proactive planning for vulnerable moment (disclosure to Isabella)

Chapter 20: Special Population Cases

Case Study 11: Substance Abuse and Recovery Motivation

Case Background

Supervisee: Malik Jefferson, 33-year-old African American male

Offense: Felony possession with intent (methamphetamine)

Sentence: 5 years probation, residential treatment program, drug testing

Risk Level: High (LSI-R score: 31)

History: Extensive substance use history beginning at age 14. Three prior drug convictions. Has been through treatment five times with multiple relapses. Recently completed 90-day residential treatment and is transitioning to outpatient. Previous relapses have typically occurred within weeks of leaving residential settings.

Criminogenic Needs: Chronic substance abuse (methamphetamine, alcohol), antisocial peers, unemployment, trauma history

Context: First post-residential meeting. Malik just completed 90 days of residential treatment and is moving into a sober living facility. Officer Terrence Williams wants to assess his genuine commitment to recovery and identify early warning signs.

Session Script

OFFICER WILLIAMS: Malik, congratulations on completing the program. That's ninety days you didn't have to do, and you did them. How does it feel to be on this side of it?

[MI Skill: Affirmation followed by open question]

MALIK: Feels weird, honestly. Good, but weird. Like, I know what to do in there. Out here, I'm not so sure.

OFFICER WILLIAMS: The structure of residential feels safer than the uncertainty of what comes next.

[MI Skill: Reflection capturing ambivalence about transition]

MALIK: Exactly. In there, everything is scheduled. Wake up, groups, meals, more groups, lights out. No decisions. Out here, I got decisions coming at me all day.

OFFICER WILLIAMS: Too many decisions without enough structure to support them.

[MI Skill: Reflection]

MALIK: And the triggers. Man, the triggers. First day out, I'm waiting for the bus and someone I used to use with walks by. Just like that. "Hey Malik, where you been?" My heart was pounding.

OFFICER WILLIAMS: That encounter caught you off guard and brought up physical reactions.

[MI Skill: Reflection on visceral response]

MALIK: It did. I got on the bus and my hands were shaking.

OFFICER WILLIAMS: What did you do with that?

[MI Skill: Open question exploring coping response]

MALIK: Called my sponsor. Soon as I sat down, I called him. He talked me through it. Reminded me to breathe. Told me to get to a meeting that night. I did.

OFFICER WILLIAMS: So in that first moment of exposure, you reached out immediately and followed through on the advice you got.

[MI Skill: Reflection highlighting effective coping sequence]

MALIK: I mean, I knew I had to. If I don't do something different, I know what happens. I've been here before.

OFFICER WILLIAMS: This isn't your first rodeo. You know the pattern.

[MI Skill: Simple reflection acknowledging experience]

MALIK: [Sighs] Five treatments. Five relapses. Each time I tell myself it's going to be different, and each time I end up the same place.

OFFICER WILLIAMS: You've had the same starting intention but the same ending result, over and over.

[MI Skill: Reflection naming frustrating pattern]

MALIK: Makes you wonder if it's even possible. Like, maybe some people just aren't meant to stay clean.

OFFICER WILLIAMS: Part of you wonders if you're one of those people who can't do this.

[MI Skill: Reflection with "part of you" language]

MALIK: Sometimes. Yeah.

OFFICER WILLIAMS: What does another part think?

[MI Skill: Open question exploring other perspective]

MALIK: [Pause] Another part thinks those five times taught me things. Like, each time I learned something about what doesn't work for me.

OFFICER WILLIAMS: Tell me what you learned that doesn't work.

[MI Skill: Elaboration question]

MALIK: Isolation. That's the big one. Every time I relapsed, I had pulled away from people first. Stopped going to meetings. Stopped calling my sponsor. Told myself I had it under control.

OFFICER WILLIAMS: Disconnection precedes relapse for you.

[MI Skill: Reflection naming pattern]

MALIK: Every time. Without fail.

OFFICER WILLIAMS: What else doesn't work?

MALIK: Thinking I can hang around certain people and not use. I can't. Maybe some people can be around drugs and say no. I'm not that person.

OFFICER WILLIAMS: You've learned your limits around exposure.

[MI Skill: Reflection on self-knowledge]

MALIK: And stress. Unmanaged stress. When things pile up and I don't have an outlet, that's when I start looking for relief.

OFFICER WILLIAMS: Stress without an outlet creates vulnerability.

[MI Skill: Reflection]

MALIK: Yeah. So I know what doesn't work. I just... struggle to do what does work, consistently.

OFFICER WILLIAMS: The knowledge is there. The consistency is the challenge.

[MI Skill: Reflection distinguishing knowing from doing]

MALIK: That's my whole life right there.

OFFICER WILLIAMS: Malik, what's different this time? Not what you hope is different, but what's actually different?

[MI Skill: Open question seeking concrete change, not aspiration]

MALIK: [Thinks] I'm tired. Really tired. Before, I still had this idea that maybe I could control it. Maybe I could use sometimes and not others. This time, I know I can't. I stopped trying to negotiate with it.

OFFICER WILLIAMS: The fantasy of controlled use is gone.

[MI Skill: Reflection on cognitive shift]

MALIK: Yeah. That's done.

OFFICER WILLIAMS: What else is different?

MALIK: My daughter. Aaliyah. She's four now. Last time I was in treatment, she was a baby. She didn't know. Now she knows something's wrong with her daddy. My mom has custody, and Aaliyah asks her why daddy can't live with them.

OFFICER WILLIAMS: [Waits in silence]

MALIK: [Voice breaking] I can't do that to her. I can't be that father who's never there. Who she's ashamed of. Who she has to explain to her friends.

OFFICER WILLIAMS: Aaliyah matters in a way that changes the equation.

[MI Skill: Reflection on deepened motivation]

MALIK: She's everything. I didn't get that before. When she was a baby, she was just... abstract. Now she's a person. A person who needs a father.

OFFICER WILLIAMS: The responsibility has become real.

[MI Skill: Simple reflection]

MALIK: Real. Yeah. [Pause] And something else that's different. This treatment... they worked with me on the trauma stuff. Things I never talked about before.

OFFICER WILLIAMS: The program addressed something deeper that previous treatments didn't touch.

[MI Skill: Reflection on new treatment element]

MALIK: I never told anyone about what happened to me as a kid. I always thought, what does that have to do with using? But now I see... that's where all of it started. Using was a way to not feel that stuff.

OFFICER WILLIAMS: Understanding the function the drugs served gives you different options.

[MI Skill: Reflection on insight about addiction function]

MALIK: It does. Because now I know what I'm actually running from. And I'm learning other ways to deal with it.

OFFICER WILLIAMS: Let me pull together what I'm hearing, Malik. You've identified what doesn't work for you: isolation, exposure to users, and unmanaged stress. You've had five previous attempts that taught you these lessons. What's different this time includes: you've given up the fantasy of controlled use, your daughter Aaliyah has become real and motivating in a new way, and you've begun addressing underlying trauma that fueled the using. The challenge isn't knowledge; it's consistency in doing what you know works.

[MI Skill: Comprehensive summary]

MALIK: Yeah.

OFFICER WILLIAMS: On a scale of zero to ten, how committed are you to staying clean during this transition period, the next three months?

[MI Skill: Commitment ruler]

MALIK: Nine.

OFFICER WILLIAMS: Nine. That's strong. What keeps it from being a ten?

[MI Skill: Exploring gap]

MALIK: Because I don't trust myself completely. I've said nine before and ended up relapsed. I know my track record. I'm committed, but I know I need help to keep that commitment.

OFFICER WILLIAMS: Your confidence in your intention is high, but you recognize that intention alone isn't enough.

[MI Skill: Reflection naming important distinction]

MALIK: Right. I need structure, accountability, people who will call me out if I start slipping.

OFFICER WILLIAMS: You're asking for support that matches your vulnerability.

[MI Skill: Reflection on appropriate help-seeking]

MALIK: I am. I can't do this alone. I've tried that. It doesn't work.

OFFICER WILLIAMS: That's one of the most important things you could possibly know.

[MI Skill: Affirmation]

MALIK: I know it now. Took me five times, but I know it.

OFFICER WILLIAMS: So let's build a structure that supports your nine. What does that look like?

[MI Skill: Open question toward planning]

MALIK: Meetings every day for the first month. Sponsor check-ins daily. No contact with anyone from the using life, period. Regular appointments with my trauma therapist. And being honest with you when things get hard.

OFFICER WILLIAMS: That's a robust recovery structure. I want to add one thing, if you're open to it.

[MI Skill: Asking permission to add

MALIK: What's that?

OFFICER WILLIAMS: A plan for when, not if, you encounter a trigger and feel the pull. What will you do in that moment?

MALIK: Call my sponsor first. If I can't reach him, call someone else from the program. If I still feel it, get to a meeting. If I still feel it after that, call you.

OFFICER WILLIAMS: You've got a sequence. Sponsor, then another program member, then meeting, then me. How will you make sure you actually follow that sequence when the pull is strong?

[MI Skill: Testing commitment with reality]

MALIK: Because the pull will always pass. I just have to survive it. Every time I relapsed, I didn't survive the pull. I gave in before it could pass. This time, I'm going to outlast it.

OFFICER WILLIAMS: Outlast the pull until it passes.

[MI Skill: Reflection on strategy]

MALIK: That's my only job. The pull will come. My job is to survive it.

Reflection

This session demonstrates MI's application to chronic substance use with multiple prior treatment failures. Malik arrived with self-doubt about his capacity to succeed given his history. Officer Williams neither minimized this history nor allowed it to dominate, instead using it as data about what Malik had learned.

The critical turning point was asking "What's different this time?" followed by "Not what you hope is different, but what's actually different." This specification invited concrete reflection rather than hopeful statements. Malik's identification of three actual differences (no controlled use fantasy, Aaliyah's developmental shift, trauma processing) represented substantive changes in his recovery infrastructure.

The commitment ruler revealed a nine, unusually high, but Malik's explanation of why not ten demonstrated sophisticated self-knowledge. His recognition that intention alone isn't enough, and his explicit request for accountability, suggested genuine humility about his needs.

The session ended with a detailed safety plan, a specific sequence for responding to triggers. Officer Williams's question "How will you make sure you actually follow that sequence?" pressed for a reality-based commitment rather than easy promises.

Outcome Analysis

Immediate through Long-term Outcomes:

- Malik maintained daily meeting attendance for full first month
- He experienced three significant trigger events in first 90 days; used support sequence each time successfully
- He had one "close call" at month 4 involving contact from ex-using partner; immediately disclosed to officer and sponsor
- His visitation with Aaliyah increased; moved from supervised to unsupervised at month 8
- He completed 18 months of probation without relapse; transferred to low-intensity supervision
- At 24-month follow-up, he remained clean and was training to become peer recovery support specialist

Case Study 12: Mental Health and Co-occurring Disorders

Case Background

Supervisee: Jennifer Walsh, 41-year-old white female

Offense: Felony assault (attacked coworker during apparent mental health crisis)

Sentence: 4 years probation, mental health treatment, no contact with victim

Risk Level: Moderate (LSI-R score: 19)

History: Diagnosed with bipolar disorder at age 22. Has been on and off medication for twenty years. Offense occurred during apparent manic episode when Jennifer accused coworker of conspiracy against her. No prior criminal history. She has been resistant to medication compliance, reporting that medications make her "feel dead inside."

Criminogenic Needs: Mental health management, medication compliance, stress management, social support

Context: Third month of supervision. Jennifer is currently stable on medication but has expressed the same ambivalence about medication that has preceded past periods of non-compliance. Officer Patricia Lane wants to address this pattern.

Session Script

OFFICER LANE: Jennifer, you're looking well today. How have things been going?

JENNIFER: Fine, I guess. Same as always. Wake up, take my pills, go to therapy, take more pills, go to bed. Exciting life.

OFFICER LANE: The routine feels monotonous.

[MI Skill: Reflection on affect]

JENNIFER: It's not a life. It's existing. I feel like a zombie half the time.

OFFICER LANE: The medication affects how alive you feel.

[MI Skill: Reflection on side effects]

JENNIFER: That's one way to put it. I used to be creative. I used to have ideas. Now I just... am.

OFFICER LANE: Something was lost when you started the medication.

[MI Skill: Reflection on perceived cost]

JENNIFER: My whole personality, maybe. Before the diagnosis, before the meds, I was a different person. I had energy. I painted. I wrote poetry. I felt things deeply. Now everything is flat.

OFFICER LANE: The person you were before feels more authentic than the person you are now.

[MI Skill: Complex reflection on identity]

JENNIFER: Exactly. Everyone acts like the medication is this gift. "You're stable now, Jennifer. You're doing so well." But what if I don't want to be stable? What if stable means boring and empty?

OFFICER LANE: Stability came at a price you're not sure was worth paying.

[MI Skill: Reflection capturing ambivalence]

JENNIFER: [Sighs] I know how this sounds. I know what happened when I wasn't medicated. But at least I felt alive.

OFFICER LANE: Help me understand that, Jennifer. What did feeling alive mean for you?

[MI Skill: Open question exploring experience]

JENNIFER: Colors were brighter. Ideas came faster than I could write them down. I'd stay up all night working on a painting because I couldn't stop, didn't want to stop. Everything mattered. Everything was urgent and important.

OFFICER LANE: There was an intensity and creative energy that felt meaningful.

[MI Skill: Reflection on positive aspects of mania]

JENNIFER: Yes. And people don't understand that. They see the bad parts, the spending, the paranoia, what happened with Lisa. But they don't see what it feels like from the inside.

OFFICER LANE: From the inside, there were experiences you valued, not just symptoms to be managed.

[MI Skill: Reflection honoring subjective experience]

JENNIFER: [Tears forming] Thank you for understanding that. Nobody ever says that. They just tell me I'm sick and need to take my meds.

OFFICER LANE: It sounds like you've felt dismissed and misunderstood about your own experience.

[MI Skill: Reflection on feeling invalidated]

JENNIFER: For twenty years. Since the diagnosis.

OFFICER LANE: Jennifer, I want to understand both sides of this completely. You've described what you valued about those unmedicated experiences. Can you also help me understand the costs?

[MI Skill: Transitioning to exploring other side]

JENNIFER: [Long pause] The costs. You want to know about Lisa.

OFFICER LANE: Only if you want to talk about it.

[MI Skill: Respecting autonomy]

JENNIFER: I thought she was plotting against me. Genuinely believed it. I saw patterns everywhere, connections that seemed so obvious. She moved my stapler, so she was trying to make me look disorganized. She talked to our boss, so she was trying to get me fired. It all made sense in my head.

OFFICER LANE: The thoughts felt completely logical at the time.

[MI Skill: Reflection on subjective experience of delusion]

JENNIFER: They did. And then I confronted her, and things escalated, and I... I hurt her. I've never hurt anyone in my life. The look on her face when I grabbed her... she was terrified. Of me.

OFFICER LANE: That image stays with you.

[MI Skill: Reflection]

JENNIFER: [Crying] I don't even remember exactly what I thought she had done. The logic that seemed so clear is gone now. All that's left is what I did.

OFFICER LANE: The thoughts that made the action seem necessary evaporated, but the action and its consequences remain.

[MI Skill: Complex reflection on aftermath]

JENNIFER: And she still works there. I don't. I can never go back. I lost my job, my reputation, my friends from work. Everyone thinks I'm dangerous now.

OFFICER LANE: The incident changed how everyone sees you.

[MI Skill: Reflection on social consequence]

JENNIFER: My family walks on eggshells around me. My sister checks in every day, but I know she's really checking to see if I'm "okay," meaning medicated. My brother stopped returning my calls after the arrest.

OFFICER LANE: Your family relationships have been affected too.

[MI Skill: Simple reflection]

JENNIFER: Everything has been affected. [Pause] I know the medication prevents episodes like that. I know it intellectually. But it's hard to remember that when I'm feeling dead inside every single day.

OFFICER LANE: Let me see if I can put together what you've shared. On one side, there's the unmedicated experience: creativity, intensity, feeling alive, colors brighter, ideas flowing. On the other side, there are the costs: the paranoia that felt logical but wasn't, hurting Lisa, losing your job, damaged relationships, everyone seeing you as dangerous. And the medication prevents the worst of the costs but also mutes the experiences you valued. You're caught between feeling dead but safe, or feeling alive but risking everything again.

[MI Skill: Summary presenting full picture]

JENNIFER: [Nods] That's exactly it. That's the choice I face every single day when I open that pill bottle.

OFFICER LANE: I can't imagine how exhausting it must be to make that choice every day.

[MI Skill: Empathic statement]

JENNIFER: It is.

OFFICER LANE: Jennifer, I'm wondering about something. You've described feeling alive before as creativity, intensity, meaning. Is medication truly the only thing standing between you and those experiences? Or might there be ways to access some of what you valued without the risks?

[MI Skill: Open question introducing alternative framing]

JENNIFER: [Pause] What do you mean?

OFFICER LANE: I'm curious whether the creativity and intensity were only possible in an unmedicated manic state, or whether there are elements you could cultivate intentionally, with support.

[MI Skill: Elaboration of alternative perspective]

JENNIFER: I... I don't know. I've assumed they were the same thing. The creativity was the mania, the mania was the creativity.

OFFICER LANE: That's how it's felt. What if that assumption isn't entirely true?

[MI Skill: Gentle challenge to fixed belief]

JENNIFER: [Thinks for a long time] I haven't painted since I've been on this medication regimen. I told myself it was because I couldn't, because the medication killed my creativity. But maybe... maybe I haven't tried.

OFFICER LANE: You haven't tested whether creativity is possible in your current state.

[MI Skill: Reflection on untested assumption]

JENNIFER: No. I just assumed it wasn't. So I stopped trying.

OFFICER LANE: What would it mean if you tried and found you could still create?

[MI Skill: Open question exploring implications]

JENNIFER: It would mean... [voice breaks] It would mean I could have both. Safety and something like the life I valued.

OFFICER LANE: That possibility moves you emotionally.

[MI Skill: Reflection on affect]

JENNIFER: It does. Because I've been mourning that person, the creative person. Like she died when I started the medication. What if she's still in there somewhere?

OFFICER LANE: What if she is?

[MI Skill: Reflecting question back]

JENNIFER: [Wipes eyes] I could try. I could get my paints out and just... try.

OFFICER LANE: That would be testing the assumption rather than accepting it as fact.

[MI Skill: Reflection framing action as experiment]

JENNIFER: Yes. [Pause] But what if I try and I can't? What if the medication really has killed that part of me?

OFFICER LANE: Then you'd know, rather than assume. And we could talk about what that means and what other options might exist.

[MI Skill: Acknowledging possible negative outcome]

JENNIFER: That's fair.

OFFICER LANE: I also want to address something else you mentioned. You said the medication makes you "feel dead inside." Have you talked to your prescriber about that specific experience?

[MI Skill: Open question about medication management]

JENNIFER: Not really. They ask if I'm having side effects, and I say yes, and they say that's normal and better than the alternative.

OFFICER LANE: So you've felt dismissed by prescribers too.

[MI Skill: Reflection connecting to earlier theme]

JENNIFER: Same as everyone else.

OFFICER LANE: What if you were more specific about what you're experiencing? "Feeling dead inside" is significant. There might be medication adjustments that address the symptoms while reducing that particular side effect.

[MI Skill: Providing information about options]

JENNIFER: I never thought they'd actually do anything about it.

OFFICER LANE: It might be worth advocating for yourself more specifically. You deserve a treatment that you can live with, not just survive.

[MI Skill: Affirmation of deservingness]

JENNIFER: [Nods] Maybe I could make a list. The specific things I'm experiencing. And ask if there are alternatives.

OFFICER LANE: That's a proactive step. Advocating for your own quality of life within treatment.

[MI Skill: Affirmation of autonomy and self-advocacy]

JENNIFER: And I could try painting. This weekend. Just to see.

OFFICER LANE: Two concrete steps: advocating with your prescriber and testing whether creativity is accessible. How are you feeling about medication compliance in the meantime?

[MI Skill: Checking in on immediate concern]

JENNIFER: I'll keep taking it. I know what's at stake if I don't. But maybe I won't feel so hopeless about it if I have something to work toward.

OFFICER LANE: Having hope for something better makes the daily choice more bearable.

[MI Skill: Reflection]

JENNIFER: It does. Thank you. This is the first time anyone's talked to me about this instead of at me.

Reflection

This session illustrates MI's application to mental health populations where medication ambivalence is common. Officer Lane began by genuinely exploring Jennifer's subjective experience of both medicated and unmedicated states, without immediately defending medication. This approach allowed Jennifer to feel heard rather than dismissed.

The key insight came when Officer Lane questioned whether creativity and mania were truly inseparable. By reframing this as an untested assumption rather than an established fact, she opened space for Jennifer to consider alternative possibilities. This intervention addressed the underlying loss that was driving medication ambivalence without arguing about medication itself.

The session also demonstrated appropriate scope awareness. Officer Lane recognized that medication adjustment was beyond her role but encouraged Jennifer to advocate more effectively with her prescriber. This maintained appropriate boundaries while still addressing the legitimate concern about quality of life.

Outcome Analysis

Immediate through Long-term Outcomes:

- Jennifer maintained medication compliance throughout supervision
- She resumed painting within one week of session; reported it was "different but not impossible"
- She advocated with prescriber and received medication adjustment that reduced flatness
- She completed community art class and reported feeling "more like herself"
- At 12-month follow-up, she reported viewing medication as "tool rather than prison"
- At 24-month follow-up, she had returned to part-time work in different field

Case Study 13: Domestic Violence Perpetrator Accountability

Case Background

Supervisee: Derek Morrison, 38-year-old white male

Offense: Felony domestic assault (strangulation of intimate partner)

Sentence: 4 years probation, batterer intervention program, no contact with victim

Risk Level: High (LSI-R score: 29)

History: Two prior domestic violence incidents with previous partners, both resulted in charges being dropped when victims recanted. This offense involved strangulation during an argument about finances. Victim sustained visible injuries and required emergency room treatment. Derek completed jail time and is now in community supervision with mandatory batterer intervention program enrollment.

Criminogenic Needs: Intimate partner violence pattern, power and control beliefs, minimization, alcohol use, anger management

Context: Fifth month of supervision. Derek has been compliant but minimizes his behavior and frequently positions himself as the "real victim" in his relationship. Officer James Okafor must balance accountability with engagement.

Session Script

OFFICER OKAFOR: Derek, how's the batterer intervention program going?

DEREK: [Shrugs] I go. I sit through it. Some of it applies to me, I guess. A lot of the guys in there are way worse than me.

OFFICER OKAFOR: You see yourself as different from the other participants.

[MI Skill: Simple reflection without agreeing or challenging]

DEREK: I am different. Some of those guys beat their wives regularly. I lost my temper one time.

OFFICER OKAFOR: One incident that was different from an ongoing pattern.

[MI Skill: Reflection of his framing]

DEREK: Exactly. Amanda and I fought all the time. It was mutual. But that night, things got out of hand. I reacted.

OFFICER OKAFOR: Help me understand what you mean by "mutual." What did the fighting typically look like?

[MI Skill: Open question seeking specifics]

DEREK: She'd yell, I'd yell. She'd throw things sometimes. Call me names. It wasn't one-sided.

OFFICER OKAFOR: There was verbal conflict and she sometimes threw things.

[MI Skill: Simple reflection]

DEREK: Right. So it wasn't like I was this abuser terrorizing an innocent victim. We both did things.

OFFICER OKAFOR: You want me to understand the context was more complicated than it might appear.

[MI Skill: Reflection of intention]

DEREK: Yes. Thank you.

OFFICER OKAFOR: Derek, I'm going to ask you something directly, and I want you to really think about it before you answer. When you and Amanda fought, when she yelled and called names and threw things, did you ever feel afraid she would seriously hurt you?

[MI Skill: Direct question introducing fear/safety dimension]

DEREK: [Pause] Afraid? No. Annoyed. Frustrated. But not afraid.

OFFICER OKAFOR: Not afraid. What about Amanda? When you yelled, when things escalated, do you think she was afraid?

[MI Skill: Parallel question shifting perspective]

DEREK: [Longer pause] I... I don't know. Maybe. Sometimes.

OFFICER OKAFOR: What made you think maybe sometimes?

[MI Skill: Elaboration question]

DEREK: The way she'd look at me. When I got really mad. She'd get... smaller. Like she was bracing for something.

OFFICER OKAFOR: She'd get smaller. Bracing.

[MI Skill: Reflection emphasizing his observation]

DEREK: Yeah. [Quieter] I used to think she was being dramatic.

OFFICER OKAFOR: Used to think. What do you think now?

[MI Skill: Exploring shift in perspective]

DEREK: [Long pause] Maybe she was actually scared.

OFFICER OKAFOR: That's significant to recognize, Derek. Even though the fighting felt mutual to you, the fear wasn't mutual.

[MI Skill: Affirmation followed by key distinction]

DEREK: [Uncomfortable] I never wanted her to be scared of me. I loved her.

OFFICER OKAFOR: You loved her and you also did things that made her afraid. Both are true.

[MI Skill: Double-sided reflection avoiding either/or]

DEREK: I just... I'd get so angry. She'd say something about money, about how I wasn't providing, and I'd see red. It wasn't thinking. It was just... reaction.

OFFICER OKAFOR: The anger would take over and you'd stop thinking.

[MI Skill: Reflection]

DEREK: Yeah.

OFFICER OKAFOR: Let me ask about the night of the assault specifically. What happened when you put your hands around her throat?

[MI Skill: Direct question about offense behavior]

DEREK: [Shifts in chair] I don't really remember clearly. We were arguing. She said something, I don't even remember what. And then... my hands were there.

OFFICER OKAFOR: You don't remember a decision to do it. It just happened.

[MI Skill: Reflection of his framing]

DEREK: Right.

OFFICER OKAFOR: How long were your hands there?

[MI Skill: Seeking specific detail]

DEREK: I don't know. A few seconds?

OFFICER OKAFOR: The police report says Amanda had petechial hemorrhaging in her eyes. That kind of hemorrhaging typically requires sustained pressure for at least ten to fifteen seconds. What do you make of that?

[MI Skill: Introducing factual information that contradicts minimization]

DEREK: [Pale] I didn't... it didn't feel that long.

OFFICER OKAFOR: It didn't feel that long. But based on her injuries, it was long enough to cut off blood flow to her brain for an extended period. Long enough that she could have died.

[MI Skill: Naming severity without lecturing]

DEREK: [Very quiet] I know.

OFFICER OKAFOR: You know she could have died.

[MI Skill: Simple reflection]

DEREK: They told me. In the batterer program. Strangulation is... one of the biggest predictors of... [can't finish]

OFFICER OKAFOR: Of lethality. The biggest predictor that a domestic violence situation will end in death.

[MI Skill: Completing the statement he couldn't]

DEREK: [Voice breaking] I could have killed her. I could have killed Amanda.

OFFICER OKAFOR: That's a heavy recognition.

[MI Skill: Acknowledging emotional weight]

DEREK: I love her. I would never want to... [trails off]

OFFICER OKAFOR: Derek, I believe you when you say you love her and would never want to kill her. And I also need you to understand that what you did that night was something that kills people. Your hands around her throat for that long. Whether you meant to or not, you were doing something that could have been lethal.

[MI Skill: Both/and statement maintaining accountability]

DEREK: [Crying now] I know. God, I know.

OFFICER OKAFOR: What does that mean for you going forward?

[MI Skill: Open question toward change]

DEREK: I can't ever let that happen again. I can't.

OFFICER OKAFOR: Say more about that.

[MI Skill: Elaboration request]

DEREK: I have to learn how to handle the anger differently. I can't just "react" anymore. Because my reaction almost killed someone.

OFFICER OKAFOR: The cost of uncontrolled anger is too high.

[MI Skill: Reflection]

DEREK: Way too high. [Pause] I've been going through the motions in that program. Thinking I'm better than those guys. But I did what those guys did. I am one of those guys.

OFFICER OKAFOR: That's a significant shift from where we started this conversation.

[MI Skill: Noting change without praising excessively]

DEREK: I came in here thinking I was different because it only happened once. But once was almost enough to kill her. Once is too much.

OFFICER OKAFOR: Once is too much. What does that mean for how you engage with the batterer program?

[MI Skill: Linking insight to behavior change]

DEREK: I need to actually learn something. Not just show up. I need to understand why I did what I did and how to make sure I never do it again.

OFFICER OKAFOR: You're committing to genuine engagement rather than compliance.

[MI Skill: Reflection of commitment]

DEREK: Yes.

OFFICER OKAFOR: And what about if you're ever in another relationship? What needs to be different?

[MI Skill: Open question about future pattern]

DEREK: I can't... I can't let anger drive my actions. I need to recognize when I'm getting to that point and remove myself. Walk away. Cool down. Whatever it takes.

OFFICER OKAFOR: Early intervention with yourself before things escalate.

[MI Skill: Reflection on strategy]

DEREK: Yes. Because by the time my hands were on her throat, it was too late to make a good decision. I have to make the good decision earlier.

OFFICER OKAFOR: That's insight that can save a life. Maybe your own, if you end up in prison. Maybe someone else's.

[MI Skill: Affirmation linking insight to stakes]

DEREK: I don't want to be that person. The person who hurts people he loves. I don't want that to be who I am.

OFFICER OKAFOR: Who do you want to be?

[MI Skill: Open question about identity]

DEREK: Someone safe. Someone a woman can trust. Someone who handles his emotions like an adult instead of... whatever that was.

OFFICER OKAFOR: Someone safe, trustworthy, emotionally mature. That's a very different image than the person who had his hands around Amanda's throat.

[MI Skill: Reflection highlighting gap between current and aspirational self]

DEREK: It is. And I have a lot of work to do to become that person.

OFFICER OKAFOR: Are you willing to do that work?

[MI Skill: Eliciting commitment]

DEREK: I have to be. The alternative is unacceptable.

Reflection

This session demonstrates MI's application to domestic violence perpetrators, a population where balancing engagement and accountability is critical. Officer Okafor did not accept Derek's minimization but also did not argue against it directly. Instead, he asked questions that led Derek to examine his own assumptions.

The key moment came when Officer Okafor asked whether Derek felt afraid during arguments, then asked the parallel question about Amanda. This simple reframe shifted the conversation from "mutual fighting" to asymmetric fear, a crucial distinction in understanding intimate partner violence.

Introducing factual information about the injury severity was done strategically, after rapport had been established and Derek had begun to examine his perspective. The information about petechial hemorrhaging and strangulation lethality created cognitive dissonance that Derek had to resolve.

The session ended with Derek articulating his own commitment to change, driven by recognition of what he almost did rather than external pressure. This self-generated motivation is more likely to produce genuine behavior change than compliance-based engagement.

Outcome Analysis

Immediate through Long-term Outcomes:

- Derek's engagement with batterer intervention program shifted; facilitator noted increased participation
- He completed program with positive evaluation
- He began individual therapy to address anger patterns and family-of-origin issues
- At 18-month follow-up, he had been in new relationship for 6 months with no incidents
- He reported using early intervention strategies regularly
- He completed probation successfully; new partner (aware of history) reported no concerning behavior

Case Study 14: Sex Offense Supervision and Denial

Case Background

Supervisee: Robert Henley, 54-year-old white male

Offense: Felony possession of child sexual abuse material (CSAM)

Sentence: 6 years probation, sex offense treatment, registration requirements, computer monitoring

Risk Level: Moderate (Static-99R score: 3)

History: No prior criminal history. Robert worked as an accountant for 30 years. He was detected through federal investigation of file-sharing networks. He has been compliant with supervision conditions but maintains he "accidentally" downloaded the material and didn't know what it was. Treatment providers report he is engaging minimally due to denial.

Criminogenic Needs: Sexual interest in minors (denied), cognitive distortions, social isolation, denial/minimization

Context: Eighth month of supervision. Treatment providers have expressed concern that Robert's denial is preventing meaningful progress. Officer Linda Vasquez must address denial while maintaining engagement.

Session Script

OFFICER VASQUEZ: Robert, I received the latest report from your treatment group. Dr. Jamison notes that you're attending regularly but not participating actively in discussions. She's concerned about the denial.

ROBERT: [Stiffens] I've explained this multiple times. I don't belong in that group. Those men are... they're pedophiles. I'm not like them.

OFFICER VASQUEZ: You see yourself as fundamentally different from the other group members.

[MI Skill: Simple reflection without arguing]

ROBERT: I am different. I made a mistake with file sharing. I downloaded files without knowing what they were. That's not the same as being attracted to children.

OFFICER VASQUEZ: An accident that got caught up in a larger investigation.

[MI Skill: Reflection of his narrative]

ROBERT: Exactly. I've tried to explain this, but no one believes me.

OFFICER VASQUEZ: That must be frustrating, feeling like your explanation isn't being heard.

[MI Skill: Reflection on emotional experience]

ROBERT: It is. Thirty years of being a law-abiding citizen, and now I'm treated like a predator.

OFFICER VASQUEZ: Robert, I want to have an honest conversation with you, if you're open to it. Not about whether you're guilty or innocent. The court has already decided that. But about what happens from here.

[MI Skill: Reframing conversation away from guilt argument]

ROBERT: What do you mean?

OFFICER VASQUEZ: I mean that regardless of how the material came to be on your computer, you're on probation for six years. You're required to complete sex offense treatment. And right now, the treatment isn't working because you're not engaging with it. So the question isn't whether you're guilty. The question is how you're going to get through the next five years.

[MI Skill: Focusing on practical reality]

ROBERT: I just have to wait it out. Attend the sessions. Do my time.

OFFICER VASQUEZ: Is that realistic? Dr. Jamison has already indicated she may not be able to certify completion if you don't engage. Without completion, you're looking at potential violation. Six years of minimal engagement, or six years that lead to treatment failure and revocation. Those are the options as I see them.

[MI Skill: Presenting honest assessment of consequences]

ROBERT: [Pale] She can do that? Not certify me?

OFFICER VASQUEZ: If you don't meet treatment goals, yes. Treatment completion isn't just attendance. It's demonstrating progress.

ROBERT: But how can I demonstrate progress on something I didn't do?

OFFICER VASQUEZ: That's the bind you're in. And I'm not here to tell you what to believe about yourself. But I am here to help you figure out how to navigate this situation.

[MI Skill: Acknowledging dilemma without resolving it]

ROBERT: [Long silence]

OFFICER VASQUEZ: Robert, let me ask you something. Setting aside how the files got there, what was your reaction when you first saw the material?

[MI Skill: Open question about behavior rather than motive]

ROBERT: [Very long pause] I... I was disturbed.

OFFICER VASQUEZ: Disturbed. Say more about that.

[MI Skill: Elaboration request]

ROBERT: It was... children. In situations no child should be in. I felt sick.

OFFICER VASQUEZ: You felt sick seeing it.

[MI Skill: Simple reflection]

ROBERT: Yes.

OFFICER VASQUEZ: And then what did you do?

[MI Skill: Continuing behavioral inquiry]

ROBERT: [Very quiet] I should have deleted it immediately.

OFFICER VASQUEZ: But you didn't.

[MI Skill: Simple statement of fact]

ROBERT: [Almost inaudible] No.

OFFICER VASQUEZ: What happened instead?

[MI Skill: Continued inquiry]

ROBERT: [Long pause] I don't know. I told myself I'd delete it later. I closed the files. I didn't look at them again.

OFFICER VASQUEZ: You closed them but didn't delete them.

[MI Skill: Reflection without judgment]

ROBERT: [Silence]

OFFICER VASQUEZ: Robert, I'm not asking you to confess to something you don't believe you did. But I am asking you to sit with something uncomfortable. You saw material that made you sick, and you didn't delete it. Whatever the explanation for that, there's something to understand there.

[MI Skill: Inviting reflection on behavior without demanding admission]

ROBERT: [Very quiet] I don't know why I didn't delete it.

OFFICER VASQUEZ: That's actually an honest answer. "I don't know why" is different from "It was an accident I knew nothing about."

[MI Skill: Noting shift toward honesty]

ROBERT: [Silence]

OFFICER VASQUEZ: The treatment program isn't asking you to label yourself a pedophile. It's asking you to understand your behavior. And there's behavior here you've just told me you don't understand yourself.

[MI Skill: Reframing treatment purpose]

ROBERT: I've spent my whole life being a good person. Following rules. Doing the right thing. I don't understand how I ended up here.

OFFICER VASQUEZ: That confusion is real. You don't recognize the person who didn't delete those files.

[MI Skill: Reflection on identity confusion]

ROBERT: [Tears forming] I don't. I really don't.

OFFICER VASQUEZ: What would it mean to try to understand that person? Not to condemn yourself, but to understand?

[MI Skill: Open question about self-examination]

ROBERT: I don't know if I can.

OFFICER VASQUEZ: What makes it so hard?

[MI Skill: Exploring barrier]

ROBERT: Because if I look at why... if I really look... I might find something I don't want to see.

OFFICER VASQUEZ: Something about yourself you'd rather not know.

[MI Skill: Reflection on fear]

ROBERT: [Nods, crying]

OFFICER VASQUEZ: Robert, that fear is understandable. And it's also keeping you stuck. The treatment is offering a space to explore these questions with support, not alone. But you have to be willing to walk through that door.

[MI Skill: Acknowledging fear while presenting option]

ROBERT: What if I find out I'm... one of them?

OFFICER VASQUEZ: What if you find out you're someone who needs to understand something about himself? That's not the same as being a monster. The men in your group are working on understanding themselves too. That's why they're there.

[MI Skill: Normalizing within group context]

ROBERT: I've spent eight months convinced I was different from them.

OFFICER VASQUEZ: And now?

[MI Skill: Open question about shift]

ROBERT: Now I'm not sure about anything.

OFFICER VASQUEZ: That uncertainty might actually be the beginning of something. Being sure you were different kept you from looking at your own behavior. Not being sure opens a door.

[MI Skill: Reframing uncertainty as opportunity]

ROBERT: I don't know if I'm ready.

OFFICER VASQUEZ: You don't have to be ready for everything. You just have to be ready for the next step. What would one small step toward engagement look like?

[MI Skill: Scaling down to manageable commitment]

ROBERT: [Thinks] Maybe... maybe talking in group. About the confusion. About not understanding my own behavior.

OFFICER VASQUEZ: Sharing the honest confusion instead of maintaining a position of certainty.

[MI Skill: Reflection on shift in group participation]

ROBERT: Yes. I could do that.

OFFICER VASQUEZ: That would be a significant change from where you've been.

[MI Skill: Affirmation without over-praising]

ROBERT: I know.

Reflection

This session demonstrates MI's application to the exceptionally challenging population of sex offense denial cases. Officer Vasquez did not attempt to break down Robert's denial through confrontation, which typically produces entrenchment. Instead, she redirected the conversation away from the guilt question toward practical consequences and behavioral exploration.

The pivotal intervention was asking about Robert's reaction when he first saw the material and what he did next. This behavioral inquiry avoided the contested territory of intent while revealing an acknowledgment he had not previously made: he saw the material, felt sick, and didn't delete it. This contradiction in his own account created cognitive dissonance.

Officer Vasquez's statement "I don't know why is different from it was an accident I knew nothing about" highlighted the shift without labeling it as confession. This gentle observation allowed Robert to recognize his own movement without feeling trapped.

The session ended with a modest commitment to share his confusion in group rather than maintain his defensive position. This incremental engagement creates possibility for treatment progress without requiring full admission.

Outcome Analysis

Immediate through Long-term Outcomes:

- Robert began participating actively in treatment group
- His therapist noted shift from "complete denial" to "partial acknowledgment"
- He disclosed early experiences of accessing adult pornography that "escalated" over time
- He acknowledged sexual arousal to CSAM material by month 14
- He completed treatment successfully at month 36
- He remained compliant through full probation term
- Polygraph examinations supported no new offenses

Case Study 15: Juvenile Justice and Adolescent Engagement

Case Background

Supervisee: Jaylen Carter, 16-year-old African American male

Offense: Aggravated assault (school fight resulting in serious injury)

Sentence: 18 months juvenile probation, anger management, community service

Risk Level: Moderate (SAVRY score: Moderate)

History: Two prior school disciplinary referrals for fighting. No prior court involvement. Jaylen comes from a single-parent household; mother works two jobs. The assault occurred after an ongoing conflict with another student involving social media insults about Jaylen's deceased father.

Criminogenic Needs: Anger management, peer conflict, emotional regulation, limited adult supervision, grief/trauma (father's death)

Context: Third month of supervision. Jaylen has been minimally communicative, providing one-word answers and viewing probation as punishment rather than support. Officer Tyrone Jackson, who specifically works with juvenile caseloads, attempts to build engagement.

Session Script

OFFICER JACKSON: What's up, Jaylen? How's it going?

JAYLEN: [Shrugs] Fine.

OFFICER JACKSON: School?

JAYLEN: Fine.

OFFICER JACKSON: Home?

JAYLEN: Fine.

OFFICER JACKSON: [Pauses, then leans back] Jaylen, we've done this three times now. I ask questions, you say fine, we both count down the minutes until you can leave. Is that really how you want to spend the next fifteen months?

[MI Skill: Meta-communication about pattern]

JAYLEN: [Looks up, slightly surprised] I don't want to be here at all.

OFFICER JACKSON: Fair enough. What would you be doing if you weren't here?

[MI Skill: Respecting honesty; redirecting to interests]

JAYLEN: I don't know. Hanging out. Playing 2K. Whatever.

OFFICER JACKSON: You play 2K? What's your team?

[MI Skill: Finding connection point]

JAYLEN: [Slight interest] Lakers. Always been Lakers.

OFFICER JACKSON: Since when?

JAYLEN: Since I was little. My dad was from LA originally. He got me into them.

OFFICER JACKSON: Your dad was a Lakers fan.

[MI Skill: Simple reflection opening door to meaningful topic]

JAYLEN: [Guard coming back up] Yeah.

OFFICER JACKSON: I read in your file that he passed away. I'm sorry about that.

JAYLEN: [Shrugs] It was two years ago.

OFFICER JACKSON: Two years isn't that long.

[MI Skill: Normalizing ongoing grief]

JAYLEN: Long enough that everyone thinks I should be over it.

OFFICER JACKSON: People think there's an expiration date on missing your dad.

[MI Skill: Reflection capturing frustration]

JAYLEN: They do. My mom, my teachers. "Jaylen, you need to move on." How am I supposed to move on?

OFFICER JACKSON: That's a real question. How are you supposed to move on from losing your father when you were fourteen?

[MI Skill: Validating question as legitimate]

JAYLEN: I don't know. I don't know how to do it.

OFFICER JACKSON: It's not something anyone teaches you.

[MI Skill: Acknowledging lack of guidance]

JAYLEN: Nobody taught me nothing. Just "be strong, man up, don't cry." That's all I hear.

OFFICER JACKSON: You've been told to push it down and keep going.

[MI Skill: Reflection on pressure to suppress]

JAYLEN: Yeah. [Pause] And I try. I do. But sometimes...

OFFICER JACKSON: Sometimes what?

[MI Skill: Invitation to continue]

JAYLEN: Sometimes I'm just... angry. All the time. At everything.

OFFICER JACKSON: The anger is always there.

[MI Skill: Simple reflection]

JAYLEN: Like right under the surface. And it doesn't take much to set it off.

OFFICER JACKSON: What set it off with Marcus? The kid from the fight?

[MI Skill: Connecting to index offense]

JAYLEN: [Jaw tightens] He said some stuff. Online. About my dad.

OFFICER JACKSON: What kind of stuff?

JAYLEN: Said my dad was a deadbeat. Said that's why he died. Because he was a crackhead who didn't care about his family.

OFFICER JACKSON: He attacked your father's memory and character.

[MI Skill: Reflection naming what was attacked]

JAYLEN: My dad wasn't a crackhead. He was sick. He had heart problems. He worked two jobs to take care of us until he couldn't work anymore.

OFFICER JACKSON: Your father was a hardworking man who got sick, and Marcus made him sound like something he wasn't.

[MI Skill: Reflection honoring truth versus insult]

JAYLEN: Yeah. And everyone saw it. He posted it where everyone could see. Laughing emojis and everything.

OFFICER JACKSON: Public humiliation of someone you love who isn't here to defend himself.

[MI Skill: Reflection on public nature and helplessness]

JAYLEN: [Eyes wet but trying not to show it] He can't defend himself. He's gone. So I had to.

OFFICER JACKSON: You felt like you were the only one who could defend your father's honor.

[MI Skill: Reflection on role he took on]

JAYLEN: Yeah. Who else was going to do it?

OFFICER JACKSON: So when you hit Marcus, you weren't just hitting some kid who annoyed you. You were defending your dad.

[MI Skill: Reframing context of violence]

JAYLEN: [Nods]

OFFICER JACKSON: That's not what the police report shows. It just shows aggravated assault. It doesn't show what was underneath.

[MI Skill: Acknowledging gap between official record and human truth]

JAYLEN: Nobody cares what was underneath. They just see another Black kid fighting.

OFFICER JACKSON: You feel like you got labeled without anyone trying to understand.

[MI Skill: Reflection on racial dimension]

JAYLEN: That's exactly what happened.

OFFICER JACKSON: Jaylen, I want to be straight with you. What Marcus said was vile. Attacking your dead father like that, publicly humiliating you, that's cruel. And I understand why you reacted the way you did. It makes sense.

[MI Skill: Validating emotional logic]

JAYLEN: [Looks at officer with surprise] You're the first adult who's said that.

OFFICER JACKSON: I can understand something and still have to tell you it created problems. Marcus almost lost an eye. You almost caught an adult felony. And none of what you did changed what Marcus said or what people think about your dad.

[MI Skill: Both validating and introducing consequences]

JAYLEN: [Quietly] I know. I know it didn't help anything.

OFFICER JACKSON: You did something that made complete emotional sense in the moment, and it backfired. Now you're on probation, you've got a record, and Marcus is probably telling people you're dangerous.

[MI Skill: Spelling out counterproductive results]

JAYLEN: He is. People are scared of me now.

OFFICER JACKSON: Is that how you want people to see you? Dangerous?

[MI Skill: Open question about identity]

JAYLEN: No. [Pause] I'm not dangerous. I just... I lost it.

OFFICER JACKSON: You lost it because something mattered to you so much that you couldn't keep it together.

[MI Skill: Reflection connecting intensity to care]

JAYLEN: My dad matters. More than anything.

OFFICER JACKSON: He does. And that means you need ways to protect his memory and honor him that don't land you in places like this or worse.

[MI Skill: Linking value to need for different strategies]

JAYLEN: [Quiet] I don't know how else.

OFFICER JACKSON: What would your dad want you to do?

[MI Skill: Invoking father's perspective]

JAYLEN: [Long pause, tears finally falling] He'd want me to be smart. He'd want me to graduate, go to college, make something of myself.

OFFICER JACKSON: How does beating up Marcus fit with making something of yourself?

[MI Skill: Connecting behavior to stated value]

JAYLEN: It doesn't. It was stupid.

OFFICER JACKSON: It was understandable and it was counterproductive.

[MI Skill: Both/and framing]

JAYLEN: Yeah.

OFFICER JACKSON: Jaylen, you're sixteen. You've got your whole life ahead of you. The question is whether you're going to let that anger drive your choices, or whether you're going to find another way to carry the pain.

[MI Skill: Presenting choice]

JAYLEN: I don't know how to carry it different.

OFFICER JACKSON: That's what we can work on. Not because the court says so, but because your dad would want you to have a future.

[MI Skill: Reframing motivation from compliance to values]

JAYLEN: [Nods] Okay.

OFFICER JACKSON: Okay meaning you're willing to actually talk to me? Not just "fine, fine, fine"?

[MI Skill: Checking for genuine commitment]

JAYLEN: [Small smile] Yeah. I'll talk.

Reflection

This session demonstrates MI's application to juvenile populations, where engagement requires meeting youth where they are and respecting their developmental context. Officer Jackson recognized that standard questioning was producing minimal engagement and directly named the pattern, which paradoxically created connection by being honest.

The breakthrough came through genuine curiosity about Jaylen's interests, which led organically to discussion of his father. Rather than treating the father's death as background information in a file, Officer Jackson explored its ongoing significance and connected it to the underlying emotional reality of the offense.

The validation of Jaylen's emotional logic was critical. By saying "What Marcus said was vile" and "I understand why you reacted," Officer Jackson communicated that he saw Jaylen as a full human being, not just an offender. This did not mean excusing the violence; the consequences and counterproductive nature were named clearly. But validation preceded accountability.

Asking "What would your dad want you to do?" introduced Jaylen's own values as the standard for behavior, far more powerful than probation requirements.

Outcome Analysis

Immediate through Long-term Outcomes:

- Jaylen's engagement transformed; officer noted "like talking to a different kid"
- He began grief counseling for father's death
- He completed anger management program with positive feedback
- He used writing and journaling to process feelings (developed in counseling)
- He graduated high school on time
- He completed probation early (12 months of 18)
- At follow-up, he was enrolled in community college and had no new incidents

Chapter 19: Supervision Cycle Cases

Case Study 16: Post-Violation Conversation

Case Background

Supervisee: Marcus Ellsworth, 34-year-old African American male (from Case Study 1)

Offense: Felony possession with intent to distribute (cocaine)

Sentence: 3 years probation

Supervision Context: Marcus, whose initial intake was covered in Case Study 1, has been doing well for six weeks. He enrolled in CBT for substance use, attended all appointments, and reconnected with his daughter Keisha. However, his most recent drug screen came back positive for cocaine.

Context: Post-positive drug screen meeting. Officer Denise Whitfield must address the violation while maintaining the relationship and therapeutic momentum established earlier.

Session Script

[Marcus enters looking defeated, won't make eye contact]

MARCUS: Just do what you got to do.

OFFICER WHITFIELD: What do you mean?

MARCUS: Lock me up. Violate me. Whatever. I messed up. I knew I would. It was only a matter of time.

OFFICER WHITFIELD: You're expecting me to send you back to prison.

[MI Skill: Reflection without confirming or denying]

MARCUS: Isn't that what happens? Dirty UA, violation, back inside. That's how it works.

OFFICER WHITFIELD: That's how it's worked before. Let me ask you something first. What happened?

[MI Skill: Distinguishing past from present; seeking understanding]

MARCUS: What difference does it make?

OFFICER WHITFIELD: It makes a difference to me. We've been building something here. Six weeks of you showing up, doing the work, connecting with Keisha. That matters. I want to understand what happened before we decide what comes next.

[MI Skill: Affirmation of progress; collaborative framing]

MARCUS: [Looks up, surprised] You're not just going to violate me?

OFFICER WHITFIELD: I'm not making any decisions until I understand what happened.

MARCUS: [Long pause] I saw my ex. Keisha's mom. She brought Keisha to meet me at the park. And after Keisha went off to play, Denise started in on me. Telling me I'm never going to change. Telling me she's going to file for full custody because she doesn't trust me. Telling me Keisha asks about me and she doesn't know what to say.

OFFICER WHITFIELD: Denise attacked your progress and threatened your relationship with Keisha.

[MI Skill: Reflection capturing emotional impact]

MARCUS: Right in front of her, too. Well, not right in front. But close enough. And I just... I lost it. Not at her. I kept my cool at the park. But afterward...

OFFICER WHITFIELD: You held it together in the moment, and then what?

[MI Skill: Noting coping, then exploring aftermath]

MARCUS: I went home and I couldn't stop thinking about it. About losing Keisha. About Denise being right, that I'm never going to change. About everything I've tried to do not mattering because one person can just take it all away.

OFFICER WHITFIELD: The thoughts were spiraling.

[MI Skill: Simple reflection]

MARCUS: Yeah. And I knew I should call my sponsor. I knew I should go to a meeting. I knew all the right things to do. But I was so deep in my head, and I just thought, "What's the point? She's right. I'm never going to change."

OFFICER WHITFIELD: In that moment, you believed Denise's version of you more than your own experience of the past six weeks.

[MI Skill: Complex reflection on cognitive distortion]

MARCUS: [Tears forming] Yeah. I forgot everything. Everything I'd been working on. Everything I felt when I was with Keisha. All I could hear was Denise saying I'm worthless.

OFFICER WHITFIELD: Marcus, I want you to hear something. Six weeks ago, in this office, you told me your daughter matters more than anything. You told me you want to be the father she deserves. You enrolled in treatment. You showed up every single time. You started reconnecting with Keisha in real ways. That's not nothing. That's not who you were before.

[MI Skill: Affirmation reminding of progress and values]

MARCUS: But I used anyway.

OFFICER WHITFIELD: Yes, you did. And I'm not going to pretend that didn't happen. But I'm also not going to pretend the six weeks didn't happen either. Both are true.

[MI Skill: Both/and framing]

MARCUS: So what happens now?

OFFICER WHITFIELD: That depends on a few things. Let me ask you: what did you learn from this?

[MI Skill: Open question inviting reflection]

MARCUS: [Thinks] That I can't handle Denise by myself. That when she gets in my head, I need to get her out fast.

OFFICER WHITFIELD: Being around Denise without support is a high-risk situation for you.

[MI Skill: Reflection naming risk factor]

MARCUS: Yeah. I knew she was a trigger, but I didn't know how bad. Until it was too late.

OFFICER WHITFIELD: What would you do differently if you could go back?

[MI Skill: Exploring alternative response]

MARCUS: Call somebody. My sponsor. My CBT counselor. You. Anybody. Before I had time to spiral.

OFFICER WHITFIELD: Interrupt the spiral before it gets too deep.

[MI Skill: Simple reflection]

MARCUS: Yeah. Because once I'm in it, I can't think straight.

OFFICER WHITFIELD: What would it take to make that call next time?

[MI Skill: Planning question]

MARCUS: Recognizing I'm in it. That's the hard part. I don't realize how bad it is until afterward.

OFFICER WHITFIELD: So we need an early warning system. What were the first signs that you were spiraling after the park?

[MI Skill: Detailed exploration of relapse chain]

MARCUS: [Thinks] My hands were shaking when I got in the car. And I was driving fast, like I just needed to get somewhere. And I kept replaying what she said. Over and over.

OFFICER WHITFIELD: Shaking hands, driving fast, mental replay. Those are warning signs that showed up before you made the decision to use.

[MI Skill: Identifying early warning signs]

MARCUS: Yeah. If I'd recognized those...

OFFICER WHITFIELD: Then what?

MARCUS: Then I could have done something different. Before it got to the point where using seemed like the only option.

OFFICER WHITFIELD: Marcus, here's what I'm going to do. I'm not going to violate you for this positive screen.

MARCUS: [Shock] What?

OFFICER WHITFIELD: I'm going to document it as an occasion for increased services rather than a violation. You'll have twice-weekly drug testing for the next two months. You'll add an extra session per week with your CBT counselor. And we're going to develop a detailed safety plan for interactions with Denise.

MARCUS: Why? Why aren't you sending me back?

OFFICER WHITFIELD: Because sending you back doesn't solve anything. You've got six weeks of genuine progress. You've got insight into what happened. You've got a daughter who needs her father. The goal isn't punishment. The goal is helping you succeed. And right now, increased support is more likely to help you succeed than incarceration.

MARCUS: [Crying openly now] Nobody's ever given me a second chance like this.

OFFICER WHITFIELD: Then let's make it count. What's your commitment?

[MI Skill: Eliciting commitment]

MARCUS: No more using. Period. And calling someone the moment I feel myself starting to spiral.

OFFICER WHITFIELD: Who's on your call list?

MARCUS: My sponsor Curtis. My counselor Dr. Reyes. You. My cousin Terrell, he's been clean for five years.

OFFICER WHITFIELD: Four people. What's the rule?

MARCUS: I call someone before I do anything else.

OFFICER WHITFIELD: Before you do anything else. Write that down somewhere you'll see it.

MARCUS: I will. [Pause] Thank you. I don't have words for this.

OFFICER WHITFIELD: The words I want are the ones you live by. Let's get to work.

Reflection

This session demonstrates MI's application to post-violation conversations, where the temptation is to respond punitively. Officer Whitfield chose to understand before acting, which revealed that the relapse occurred in the context of significant emotional threat (custody implications) and that Marcus had insight into what went wrong.

The decision not to violate was not based on leniency but on strategic assessment: Marcus had genuine progress, demonstrated insight, and a clear pathway to increased support. Incarceration would have interrupted treatment, separated him from Keisha, and likely reinforced the belief that he was unable to change.

The session established concrete increased structure (more testing, more counseling, safety plan) while maintaining the therapeutic relationship. The emotional impact of receiving an unexpected second chance created powerful motivation for Marcus to make it count.

Outcome Analysis

Subsequent Outcomes:

- Marcus maintained negative drug screens for remainder of probation
- He developed detailed safety plan for co-parenting contact
- His custody situation stabilized; maintained consistent visitation
- He became peer support in his CBT group
- He completed probation successfully
- At 2-year follow-up, he had no new charges and maintained employment

Case Study 17: Case Planning Session

Case Background

Supervisee: Michelle Torres, 27-year-old Latina female

Offense: Felony theft (employee theft over extended period)

Sentence: 3 years probation, restitution of $15,000

Risk Level: Low-Moderate (LSI-R score: 14)

History: No prior criminal history. Michelle worked as assistant manager at a retail store and stole merchandise over 18 months, totaling approximately $15,000 in value. She was caught on surveillance and confessed fully. She has been compliant with supervision but lacks clear goals beyond "getting through probation."

Context: First formal case planning session, third month of supervision. Officer Sandra Kim wants to develop a meaningful case plan that goes beyond compliance checkboxes.

Session Script

OFFICER KIM: Michelle, today I'd like us to work together on your case plan. This is the document that guides what we focus on during your supervision. I want it to reflect your goals, not just what the court ordered.

[MI Skill: Collaborative framing]

MICHELLE: Okay. I guess my goal is to just get through this and put it behind me.

OFFICER KIM: Getting through and moving on. That's understandable. What would "putting it behind you" look like?

[MI Skill: Elaboration question]

MICHELLE: I don't know. Just... not having this hanging over me anymore. Being able to apply for jobs without having to check the felony box.

OFFICER KIM: The conviction creates obstacles you want to get past.

[MI Skill: Reflection]

MICHELLE: It does. I had a good job before this. Now I can't even get interviews.

OFFICER KIM: The job search has been discouraging.

[MI Skill: Simple reflection]

MICHELLE: Very. I've applied to maybe fifty places. Three callbacks. No offers.

OFFICER KIM: Fifty applications, three callbacks. That's a lot of rejection.

[MI Skill: Reflection acknowledging effort and disappointment]

MICHELLE: It makes me wonder if I'll ever work again. In retail, everyone does background checks now. And the minute they see theft conviction, forget it.

OFFICER KIM: Retail feels closed off because of the nature of your offense.

[MI Skill: Reflection on specific barrier]

MICHELLE: It does. And that's all I know. I've been in retail since I was sixteen.

OFFICER KIM: Let me ask you something. Before all this happened, when you thought about your future, what did you see?

[MI Skill: Open question exploring pre-offense aspirations]

MICHELLE: [Thinks] I don't know. I guess I figured I'd keep moving up in retail management. Maybe have my own store someday.

OFFICER KIM: Your own store. Like franchise ownership?

[MI Skill: Elaboration]

MICHELLE: Maybe. Or just being a store manager at a big company. Having people work for me instead of always working for someone else.

OFFICER KIM: Leadership and autonomy were important to you.

[MI Skill: Reflection on values]

MICHELLE: Yeah. I was good at it. My numbers were always strong. Employees liked working with me.

OFFICER KIM: Those are real skills: driving results and managing people well. What made you good at it?

[MI Skill: Affirmation and elaboration question]

MICHELLE: I actually cared about the people on my team. I didn't just boss them around. I helped them solve problems, advocated for them with upper management. And I'm organized. I can keep track of a million things at once.

OFFICER KIM: Genuine investment in your team, problem-solving, advocacy, organizational skills. That's a strong skill set. It's not limited to retail.

[MI Skill: Reflecting skills and introducing transferability]

MICHELLE: [Pause] I never thought about it outside of retail. That's just where I ended up.

OFFICER KIM: What if you thought about it differently? What other fields value leadership, organization, and caring about people?

[MI Skill: Open question expanding possibilities]

MICHELLE: I don't know. Healthcare? But you need degrees for that.

OFFICER KIM: Some healthcare roles, yes. What about others?

MICHELLE: [Thinks] Social services maybe? My aunt works for a nonprofit and she's always saying they need organized people.

OFFICER KIM: Nonprofit work. That's an interesting direction. How does a theft conviction play in that world?

[MI Skill: Reality-testing without dismissing]

MICHELLE: I don't know. Maybe better than retail? They're probably not worried I'm going to steal their donations.

OFFICER KIM: The nature of the offense might matter less in a different context.

[MI Skill: Reflection affirming logic]

MICHELLE: Maybe. But I don't have any experience in nonprofits.

OFFICER KIM: Not directly. But you have transferable skills. And there are ways to get experience while building your record of changed behavior.

[MI Skill: Introducing possibilities]

MICHELLE: Like volunteering?

OFFICER KIM: That's one option. It's also something that could look good when you eventually apply for expungement. Community contribution, giving back.

[MI Skill: Connecting to long-term benefit]

MICHELLE: I hadn't thought about expungement.

OFFICER KIM: It's years away, but it's something to work toward. The court will look at what you did during supervision. If you just survived it, that's one thing. If you used it to genuinely turn things around, that's another.

[MI Skill: Framing supervision as opportunity]

MICHELLE: So what would turning things around look like?

OFFICER KIM: That's what I want us to figure out together. Based on what you've said, here's what I'm hearing as potential goals: finding stable employment, preferably in a field where your skills transfer and your conviction is less of a barrier. Building a track record of community contribution. Developing financial stability to manage the restitution. And positioning yourself for eventual expungement. How does that sound as a framework?

[MI Skill: Summary reflecting back goals with additions]

MICHELLE: It sounds... actually purposeful. Not just waiting for time to pass.

OFFICER KIM: What if this supervision period became the foundation for a different life direction rather than just something to get through?

[MI Skill: Reframing supervision as opportunity]

MICHELLE: I like that. I've been so focused on what I lost that I haven't thought about what I could build.

OFFICER KIM: What's one step you could take in the next month toward that building?

[MI Skill: Moving toward action]

MICHELLE: I could talk to my aunt about her nonprofit. Maybe volunteer there to start.

OFFICER KIM: That would address multiple goals at once: experience, community contribution, networking. What else?

MICHELLE: I could stop applying just to retail jobs. Maybe look at admin positions, office management. My skills should work there too.

OFFICER KIM: Expanding your job search based on skills rather than industry.

[MI Skill: Reflection]

MICHELLE: Yeah. And maybe... I could take a class? There's a project management certificate at the community college. That might help me stand out.

OFFICER KIM: Professional development that's relevant to multiple career paths. Michelle, you just developed a substantial case plan in the past few minutes. How does it feel?

[MI Skill: Process observation]

MICHELLE: [Slight smile] Like maybe there's actually a way forward. Not just treading water.

OFFICER KIM: Let me write this up as our formal case plan. Goals: stable employment in a field with transferable skills, community contribution through volunteering, financial stability including restitution management, and professional development through coursework. Action steps: contact aunt about volunteer opportunities, expand job search beyond retail, and research project management certificate. Does that capture it?

[MI Skill: Summary and documentation]

MICHELLE: It does. It actually does.

Reflection

This session demonstrates MI's application to case planning, transforming a potentially routine bureaucratic process into meaningful goal exploration. Officer Kim began by acknowledging Michelle's stated goal of "getting through" but explored what that actually meant, leading to deeper aspirations.

The critical shift came when Officer Kim reflected Michelle's skills as transferable rather than industry-specific. This reframe opened possibilities Michelle had not considered, moving her from hopelessness about retail barriers to curiosity about alternative paths.

The case plan that emerged was generated by Michelle, not imposed by the officer. Volunteering, expanding job search, and pursuing education were all her ideas, making them intrinsically motivated goals rather than compliance requirements.

Outcome Analysis

Intermediate through Long-term Outcomes:

- Michelle began volunteering at aunt's nonprofit within two weeks
- She obtained admin position at healthcare company at month 5
- She completed project management certificate at month 12
- She was promoted to office manager at month 18
- Her restitution was paid in full at month 30 (ahead of schedule)
- She applied for expungement immediately upon eligibility

Case Study 18: Routine Office Visit with Stalled Progress

Case Background

Supervisee: Thomas Brennan, 42-year-old white male

Offense: Felony DUI (third offense)

Sentence: 4 years probation, ignition interlock device, substance abuse treatment

Risk Level: Moderate (LSI-R score: 21)

History: Two prior DUI convictions. Thomas completed residential treatment at month 3 and has been in outpatient since. He attends sessions and tests negative, but treatment providers describe him as "going through the motions." Officer David Reyes has noticed similar stagnation in their interactions.

Context: Month 10 routine office visit. Thomas arrives, completes the standard check-in, and seems ready to leave. Officer Reyes decides to address the stagnation.

Session Script

OFFICER REYES: Thomas, before you go, I want to check in with you about something. We've been doing this for almost a year now. Everything is technically fine. You're compliant, testing clean, attending treatment. But I'm wondering how you're actually doing.

[MI Skill: Moving beyond compliance to connection]

THOMAS: I'm fine. Why?

OFFICER REYES: "Fine" is what you always say. I'm curious if there's more underneath.

[MI Skill: Expressing curiosity about authentic experience]

THOMAS: What do you want me to say? I'm doing what I'm supposed to do.

OFFICER REYES: You're doing what you're supposed to do. And is that all you want from this experience? Just doing what you're supposed to?

[MI Skill: Open question challenging minimal engagement]

THOMAS: [Pause] What else is there?

OFFICER REYES: That's a genuine question. For some people, probation is just something to survive. For others, it becomes an opportunity to make real changes. Which is it for you?

[MI Skill: Presenting options]

THOMAS: [Sighs] Honestly? I don't know anymore. When I first got out of treatment, I was motivated. I was going to do things differently. But now... it all just feels like routine. Go to meetings, talk to the counselor, pee in a cup, come here. Repeat.

OFFICER REYES: The initial motivation faded and it's become mechanical.

[MI Skill: Reflection]

THOMAS: Yeah. And I don't even know if I'm staying sober because I want to or because I don't have a choice. The interlock is on my car. I get tested all the time. I couldn't drink even if I wanted to.

OFFICER REYES: The external controls are doing the work, and you're not sure what's inside.

[MI Skill: Complex reflection on extrinsic vs. intrinsic motivation]

THOMAS: Exactly. What happens when the interlock comes off? When I'm done with probation? Will I go right back to drinking?

OFFICER REYES: That's an important question you're asking yourself. What do you think?

[MI Skill: Exploring rather than reassuring]

THOMAS: I don't know. Sometimes I think I've genuinely changed. Other times I think I'm just white-knuckling it because I have no other option.

OFFICER REYES: Two different stories about what's happening inside you.

[MI Skill: Reflection on internal ambiguity]

THOMAS: Yeah.

OFFICER REYES: What would help you know which one is true?

[MI Skill: Open question toward self-assessment]

THOMAS: [Thinks] I don't know. Maybe... if I actually chose it? Instead of just having it chosen for me?

OFFICER REYES: Making a deliberate choice rather than defaulting to compliance.

[MI Skill: Reflection]

THOMAS: But I don't know how to do that. Everything is structured for me. The supervision, the treatment, the testing. Where's the choice?

OFFICER REYES: You feel like the system has removed your agency and you're just a passenger.

[MI Skill: Reflection on loss of autonomy]

THOMAS: That's it exactly. Even the good things don't feel like mine. They feel like the system's.

OFFICER REYES: Thomas, what if you created something that was yours? Something you chose, not because it was required, but because you wanted it?

[MI Skill: Introducing possibility of autonomous action]

THOMAS: Like what?

OFFICER REYES: I don't know. What matters to you? What did you care about before the drinking took over?

[MI Skill: Open question about values and interests]

THOMAS: [Long pause] I used to coach my son's baseball team. Back when he was in little league. Before the divorce. Before everything fell apart.

OFFICER REYES: Baseball coaching. Tell me about that.

[MI Skill: Elaboration request]

THOMAS: Those kids looked up to me. I taught them about the game, about teamwork, about how to lose with grace and win without being a jerk. It was the best I ever felt about myself.

OFFICER REYES: Mentoring young people and being looked up to. That meant something real to you.

[MI Skill: Reflection on meaning]

THOMAS: It did. And then I lost it. The divorce, moving away, no time, no energy. Just work and drinking.

OFFICER REYES: What would it mean to reconnect with something like that now?

[MI Skill: Open question about renewal]

THOMAS: I don't know if I could. Who's going to let a guy with three DUIs coach kids?

OFFICER REYES: That's a real concern. There might be background check issues. But is that the only way to mentor young people?

[MI Skill: Acknowledging barrier while exploring alternatives]

THOMAS: [Thinks] I guess not. There's probably other ways.

OFFICER REYES: What comes to mind?

THOMAS: Maybe tutoring? Or volunteering somewhere that works with at-risk youth? I came from a rough background myself. I understand those kids.

OFFICER REYES: Using your experience to help young people who might be heading down a similar path.

[MI Skill: Reflection connecting past to potential contribution]

THOMAS: Yeah. [Pause] That would actually feel like something. Not just going through the motions.

OFFICER REYES: Not just compliance. Purpose.

[MI Skill: Naming what was missing]

THOMAS: Purpose. That's what I've been missing.

OFFICER REYES: Thomas, what if finding that purpose became part of your work here? Not a requirement, but something you chose to pursue because it matters to you?

[MI Skill: Offering reframe of supervision purpose]

THOMAS: I'd want that. Something that's actually mine.

OFFICER REYES: What's one step you could take to explore this?

[MI Skill: Moving toward action]

THOMAS: I could look into volunteer opportunities. Youth mentoring programs. See what's out there.

OFFICER REYES: Will you do that before our next meeting?

[MI Skill: Eliciting commitment]

THOMAS: Yeah. I will.

OFFICER REYES: Good. And Thomas, the question you asked, whether you'll go back to drinking when the interlock comes off, that's the right question. Finding something that matters to you, something that's yours, might be the thing that makes the answer different from what you're afraid it will be.

[MI Skill: Connecting purpose to long-term sobriety]

THOMAS: [Nods] I hope so.

Reflection

This session demonstrates MI's application to stalled progress during routine supervision. Thomas was technically compliant but emotionally disengaged, going through the motions without genuine investment. Officer Reyes recognized this pattern and addressed it directly.

The key insight was Thomas's articulation that external controls were doing the work of sobriety, leaving him uncertain about his internal motivation. By exploring this honestly rather than offering reassurance, Officer Reyes helped Thomas identify what was missing: a sense of choice and purpose.

The emergence of youth mentoring as a meaningful goal came from Thomas's own history. Officer Reyes did not suggest volunteering; he asked what mattered to Thomas and explored the answer. This client-generated direction carries more motivational weight than any officer recommendation.

Outcome Analysis

Subsequent Outcomes:

- Thomas connected with youth mentoring program within two weeks
- He became regular mentor to two teenage boys with similar backgrounds
- His treatment engagement improved; counselor noted increased participation
- He articulated sobriety as necessary for mentoring credibility
- He completed probation successfully
- At follow-up, he remained sober and continued mentoring, calling it "the reason I stay straight"

Case Study 19: Crisis Intervention and Safety Planning

Case Background

Supervisee: Amanda Chen, 29-year-old Asian American female

Offense: Prescription fraud (forged prescriptions for benzodiazepines)

Sentence: 2 years probation, substance abuse treatment

Risk Level: Low (LSI-R score: 11)

History: No prior criminal history. Amanda works as a paralegal. She developed benzodiazepine dependency following a traumatic sexual assault three years ago. She was caught forging prescriptions when her doctor reduced her supply. She disclosed the assault during treatment intake but has not addressed it in depth.

Context: Month 8. Amanda missed her previous appointment without explanation and arrives today visibly distressed. Officer Patricia Yang is immediately concerned.

Session Script

[Amanda enters looking disheveled, eyes red from crying, hands shaking]

OFFICER YANG: Amanda, I can see something is wrong. What's happening?

[MI Skill: Direct acknowledgment of distress]

AMANDA: [Barely audible] I can't do this anymore.

OFFICER YANG: Can't do what?

[MI Skill: Clarification without assumptions]

AMANDA: Any of it. Life. Pretending to be okay. I'm not okay.

OFFICER YANG: You're not okay. Tell me what's going on.

[MI Skill: Reflection followed by open invitation]

AMANDA: [Crying] I saw him. Last week. He was at a restaurant I went to. Sitting there like nothing ever happened. Laughing with his friends.

OFFICER YANG: You saw the person who assaulted you.

[MI Skill: Simple reflection with implicit understanding]

AMANDA: [Nods, crying harder] And everything came back. All of it. The nightmares started again. I can't sleep. I can't eat. I can't function.

OFFICER YANG: The encounter triggered everything you've been trying to manage.

[MI Skill: Reflection on trauma response]

AMANDA: I've been drinking. I know I'm not supposed to, but I needed something. The benzos were the only thing that ever helped with the anxiety, and I can't have those anymore, so I've been drinking to sleep.

OFFICER YANG: You've been drinking to cope with what's been happening since you saw him.

[MI Skill: Non-judgmental reflection of self-medication]

AMANDA: I know it's wrong. I know I could get violated. But I just wanted to stop feeling this way.

OFFICER YANG: Amanda, I'm less concerned about the drinking right now than I am about you. When you said you "can't do this anymore," what did you mean?

[MI Skill: Prioritizing safety assessment]

AMANDA: [Long pause] Sometimes I think everyone would be better off without me. I'm a burden. A mess. I can't even follow basic probation conditions.

OFFICER YANG: You've had thoughts that people would be better off if you weren't here.

[MI Skill: Reflection for clarification]

AMANDA: [Whispers] Yes.

OFFICER YANG: Amanda, I need to ask you directly: Are you thinking about hurting yourself?

[MI Skill: Direct suicide assessment]

AMANDA: [Crying] I don't know. I'm not planning anything. But sometimes I just wish I could disappear.

OFFICER YANG: You're not planning anything specific, but you're having thoughts of not existing. How often do these thoughts come?

[MI Skill: Assessing frequency]

AMANDA: Every day. Since I saw him.

OFFICER YANG: Every day for a week. That's a lot to carry. Have you told anyone else about these thoughts?

[MI Skill: Assessing support]

AMANDA: No. I couldn't. What would I even say?

OFFICER YANG: Amanda, I'm really glad you came in today. You could have missed this appointment too. Instead, you're here, telling me what's happening. That matters.

[MI Skill: Affirmation of help-seeking]

AMANDA: [Crying] I didn't know what else to do.

OFFICER YANG: Coming here was exactly the right thing. Now let me help you. First, I want to make sure you're safe. You said you're not planning anything, but the thoughts are constant. Do you have access to anything that could hurt you at home?

[MI Skill: Means restriction assessment]

AMANDA: Just pills. Over-the-counter stuff. Lots of Tylenol.

OFFICER YANG: I'd like you to get rid of that today. Can you do that?

[MI Skill: Concrete safety step]

AMANDA: [Nods] Yes. I can throw it out.

OFFICER YANG: Good. Now, the drinking. You've been using it to cope because the benzos aren't available. What we need is a safer way to manage what you're experiencing. The trauma response you're having needs proper treatment.

[MI Skill: Reframing toward appropriate intervention]

AMANDA: I was supposed to do trauma therapy. My treatment provider kept telling me. But I was afraid.

OFFICER YANG: Afraid of what?

[MI Skill: Exploring barrier]

AMANDA: Of having to talk about it. Of reliving it. It's easier to not think about it.

OFFICER YANG: Avoiding it felt safer. But then you saw him, and all the avoidance couldn't protect you.

[MI Skill: Reflection on limitations of avoidance]

AMANDA: [Nods] It all came flooding back anyway.

OFFICER YANG: What if the trauma therapy could help you not be so vulnerable to those floods? What if you could have an encounter like that and not be devastated for weeks?

[MI Skill: Presenting potential benefit of treatment]

AMANDA: Is that possible?

OFFICER YANG: For many people, yes. It's not about forgetting or being okay with what happened. It's about the memory losing its power to hijack your life.

[MI Skill: Psychoeducation about trauma treatment]

AMANDA: I want that. I want this thing to stop running my life.

OFFICER YANG: That's exactly what trauma therapy can help with. I want to help you connect with a therapist who specializes in this, today, not someday.

[MI Skill: Immediate action orientation]

AMANDA: Today?

OFFICER YANG: Today. I'm going to give you three names. I want you to call all three from this office before you leave, and set up an intake with whoever can see you first.

[MI Skill: Concrete action with immediate implementation]

AMANDA: Okay. I can do that.

OFFICER YANG: And I want us to talk about what you're going to do tonight. When you go home. When the thoughts come.

[MI Skill: Developing safety plan]

AMANDA: I don't know.

OFFICER YANG: Let's figure it out together. Who can you call if the thoughts get bad?

AMANDA: My sister. She doesn't know everything, but she's always there for me.

OFFICER YANG: Can you tell her what's happening?

AMANDA: I could tell her I'm struggling. I don't have to tell her everything.

OFFICER YANG: Partial honesty is okay right now. Just enough for her to know you need support. Will you call her tonight?

AMANDA: Yes.

OFFICER YANG: What else helps when you're overwhelmed? Besides alcohol.

AMANDA: My cat. Holding my cat. Sometimes that helps.

OFFICER YANG: Your cat. Anything else?

AMANDA: Hot showers. Music. Sometimes walking helps.

OFFICER YANG: So your safety plan for tonight: call your sister, be with your cat, hot shower, music, walking. And if the thoughts get really bad?

AMANDA: Call my sister? Or you?

OFFICER YANG: Yes, call your sister or call me. I'm going to give you my cell number for emergencies. And there's the crisis line, 988, if you can't reach either of us.

AMANDA: [Takes deep breath] Okay. I can do this.

OFFICER YANG: Yes, you can. And Amanda? You came in here today because part of you wants to live, even when another part doesn't. Hold onto that part.

[MI Skill: Affirmation of survival instinct]

AMANDA: [Nods, still crying but calmer]

Reflection

This session demonstrates crisis intervention within a supervision context. Officer Yang recognized immediately that standard supervision conversation was not appropriate given Amanda's presentation. She prioritized safety assessment and immediate stabilization over compliance concerns.

The session followed crisis intervention best practices: acknowledging distress, assessing suicidal ideation directly, evaluating means access, developing a concrete safety plan, and connecting to immediate treatment. Officer Yang did not lecture about alcohol use; she named it as understandable coping and focused on establishing safer alternatives.

The connection to trauma therapy reframed the intervention as hopeful rather than punitive. Amanda had been avoiding trauma treatment out of fear, but the officer presented it as a path to freedom from the trauma's power.

Outcome Analysis

Subsequent Outcomes:

- Amanda connected with trauma therapist within three days
- She began EMDR treatment and engaged fully
- Her suicidal ideation decreased significantly within one month
- She disclosed assault to her sister, who provided ongoing support

- She had one drinking episode during particularly difficult therapy session; addressed without violation
- She completed probation successfully
- At follow-up, she reported trauma symptoms significantly reduced and no ongoing suicidal ideation

Case Study 20: Successful Termination and Transition

Case Background

Supervisee: James Porter, 36-year-old white male

Offense: Felony embezzlement

Sentence: 4 years probation, restitution of $32,000

Supervision History: James has been on supervision for 3 years and 10 months. He completed all requirements, paid full restitution, maintained employment throughout, completed financial management coursework, and has had no violations. He is two months from scheduled termination.

Context: Final substantive meeting before termination. Officer Robert Martinez wants to conduct a meaningful closing session that consolidates gains and supports sustainable success.

Session Script

OFFICER MARTINEZ: James, it's hard to believe we're almost at the end. Two months left. How are you feeling?

JAMES: [Smiles] Honestly? A little surreal. Four years felt like forever when it started. Now I can see the finish line.

OFFICER MARTINEZ: The end is in sight. What's that like?

[MI Skill: Open question about experience]

JAMES: Mostly good. Relieved. Proud, I think. Nervous too.

OFFICER MARTINEZ: Tell me about the nervous part.

[MI Skill: Exploring ambivalent feeling]

JAMES: I've had structure for four years. Someone to report to. Something to work toward. In two months, that's all gone. It's just me.

OFFICER MARTINEZ: The structure has been a container, and you're wondering what happens when it's removed.

[MI Skill: Reflection on function of supervision]

JAMES: Yeah. What if I need it? What if the structure was the only thing keeping me on track?

OFFICER MARTINEZ: That's a version of a question a lot of people ask near the end. Let me turn it back to you: what do you think?

[MI Skill: Reflecting question rather than answering]

JAMES: [Thinks] I don't think so. I mean, the structure helped at the beginning. But somewhere along the way, it stopped being about the structure and started being about who I wanted to be.

OFFICER MARTINEZ: There was a shift from external motivation to internal motivation.

[MI Skill: Reflection on motivation change]

JAMES: Yeah. The first year, I was definitely doing things because I had to. Checking boxes. But by the second year, I started actually wanting the life I was building. The good job. The stability. The self-respect.

OFFICER MARTINEZ: The compliance became genuine commitment.

[MI Skill: Reflection on transformation]

JAMES: I guess it did.

OFFICER MARTINEZ: When did you notice that shift?

[MI Skill: Elaboration question]

JAMES: Probably when I paid off the restitution early. I could have just made the minimum payments, but I wanted it done. I wanted to be completely free of what I'd done. That was for me, not for probation.

OFFICER MARTINEZ: Paying it off early was about closing a chapter in your own story, not satisfying a condition.

[MI Skill: Reflection on meaning]

JAMES: Exactly.

OFFICER MARTINEZ: James, I want to take a few minutes to look back at where you started and where you are now. When you first came into my office four years ago, what was going on for you?

[MI Skill: Inviting retrospective reflection]

JAMES: [Takes breath] I was terrified. Ashamed. I couldn't believe I'd done what I did. I kept thinking my life was over. That I'd never work in finance again, never be respected again, never be able to look my family in the eye again.

OFFICER MARTINEZ: Terror, shame, a sense that everything was ruined.

[MI Skill: Reflection on initial state]

JAMES: Yeah. I couldn't see any future worth having.

OFFICER MARTINEZ: And now?

JAMES: Now I have a job I'm proud of. Not in finance, but honest work where I'm valued. My wife stayed with me, and we're stronger than before. My kids know what happened, age-appropriately, and they know their dad made a mistake and worked to make it right.

OFFICER MARTINEZ: A life rebuilt with integrity.

[MI Skill: Simple reflection]

JAMES: It took work. A lot of work. But yeah. I have a life I'm proud of now.

OFFICER MARTINEZ: What made the difference? Between the person who walked in four years ago and the person sitting here today?

[MI Skill: Open question about change mechanism]

JAMES: [Thinks] Honesty. I finally got honest with myself about why I did what I did. It wasn't just about the money. It was about proving something, feeling important, keeping up with people who had more. Once I understood that, I could address it.

OFFICER MARTINEZ: Understanding the "why" let you change the pattern.

[MI Skill: Reflection on insight leading to change]

JAMES: And accountability. Having to face what I did every month, report on my progress, answer questions. It was uncomfortable, but it kept me honest.

OFFICER MARTINEZ: The discomfort of accountability served a purpose.

[MI Skill: Reflection reframing accountability positively]

JAMES: It did. And... this might sound strange... but these conversations helped. Having someone who actually seemed to want me to succeed. Not just someone waiting for me to fail.

OFFICER MARTINEZ: The relationship mattered.

[MI Skill: Reflection on therapeutic alliance]

JAMES: It really did. You treated me like a person, not just a case number. That made me want to prove I deserved that treatment.

OFFICER MARTINEZ: Thank you for saying that, James. It's meant a lot to me too, watching you do this work.

[MI Skill: Appropriate self-disclosure of positive regard]

JAMES: [Nods]

OFFICER MARTINEZ: As we approach the end, I want to ask you about the future. What are the potential challenges that could threaten the life you've built?

[MI Skill: Relapse prevention planning]

JAMES: [Considers] Financial stress. That's always a risk. When money gets tight, old thinking can creep back in. "There's an easier way. No one would know."

OFFICER MARTINEZ: You know that voice. How will you handle it when it shows up?

[MI Skill: Coping planning]

JAMES: Remember what it cost me. The shame, the fear, almost losing everything. No amount of money is worth going back to that.

OFFICER MARTINEZ: The memory of consequences as protection.

[MI Skill: Reflection on deterrent function]

JAMES: And talking to Sarah. My wife. Keeping her in the loop about finances. No secrets. That was part of the problem before. I was hiding things.

OFFICER MARTINEZ: Transparency with your wife as a safeguard.

[MI Skill: Reflection on relational accountability]

JAMES: Yes.

OFFICER MARTINEZ: What else might be a challenge?

JAMES: Pride. Wanting to look successful. Comparing myself to people who have more. I have to stay grounded in what actually matters, not what looks impressive.

OFFICER MARTINEZ: Keeping your values front and center rather than external measures of success.

[MI Skill: Reflection on values orientation]

JAMES: Yeah.

OFFICER MARTINEZ: James, I have confidence in you. But I want to give you one piece of advice for after this ends. Life will present situations where the old patterns are tempting. Not in obvious ways, but in subtle ones. "Just this once. Just a small thing. No one will know." When that voice comes, and it will come, remember this conversation. Remember who you've worked to become. And call someone before you act.

[MI Skill: Anticipatory guidance]

JAMES: I will. I don't want to go back to who I was.

OFFICER MARTINEZ: You're not that person anymore. But he's not gone. He's a part of you that you've learned to manage. Keep managing him.

[MI Skill: Realistic framing of change]

JAMES: I understand.

OFFICER MARTINEZ: Is there anything else you want to talk about as we close this chapter?

[MI Skill: Open invitation for final topics]

JAMES: I just want to say thank you. This process could have been punitive and dehumanizing. Instead, it was... I don't know... redemptive? I came out better than I went in. That's not nothing.

OFFICER MARTINEZ: You did the work, James. I just created space for it.

[MI Skill: Attributing success to client]

JAMES: [Nods] I'm ready for what comes next.

OFFICER MARTINEZ: I believe you are. Good luck, James. Truly.

Reflection

This termination session demonstrates how to close supervision in a way that consolidates gains, plans for future challenges, and honors the work done. Officer Martinez guided James through a retrospective review that allowed him to articulate his own transformation, creating a narrative of change he could carry forward.

The exploration of future challenges (financial stress, pride, comparison) established a relapse prevention framework without being heavy-handed. James identified his own vulnerabilities and coping strategies, demonstrating internalized self-management.

The session balanced confidence in James's growth with realistic acknowledgment that old patterns remain part of him. The phrase "He's a part of you that you've learned to manage" normalized ongoing vigilance without undermining confidence.

Outcome Analysis

Post-Supervision Outcomes (2-year follow-up):

- James maintained employment with one promotion
- No financial irregularities or legal issues
- He reported one significant financial stress period; used identified coping strategies successfully
- His marriage remained strong
- He began volunteering with white-collar crime rehabilitation program
- He described supervision experience as "turning point" in his life

---

Complete Mi Skills Summary Across All Case Studies

Skills Frequency Analysis

Skill	Total Uses (Across 20 Cases)	Average Per Session
Simple Reflections	187	9.4
Complex Reflections	168	8.4
Open Questions	142	7.1
Affirmations	67	3.4
Summaries	48	2.4
Autonomy Support	43	2.2
Strategic Silence	26	1.3
Permission Seeking	21	1.1
Double-Sided Reflections	18	0.9

Key Patterns Observed

Reflection Ratio: Across all sessions, reflections outnumbered questions approximately 2.5:1, consistent with MI best practices emphasizing listening over questioning.

Affirmation Frequency: Affirmations were used strategically rather than liberally, averaging 3.4 per session. They were deployed at moments of genuine client strength or progress rather than as generic encouragement.

Summary Timing: Summaries appeared most frequently at transition points within sessions and near session conclusions, serving to consolidate material and move conversations forward.

Autonomy Support: Phrases emphasizing client choice and control appeared consistently across populations and contexts, including resistant clients, mandated treatment, and crisis situations.

Population-Specific Adaptations

Resistant Clients: Higher use of rolling with resistance, more strategic affirmations, emphasis on non-defensive responses to provocation.

Substance Abuse: Increased use of importance/confidence rulers, more detailed exploration of ambivalence, integration of change talk types (DARN-CAT).

Domestic Violence: Careful balance of validation and accountability, specific attention to fear differentials, persistent connection to behavior consequences.

Sex Offense: Strategic redirection from guilt arguments to behavioral exploration, graduated approach to engagement, acceptance of partial acknowledgment.

Juvenile: Development of rapport through genuine interest, integration of developmental context, connection to identity formation goals.

Mental Health: Exploration of medication ambivalence without defending medication, validation of subjective experience, introduction of alternative framings.

Conclusion

These twenty case studies demonstrate that Motivational Interviewing principles and techniques can be effectively adapted across the full range of criminal justice supervision contexts. From initial resistant intakes to successful terminations, from routine office visits to crisis interventions, the core MI approach of empathic engagement, strategic questioning, and selective reflection consistently produces more productive conversations than confrontational or purely compliance-focused approaches.

The cases illustrate several overarching themes:

Meeting clients where they are requires genuine curiosity about their perspectives, even perspectives the officer may disagree with or find problematic. Validation of emotional experience does not equal endorsement of behavior.

Change talk must be evoked, not argued. In every case where genuine progress occurred, the client articulated their own reasons for change rather than being persuaded by officer arguments.

Resistance signals engagement failure, not client deficiency. When clients became defensive or argumentative, effective responses involved the officer adjusting their approach rather than increasing pressure.

Progress is rarely linear. Setbacks, violations, and stalled periods are normal parts of the change process. How these moments are handled often determines long-term outcomes.

The relationship is the vehicle for change. Across all twenty cases, the quality of the working alliance emerged as a critical factor in client engagement and eventual success.

These case studies are intended as learning tools for officers seeking to enhance their MI skills. Each demonstrates not just what to say, but how to think about the person, the situation, and the possibilities for change that exist even in challenging circumstances.

Appendix A: Quick Reference MI Skills

This appendix provides quick reference materials for MI skills discussed throughout the text. These summaries are intended for use after reading the full chapters, not as substitutes for comprehensive understanding.

A.1 OARS Summary

Open Questions

- Invite elaboration rather than yes/no responses
- Begin with "what," "how," "tell me about," "help me understand"
- Examples: "What's been happening with you?" "How do you see your situation?" "Tell me about your week."
- Avoid: Leading questions that suggest the "right" answer

Affirmations

- Recognize strengths, efforts, and values without praising
- Focus on specific observations rather than general approval
- Examples: "You showed up even though this is difficult." "That took effort." "You're thinking seriously about your situation."
- Avoid: Patronizing praise or hollow encouragement

Reflections

- Statements (not questions) that capture what the person said or meant
- Simple reflections repeat or slightly rephrase content
- Complex reflections add underlying meaning, emotion, or connection
- Examples: "You're frustrated with how things have gone." "Part of you wants things to change."
- Aim for 2:1 reflection-to-question ratio

Summaries

- Collect multiple elements that have emerged in conversation
- Collecting summaries gather what has been said
- Linking summaries connect related themes
- Transitional summaries mark movement to new topics
- End with "What else?" or "What am I missing?"

A.2 Change Talk Types

DARN (Preparatory Change Talk)

Desire: Wanting, wishing, liking

- "I want to stop getting in trouble."
- "I wish things were different."

Ability: Can, could, able to

- "I could probably cut back if I tried."
- "I've done it before."

Reasons: Why change would be good

- "Because I'm tired of this."
- "It would help my family."

Need: Necessity, urgency

- "I have to do something different."
- "Things can't go on like this."

CAT (Mobilizing Change Talk)

Commitment: Will, going to, promise

- "I'm going to stop."
- "I will go to treatment."

Activation: Ready, willing, prepared

- "I'm ready to make changes."
- "I'm willing to try."

Taking Steps: Actions already taken

- "I've already started looking for work."
- "I called the treatment center."

A.3 Responding to Sustain Talk

Simple Reflection: Acknowledge without amplifying

- Person: "I don't have a problem."
- Response: "You don't see this as a problem."

Double-Sided Reflection: Include both sides

- "Part of you sees this working fine, and part of you notices it's caused some problems."

Amplified Reflection: Strategic emphasis (use carefully)

- Person: "I can control my drinking."
- Response: "You have complete control over it."

Shifting Focus: Move to different territory

- "We keep coming back to this. What else is going on for you right now?"

A.4 Common Phrases

Opening Conversations

- "What brings you in today?"
- "What's been happening since we last met?"
- "How can I be most helpful today?"

Exploring Ambivalence

- "On the one hand... and on the other hand..."
- "Help me understand how you see this."
- "What concerns you about your current situation?"

Evoking Change Talk

- "What would you like to see different?"
- "How important is this to you, on a scale of 0-10?"
- "What would be good about making this change?"

Responding to Change Talk

- "Tell me more about that."
- "What else?"
- "That sounds important to you."

Managing Discord

- "I think we've gotten into an argument here."
- "I may have pushed too hard. Let me step back."
- "What you do is ultimately your choice."

Appendix B: Sample Dialogues

This appendix provides annotated dialogue examples illustrating MI application in criminal justice contexts.

B.1 Initial Interview Excerpt

Context: First supervision contact following sentencing for drug possession

Officer: What's your understanding of why you're here today? [Open question inviting supervisee's perspective]

Marcus: I got caught with some stuff and now I have to do probation.

Officer: So you're on probation for possession. [Simple reflection] What's your sense of how things got to this point? [Open question exploring context]

Marcus: Just bad luck, really. I was in the wrong place.

Officer: You see it as mostly circumstantial. [Reflection without arguing] Help me understand what a typical day was like for you before this happened. [Open question gathering information while building rapport]

Marcus: I mean, I work. I've got a job at the warehouse. I just use a little to unwind. It's not like I'm some addict.

Officer: You work, you're not unemployed or homeless. And you use occasionally to relax. [Reflection acknowledging his perspective] What worries you, if anything, about your current situation? [Open question that might evoke change talk]

Marcus: [Pause] I guess... I don't want to lose my job. If they find out about this, I could get fired. And my mom was pretty upset.

Officer: Losing your job concerns you, and disappointing your mom. [Reflection of change talk] Those relationships matter to you. [Affirmation connecting to values]

Commentary: The officer avoids lecturing about drug use, instead gathering information and building rapport. When Marcus offers hints of concern (job, mother), the officer reflects and affirms these without pushing. This creates foundation for future motivation exploration.

B.2 Routine Visit Brief MI

Context: 15-minute check-in, supervisee has been compliant but minimally engaged

Officer: What's been happening since we last met? [Open question]

Ianthe: Nothing really. Same stuff.

Officer: Things have been pretty routine. [Reflection of minimal response] What's been the hardest part of this past couple weeks? [Open question that might reveal concerns]

Ianthe: I don't know. Probably the curfew. It's hard to explain to people why I have to leave.

Officer: Having to explain yourself is uncomfortable. [Reflection] What do people think is going on? [Follow-up exploring the concern]

Ianthe: They probably think I'm a criminal or something.

Officer: You're worried about how people see you. [Reflection] What would you want them to know about you? [Open question connecting to identity]

Ianthe: That I made a mistake. I'm not a bad person. I'm trying to get through this.

Officer: You want people to see that this one situation doesn't define who you are. You're working toward something better. [Complex reflection adding meaning]

Commentary: Even in a brief contact, the officer uses open questions and reflections to move beyond surface-level check-in. The conversation reveals concerns about identity and reputation that could inform future discussions.

B.3 Violation Conversation

Context: Supervisee tested positive for marijuana after three months of clean tests

Officer: I got your drug test results. Help me understand what happened. [Direct acknowledgment followed by open question]

Julius: [Sighs] I slipped up. I know I shouldn't have.

Officer: You used, and you're acknowledging it. [Reflection of both behavior and accountability] What was going on for you when that happened? [Exploring circumstances without interrogating]

Julius: It was my brother's birthday party. Everyone was smoking. I thought one time wouldn't matter.

Officer: You were in a situation where everyone was using, and it was hard to stay outside of that. [Reflection showing understanding of context]

Julius: Yeah. I didn't plan to use. It just happened.

Officer: It caught you off guard. [Simple reflection] Looking back, what could have helped you make a different choice? [Inviting his own problem-solving]

Julius: I don't know. Maybe not going? Or leaving earlier?

Officer: You're seeing some options you didn't see in the moment. [Affirmation of reflection] I have to report this positive test. That's part of my job and I want to be straight with you about it. [Transparency about enforcement role] What I'm more concerned about is what happens next. Three months of progress doesn't disappear because of one slip. [Perspective] What do you want to do from here? [Returning focus to his choice]

Commentary: The officer addresses the violation directly, explores circumstances without excusing, and maintains MI spirit while being transparent about enforcement obligations. The conversation ends focused forward rather than dwelling on failure.

B.4 Post Relapse Conversation

Context: Supervisee disclosed using cocaine after six months clean

Officer: Thank you for telling me. That took courage when you could have kept it hidden. [Affirmation of honesty] What happened? [Open exploration]

Salome: My ex called out of nowhere. We talked, and then we met up, and before I knew it...

Officer: Contact with your ex triggered something, and things escalated from there. [Reflection without judgment]

Salome: I know I was stupid. Six months down the drain.

Officer: You're being hard on yourself. [Reflection of self-criticism] Here's how I see it: six months ago you were using daily. You'd lost your apartment. Your kids weren't talking to you. Today, one use in six months. You have housing. You're rebuilding with your kids. [Providing perspective] How do you see those two situations? [Inviting her to compare rather than telling her what to think]

Salome: [Pause] I guess I have made progress.

Officer: And one slip doesn't erase that progress. [Statement without being preachy] What do you want to do now? [Forward focus]

Salome: I need to call my sponsor. And I probably shouldn't have any contact with my ex.

Officer: You're already thinking about what would help you get back on track. [Affirmation of planning]

Commentary: The officer responds to relapse disclosure with support rather than punishment, puts the slip in context of overall progress, and helps the supervisee develop her own recovery plan.

Appendix C: Assessment and Planning Tools

This appendix provides templates and forms for MI-informed practice.

C.1 MI Informed Case Plan Template

Supervisee Name: ____________________ **Date**: _______________

Officer Name: ____________________ **Review Date**: _______________

Supervisee's Stated Goals (in their own words):

1. ______________________________
2. ______________________________
3. ______________________________

Court-Ordered Conditions:

- ______________________________
- ______________________________
- ______________________________

Connection Between Goals and Conditions (how requirements serve supervisee's own goals):

____

____

Prioritized Focus Areas (collaboratively determined):

1. ______________________________ Target date: __________
2. ______________________________ Target date: __________
3. ______________________________ Target date: __________

Supervisee's Strengths and Resources:

____

____

Potential Barriers and Plans to Address:

Barrier Plan

Supervisee Signature: _________________ **Date**: _____________ **Officer Signature**: _________________ **Date**: _____________

C.2 Change Talk Tracking Form

Supervisee: _________________ **Date**: _____________

Instructions: During or immediately after contact, note instances of change talk and how you responded.

Change Talk Heard	Type (D/A/R/N/C/A/T)	Your Response	Response Type (E/A/R/S)

Sustain Talk Heard and Response:

Reflection: What went well? What would you do differently?

C.3 Self Assessment Checklist

Instructions: Complete after recorded sessions to assess MI skill use.

OARS Skills

- [ ] Asked at least 3 open questions
- [ ] Offered at least 5 reflections
- [ ] Provided at least 1 genuine affirmation
- [ ] Offered at least 1 summary
- [ ] Maintained 2:1 reflection-to-question ratio

MI Spirit

- [ ] Treated supervisee as partner, not object

- [ ] Expressed genuine curiosity about their perspective
- [ ] Supported their autonomy even when disagreeing
- [ ] Showed compassion for their situation

Change Talk

- [ ] Heard change talk when it occurred
- [ ] Responded to change talk with EARS
- [ ] Avoided arguing against sustain talk

Discord Management

- [ ] Noticed when discord emerged
- [ ] Adjusted approach rather than escalating
- [ ] Maintained collaborative spirit despite challenges

Overall Rating (1-10): _____ **Date**: _____________

C.4 Supervision Meeting Agenda

Purpose: Structured format for supervision meetings focused on MI development

Opening (5 minutes)

- Review tracked contacts since last meeting
- Identify one success and one challenge

Recorded Session Review (15 minutes)

- Listen to selected 5-minute segment
- Discuss specific skill use and spirit
- Identify alternatives that could have been used

Case Consultation (15 minutes)

- Present challenging case using MI framework
- Apply chapter concepts to understand the case
- Develop MI-informed strategies

Skill Development Planning (10 minutes)

- Set specific skill focus for coming week
- Identify tracking method

- Schedule next meeting

Supervisor Notes: ____

Appendix D: Resources for Learning

This appendix lists resources for continued MI learning and professional development.

D.1 Books and Training Manuals

Miller, W. R., & Rollnick, S. (2013). *Motivational interviewing: Helping people change* (3rd ed.). Guilford Press. The definitive text on MI from its developers. Essential reading for serious practitioners.

Stinson, J. D., & Clark, M. D. (2017). *Motivational interviewing with offenders: Engagement, rehabilitation, and reentry*. Guilford Press. Specific application to criminal justice populations with extensive examples.

Rosengren, D. B. (2018). *Building motivational interviewing skills: A practitioner workbook* (2nd ed.). Guilford Press. Practical exercises for skill development with self-assessment tools.

Walters, S. T., Clark, M. D., Gingerich, R., & Meltzer, M. L. (2007). *Motivating offenders to change: A guide for probation and parole*. National Institute of Corrections. Free government publication specifically for community corrections.

D.2 Training and Professional Development

MINT (Motivational Interviewing Network of Trainers) The international professional organization for MI practitioners and trainers. Website provides trainer directory, training events, and resources.

Regional Training Events MINT sponsors regional Forums and international conferences providing advanced training opportunities.

University-Based Programs Several universities offer MI certificate programs and continuing education courses.

Online Resources Video examples, webinars, and online courses available through various providers. Quality varies; prioritize MINT-affiliated or university-sponsored content.

D.3 Fidelity Instruments

MITI (Motivational Interviewing Treatment Integrity) Standardized coding system for assessing MI quality. Version 4.2 is current. Requires trained raters for formal use but can inform self-assessment.

MISC (Motivational Interviewing Skill Code) Research coding system that provides detailed behavior counts. More complex than MITI.

MIA-STEP Assessment tool specifically developed for criminal justice settings.

Appendix E: Research Summary Tables

This appendix summarizes key research findings referenced throughout the text.

E.1 MI in Criminal Justice

Study	Population	Intervention	Findings
Walters et al. (2010)	Probationers	MI supervision vs. standard	Improved treatment participation, especially high-risk
Brown et al. (2015)	DWI recidivists	30-min brief MI	Delayed subsequent arrests nearly 5 years
Anstiss et al. (2011)	Prison population	Brief MI	Reduced reconviction, increased readiness
McMurran (2009)	Review	MI as preparation for treatment	Improved engagement across populations
Soleymani et al. (2018)	IPV perpetrators	MI with BIP	Improved treatment completion

E.2 MI Effectiveness by Population

Population	Evidence Level	Key Findings
Substance use	Strong	Original MI application; multiple meta-analyses support
DUI/DWI	Strong	Brief interventions produce lasting effects
IPV perpetrators	Moderate	Improves engagement; recidivism evidence limited
Sex offenders	Limited	Promising for engagement; requires adaptation
High-risk offenders	Moderate	Relationship quality predicts outcomes
Reentry	Limited	Promising; more research needed

E.3 Training Effectiveness

Finding	Source	Implication
Workshop alone has minimal lasting effect	Schwalbe et al. (2014)	Ongoing support required
Coaching improves skill retention	Madson et al. (2009)	Budget for post-training support
Skills decay without maintenance	Multiple studies	Plan for ongoing development
Feedback improves outcomes	Moyers et al. (2016)	Build feedback into supervision

Glossary of Terms

Affirmation: An MI-consistent statement that recognizes and acknowledges something positive about the client, such as their strengths, efforts, intentions, or values.

Ambivalence: The simultaneous presence of competing motivations, typically wanting to change and wanting to stay the same. Central to MI's understanding of motivation.

Change Talk: Client language that favors movement toward change, including statements of desire, ability, reasons, need, commitment, activation, and taking steps.

Compassion Fatigue: Emotional exhaustion resulting from ongoing exposure to others' suffering, particularly affecting helping professionals.

Complex Reflection: A reflection that adds meaning, emotion, or connection beyond what the client explicitly stated.

Discord: Disharmony in the therapeutic relationship, typically signaled by client arguing, defensiveness, or disengagement. Distinguished from sustain talk.

Engaging: The first of MI's four processes, involving establishing a working relationship and understanding the client's perspective.

Evoking: The third of MI's four processes, involving drawing out the client's own motivations for change.

Focusing: The second of MI's four processes, involving developing a specific direction for the conversation.

MITI (Motivational Interviewing Treatment Integrity): A standardized coding system for assessing MI quality based on recorded sessions.

MINT (Motivational Interviewing Network of Trainers): The international professional organization for MI practitioners and trainers.

OARS: Acronym for the four fundamental MI skills: Open questions, Affirmations, Reflections, and Summaries.

Open Question: A question that invites elaboration rather than a yes/no or single-word response.

Partnership: One of the four elements of MI spirit, involving collaboration with rather than power over the client.

Planning: The fourth of MI's four processes, involving developing a specific change plan when readiness emerges.

Reflection: An MI skill involving statements (not questions) that capture and return something the client has said, thought, or felt.

Reflection-to-Question Ratio: The proportion of reflections to questions in a conversation, with skilled MI practice typically showing more reflections than questions.

Righting Reflex: The natural desire of helping professionals to fix problems, correct errors, and tell clients what to do.

Simple Reflection: A reflection that repeats or slightly rephrases what the client said without adding interpretation.

Spirit of MI: The underlying approach of MI, characterized by partnership, acceptance, compassion, and evocation.

Stages of Change: A model describing the stages through which people move when changing behavior: precontemplation, contemplation, preparation, action, and maintenance.

Summary: An MI skill involving collecting multiple elements from a conversation and returning them to the client.

Sustain Talk: Client language that favors the status quo, including arguments for not changing.

Working Alliance: The collaborative relationship between practitioner and client that predicts outcomes across helping modalities.

References

Amrhein, P. C., Miller, W. R., Yahne, C. E., Palmer, M., & Fulcher, L. (2003). Client commitment language during motivational interviewing predicts drug use outcomes. *Journal of Consulting and Clinical Psychology, 71*(5), 862–878. doi:10.1037/0022-006X.71.5.862

Andrews, D. A., & Bonta, J. (2010). *The psychology of criminal conduct* (5th ed.). Anderson Publishing.

Anstiss, B., Polaschek, D. L. L., & Wilson, M. (2011). A brief motivational interviewing intervention with prisoners: When you lead a horse to water, can it drink for itself? *Psychology, Crime & Law, 17*(8), 689–710. doi:10.1080/10683160903524325

Asch, S. E. (1946). Forming impressions of personality. *Journal of Abnormal and Social Psychology, 41*(3), 258–290. doi:10.1037/h0055756

Babor, T. F., Higgins-Biddle, J. C., Saunders, J. B., & Monteiro, M. G. (2001). *AUDIT: The Alcohol Use Disorders Identification Test: Guidelines for use in primary care* (2nd ed.). World Health Organization.

Brehm, S. S., & Brehm, J. W. (1981). *Psychological reactance: A theory of freedom and control*. Academic Press.

Brown, T. G., Ouimet, M. C., Eldeb, M., Tremblay, J., Vingilis, E., Nadeau, L., Pruessner, J., & Bhatti, J. A. (2015). A randomized controlled trial of brief motivational interviewing in impaired driving recidivists: A 5-year follow-up of traffic offenses and crashes. *Alcoholism: Clinical and Experimental Research, 39*(6), 1088–1096. doi:10.1111/acer.12716

Carey, S. M., Mackin, J. R., & Finigan, M. W. (2012). What works? The ten key components of drug court: Research-based best practices. *Drug Court Review, 8*(1), 6–42.

Cavaiola, A. A., Strohmetz, D. B., & Abreo, S. D. (2007). Characteristics of DUI recidivists: A 12-year follow-up study of first-time DUI offenders. *Addictive Behaviors, 32*(4), 855–861. doi:10.1016/j.addbeh.2006.06.029

Clark, M. D. (2005). Motivational interviewing for probation staff: Increasing the readiness to change. *Federal Probation, 69*(2), 22–28.

Clark, M. D. (2006). Entering the business of behavior change: Motivational interviewing for probation staff. *Perspectives, 30*(1), 38–45.

Deci, E. L., & Ryan, R. M. (2000). The "what" and "why" of goal pursuits: Human needs and the self-determination of behavior. *Psychological Inquiry, 11*(4), 227–268. doi:10.1207/S15327965PLI1104_01

Durose, M. R., Cooper, A. D., & Snyder, H. N. (2014). *Recidivism of prisoners released in 30 states in 2005: Patterns from 2005 to 2010*. Bureau of Justice Statistics.

Eckhardt, C. I., Murphy, C. M., Whitaker, D. J., Sprunger, J., Dykstra, R., & Woodard, K. (2013). The effectiveness of intervention programs for perpetrators and victims of intimate partner violence. *Partner Abuse, 4*(2), 196–231. doi:10.1891/1946-6560.4.2.196

Figley, C. R. (1995). Compassion fatigue as secondary traumatic stress disorder: An overview. In C. R. Figley (Ed.), *Compassion fatigue: Coping with secondary traumatic stress disorder in those who treat the traumatized* (pp. 1–20). Brunner/Mazel.

Gaume, J., Gmel, G., Faouzi, M., & Daeppen, J.-B. (2008). Counsellor behaviours and patient language during brief motivational interventions: A sequential analysis of speech. *Addiction, 103*(11), 1793–1800. doi:10.1111/j.1360-0443.2008.02337.x

Ginsburg, J. I. D., Mann, R. E., Rotgers, F., & Weekes, J. R. (2002). Motivational interviewing with criminal justice populations. In W. R. Miller & S. Rollnick (Eds.), *Motivational interviewing: Preparing people for change* (2nd ed., pp. 333–346). Guilford Press.

Hanson, R. K., & Morton-Bourgon, K. E. (2005). The characteristics of persistent sexual offenders: A meta-analysis of recidivism studies. *Journal of Consulting and Clinical Psychology, 73*(6), 1154–1163. doi:10.1037/0022-006X.73.6.1154

Hettema, J., Steele, J., & Miller, W. R. (2005). Motivational interviewing. *Annual Review of Clinical Psychology, 1*, 91–111. doi:10.1146/annurev.clinpsy.1.102803.143833

Kaeble, D. (2021). *Probation and parole in the United States, 2020*. Bureau of Justice Statistics.

Kennealy, P. J., Skeem, J. L., Manchak, S. M., & Eno Louden, J. (2012). Firm, fair, and caring officer-offender relationships protect against supervision failure. *Law and Human Behavior, 36*(6), 496–505. doi:10.1037/h0093935

Lewis, K. R., Lewis, L. S., & Garby, T. M. (2013). Surviving the trenches: The personal impact of the job on probation officers. *American Journal of Criminal Justice, 38*, 67–84. doi:10.1007/s12103-012-9165-3

Lundahl, B., & Burke, B. L. (2009). The effectiveness and applicability of motivational interviewing: A practice-friendly review of four meta-analyses. *Journal of Clinical Psychology, 65*(11), 1232–1245. doi:10.1002/jclp.20638

Lundahl, B. W., Kunz, C., Brownell, C., Tollefson, D., & Burke, B. L. (2010). A meta-analysis of motivational interviewing: Twenty-five years of empirical studies. *Research on Social Work Practice, 20*(2), 137–160. doi:10.1177/1049731509347850

Madson, M. B., Loignon, A. C., & Lane, C. (2009). Training in motivational interviewing: A systematic review. *Journal of Substance Abuse Treatment, 36*(1), 101–109. doi:10.1016/j.jsat.2008.05.005

Marlatt, G. A., & Gordon, J. R. (1985). *Relapse prevention: Maintenance strategies in the treatment of addictive behaviors*. Guilford Press.

Marshall, W. L., Serran, G. A., Fernandez, Y. M., Mulloy, R., Mann, R. E., & Thornton, D. (2005). Therapist characteristics in the treatment of sexual offenders: Tentative data on their relationship with indices of behaviour change. *Journal of Sexual Aggression, 9*(1), 25–30. doi:10.1080/355260031000137940

Maslach, C., & Leiter, M. P. (2016). Understanding the burnout experience: Recent research and its implications for psychiatry. *World Psychiatry, 15*(2), 103–111. doi:10.1002/wps.20311

McLellan, A. T., Lewis, D. C., O'Brien, C. P., & Kleber, H. D. (2000). Drug dependence, a chronic medical illness: Implications for treatment, insurance, and outcomes evaluation. *JAMA, 284*(13), 1689–1695. doi:10.1001/jama.284.13.1689

McMurran, M. (2009). Motivational interviewing with offenders: A systematic review. *Legal and Criminological Psychology, 14*(1), 83–100. doi:10.1348/135532508X278326

Miller, W. R. (1983). Motivational interviewing with problem drinkers. *Behavioural Psychotherapy, 11*(2), 147–172. doi:10.1017/S0141347300006583

Miller, W. R., Benefield, R. G., & Tonigan, J. S. (1993). Enhancing motivation for change in problem drinking: A controlled comparison of two therapist styles. *Journal of Consulting and Clinical Psychology, 61*(3), 455–461. doi:10.1037/0022-006X.61.3.455

Miller, W. R., & Moyers, T. B. (2006). Eight stages in learning motivational interviewing. *Journal of Teaching in the Addictions, 5*(1), 3–17. doi:10.1300/J188v05n01_02

Miller, W. R., & Rollnick, S. (2013). *Motivational interviewing: Helping people change* (3rd ed.). Guilford Press.

Miller, W. R., Sovereign, R. G., & Krege, B. (1988). Motivational interviewing with problem drinkers: II. The drinker's check-up as a preventive intervention. *Behavioural Psychotherapy, 16*(4), 251–268. doi:10.1017/S0141347300014129

Mitchell, O., Wilson, D. B., Eggers, A., & MacKenzie, D. L. (2012). Assessing the effectiveness of drug courts on recidivism: A meta-analytic review of traditional and non-traditional drug courts. *Journal of Criminal Justice, 40*(1), 60–71. doi:10.1016/j.jcrimjus.2011.11.009

Moyers, T. B. (2014). The relationship in motivational interviewing. *Psychotherapy, 51*(3), 358–363. doi:10.1037/a0036910

Moyers, T. B., & Martin, T. (2006). Therapist influence on client language during motivational interviewing sessions. *Journal of Substance Abuse Treatment, 30*(3), 245–251. doi:10.1016/j.jsat.2005.12.003

Moyers, T. B., Martin, T., Houck, J. M., Christopher, P. J., & Tonigan, J. S. (2009). From in-session behaviors to drinking outcomes: A causal chain for motivational interviewing. *Journal of Consulting and Clinical Psychology, 77*(6), 1113–1124. doi:10.1037/a0017189

Moyers, T. B., Rowell, L. N., Manuel, J. K., Ernst, D., & Houck, J. M. (2016). The Motivational Interviewing Treatment Integrity Code (MITI 4): Rationale, preliminary reliability and validity. *Journal of Substance Abuse Treatment, 65*, 36–42. doi:10.1016/j.jsat.2016.01.001

Murphy, C. M., Linehan, E. L., Reyner, J. C., Musser, P. H., & Taft, C. T. (2012). Moderators of response to motivational interviewing for partner-violent men. *Journal of Family Violence, 27*(7), 671–680. doi:10.1007/s10896-012-9460-2

Murphy, C. M., & Meis, L. A. (2008). Individual treatment of intimate partner violence perpetrators. *Violence and Victims, 23*(2), 173–186. doi:10.1891/0886-6708.23.2.173

Murray, J., Farrington, D. P., & Sekol, I. (2012). Children's antisocial behavior, mental health, drug use, and educational performance after parental incarceration: A systematic review and meta-analysis. *Psychological Bulletin, 138*(2), 175–210. doi:10.1037/a0026407

Musser, P. H., Semiatin, J. N., Taft, C. T., & Murphy, C. M. (2008). Motivational interviewing as a pregroup intervention for partner-violent men. *Violence and Victims, 23*(5), 539–557. doi:10.1891/0886-6708.23.5.539

National Association of Drug Court Professionals. (2015). *Adult drug court best practice standards* (Vol. 2). National Association of Drug Court Professionals.

National Institute of Corrections. (2019). *Thinking for a Change: Integrated cognitive behavior change program*. U.S. Department of Justice.

Pew Center on the States. (2011). *State of recidivism: The revolving door of America's prisons*. The Pew Charitable Trusts.

Pinto e Silva, T., Gouveia, C., Santirso, F. A., Cunha, O., & Caridade, S. (2025). Effectiveness of motivational interviewing with justice-involved people: A systematic review and meta-analysis. *Psychosocial Intervention, 34*(2), 89–102. doi:10.5093/pi2025a8

Prochaska, J. O., & DiClemente, C. C. (1983). Stages and processes of self-change of smoking: Toward an integrative model of change. *Journal of Consulting and Clinical Psychology, 51*(3), 390–395. doi:10.1037/0022-006X.51.3.390

Rollnick, S., Miller, W. R., & Butler, C. C. (2008). *Motivational interviewing in health care: Helping patients change behavior*. Guilford Press.

Schwalbe, C. S., Oh, H. Y., & Zweben, A. (2014). Sustaining motivational interviewing: A meta-analysis of training studies. *Addiction, 109*(8), 1287–1294. doi:10.1111/add.12558

Serran, G. A., Fernandez, Y., Marshall, W. L., & Mann, R. E. (2003). Process issues in treatment: Application to sexual offender programs. *Professional Psychology: Research and Practice, 34*(4), 368–374. doi:10.1037/0735-7028.34.4.368

Skeem, J. L., Eno Louden, J., Polaschek, D., & Camp, J. (2007). Assessing relationship quality in mandated community treatment: Blending care with control. *Psychological Assessment, 19*(4), 397–410. doi:10.1037/1040-3590.19.4.397

Skeem, J. L., & Manchak, S. M. (2008). Back to the future: From Klockars' model of effective supervision to evidence-based practice in probation. *Journal of Offender Rehabilitation, 47*(3), 220–247. doi:10.1080/10509670802134069

Soleymani, S., Britt, E., & Wallace-Bell, M. (2018). Motivational interviewing for enhancing engagement in intimate partner violence (IPV) treatment: A review of the literature. *Aggression and Violent Behavior, 40*, 119–127. doi:10.1016/j.avb.2018.05.005

Stinson, J. D., & Clark, M. D. (2017). *Motivational interviewing with offenders: Engagement, rehabilitation, and reentry*. Guilford Press.

Taxman, F. S. (2008). No illusions: Offender and organizational change in Maryland's proactive community supervision efforts. *Criminology & Public Policy, 7*(2), 275–302. doi:10.1111/j.1745-9133.2008.00508.x

Taxman, F. S., Perdoni, M. L., & Caudy, M. (2013). The plight of providing appropriate substance abuse treatment services to offenders: Modeling the gaps in service delivery. *Victims & Offenders, 8*(1), 70–93. doi:10.1080/15564886.2012.747459

Travis, J., Western, B., & Redburn, S. (Eds.). (2014). *The growth of incarceration in the United States: Exploring causes and consequences*. National Academies Press. doi:10.17226/18613

Trotter, C. (2015). *Working with involuntary clients: A guide to practice* (3rd ed.). Routledge.

Vasilaki, E. I., Hosier, S. G., & Cox, W. M. (2006). The efficacy of motivational interviewing as a brief intervention for excessive drinking: A meta-analytic review. *Alcohol and Alcoholism, 41*(3), 328–335. doi:10.1093/alcalc/agl016

Vera Institute of Justice. (2019). *The price of prisons: Examining state spending trends, 2010–2015*. Vera Institute of Justice.

Viglione, J. (2019). The risk-need-responsivity model: How do probation officers implement the principles of effective intervention? *Criminal Justice and Behavior, 46*(5), 655–673. doi:10.1177/0093854818807505

Walters, S. T., Alexander, M., & VanBenschoten, S. W. (2008). Motivational interviewing training in criminal justice: Development of a model plan. *Federal Probation, 72*(2), 61–66.

Walters, S. T., Clark, M. D., Gingerich, R., & Meltzer, M. L. (2007). *Motivating offenders to change: A guide for probation and parole*. National Institute of Corrections.

Walters, S. T., Vader, A. M., Nguyen, N., Harris, T. R., & Eells, J. (2010). Motivational interviewing as a supervision strategy in probation: A randomized effectiveness trial. *Journal of Offender Rehabilitation, 49*(5), 309–323. doi:10.1080/10509674.2010.489455

Ward, T., & Stewart, C. A. (2003). The treatment of sex offenders: Risk management and good lives. *Professional Psychology: Research and Practice, 34*(4), 353–360. doi:10.1037/0735-7028.34.4.353

Wexler, D. B., & Winick, B. J. (Eds.). (1996). *Law in a therapeutic key: Developments in therapeutic jurisprudence*. Carolina Academic Press.

Wild, T. C., Cunningham, J. A., & Ryan, R. M. (2006). Social pressure, coercion, and client engagement at treatment entry: A self-determination theory perspective. *Addictive Behaviors, 31*(10), 1858–1872. doi:10.1016/j.addbeh.2006.01.002

www.ingramcontent.com/pod-product-compliance
Lightning Source LLC
LaVergne TN
LVHW080022210926
848481LV00011B/3084
* 9 7 8 1 9 2 3 6 4 6 5 9 9 *